Godly Directions in a Time of Plague

by
John Hooper (1495–1555)
Lancelot Andrewes (1555–1626)
William Crashaw (1572–1626)
Henry Burton (1579–1648)
John Owen (1616–1683)
Thomas Manton (1620–1677)
Thomas Draxe (d. 1618)
with chapters by C. Matthew McMahon

Copyright Information

Godly Directions in a Time of Plague by John Hooper, Lancelot Andrewes, William Crashaw, Henry Burton, John Owen, Thomas Manton and Thomas Draxe, with chapters by C. Matthew McMahon
Edited by Therese B. McMahon

This Print Edition, 2020
Electronic Edition, 2020

Manufactured in the United States of America

ISBN: 978-1-62663-355-1
eISBN: 978-1-62663-354-4

Table of Contents

Preface to the Work
by C. Matthew McMahon Ph.D., Th.D.

"But it shall come to pass, if thou wilt not hearken unto the voice of the LORD thy God, to observe to do all his commandments and his statutes which I command thee this day; that all these curses shall come upon thee, and overtake thee ... the LORD shall make the pestilence cleave unto thee, until he have consumed thee from off the land, whither thou goest to possess it," (Deut. 28:15, 21).

It is important in a day of plague, that the church engage in occasional repentance, in all humility, with fasting and prayer, casting off all wayward sins, and confessing long held sins, even back as far as a generation (see Leviticus 26). In not keeping the commandments of God, after a time, God will send sword, famine and plagues on his people to chastise them with his rod of correction. He does this for their *good*, though it might not feel that way at the time. In the last fifty or sixty years, this has happened in minimal amounts, in random areas, until now, where the coronavirus has spread over the whole face of the earth. Currently, two million are infected, 120,000 have died, and there are springing up various other difficulties and frowning providences making this plague all the more difficult. Will the church of Jesus Christ turn to God in this hour and repent?

Out of the word of God we know the very cause of this horrible coronavirus plague. Yes, it covers the entire earth, now coupled (at this point) with famines, plagues of locusts (in Africa), and other natural disasters (tornados and sever weather, drought, and other such unexpected works sent from God's throne) commanded by Christ as the Lord of Hosts. We know it is the fault of all *our* sins, *the sins of the church*. Did you think it was because of someone else?

The church ought not to play the blame game, and point the finger at the wickedness of the media, the depravity of Hollywood, the evils of government, the wickedness of ungodly laws throughout the land, persecution of the church, or even a host of national sins that they think *might* be the cause (and those certainly are thrown into the mix as secondary works that God may in fact judge by this terrible plague). Certainly, all these, are dreadful in their heinous sinfulness against God's Law and against God's Christ. However, one must consider, it is undeniable that the world *always* acts like the world. But it is far worse when *the church* acts like the world and engages in unbelief, disobedience and unthankfulness in their standing before the Lord and his gracious covenant. God has a quarrel with his church whenever they sin against him, and they are doing it now, for we see the plague across the face of the earth. In fact, they have been sinning for decades. The church must repent for all her sins, and seek a thorough reformation of life and worship, for we know that judgment begins at the house of God *first* (1 Peter 4:17).

If the church will be preserved and delivered from this horrible plague, and all its concomitant effects, it is important that they consider that God does this for

5

our good, and for our sanctification. It is true, impenitent covenant breakers will bock at this, but the tender hearts of his true church will press towards a biblical reformation. If we acknowledge our sins, and cast them away by the blood of Christ, come to God in humility, confession, prayer and fasting in amendment of life and true repentance for our waywardness and covenant breaking sins, God will be merciful and stop the plague. Do *you* believe that? He will stop it dead in its horrible track. But, if we continue in our evil course, and continue in our neglect of his word, continue in our abominable ways of depraved worship, reject his covenant, and make arguments against his word, he will not cease with the judgments he has sent to his church. What will the church do in a time like this?

This very timely and advantageous work you have in your hand, reader, is truly a godly help to Christ's church, a present help in a time of plague. It is filled with *godly directions* from various authors who took time to thoughtfully set down such biblical directions. The church must take time to consider these things when God's judgments come against his people. These authors are all of one mind, though they lived at different times over a span of almost 200 years. This is because all godly directions taken from careful Scriptural study will always end up in the same place. It is true, each writer deals with various texts, from various angles. But, still, their conclusions are the same, and they all offer the church today godly directions that will deliver the church from under the heavy hand of God's judgments.

The authors are well known to those who have taken an interest in the preachers of old, and in times of reformation. The works included have been chosen to be helpful, not overbearing. More could certainly be added (having whole books written on this subject). There are four sermons, one by John Hooper (on Mark 1:15) which is a shortened homily, a sermon by Lancelot Andrewes (on Psa. 106:29–30), one by John Owen (on 2 Timothy 3:1) and one by Thomas Manton (on Psalm 119:67). There is an extended prayer given by William Crashaw (which is *amazing*) coupled by an exhortation given by him, as well as an extended exhortation by Henry Burton on self-denial and humiliation (on Luke 9:23). Finally, Thomas Draxe sets down a series of simple questions and answers to the difficulty of a plague. In all of these the church around the world would do well to heed their godly directions in this time, that God would hear from heaven, and forgive their sin and heal their land (2 Chron. 7:14ff).

In Christ's Immeasurable Kindness,
C. Matthew McMahon, Ph.D., Th.D.
April, 2020, from my study.

Meet the Authors

Edited by C. Matthew McMahon, Ph.D., Th.D.

John Hooper (1495–1555) was an Anglican Bishop of Gloucester and Worcester, and burned at the stake as a martyr under Bloody Mary. Hooper was involved with the stalwart wing of English Protestantism. He approved of the *Consensus Tigurinus* negotiated in 1549 between the Zwinglians and Calvinists of Switzerland. It was this form of religion that he labored to spread in England. His views had considerable influence on the Puritans of Elizabeth's reign, when many editions of his works were published. Two volumes of Hooper's writings are included in the Parker Society's publications and another edition appeared at Oxford in 1855. In 1550 he translated *book 2* of Tertullian's "Ad Uxorem" (To his wife), which is the first English translation of any of Tertullian's works.

Lancelot Andrewes (1555– 1626) was an English bishop and scholar, who held high positions in the church of England during the reigns of Elizabeth I and James I. During James's reign, Andrewes served successively as Bishop of Chichester, of Ely, and of Winchester and oversaw the translation of the King James Version of the Bible (or Authorized Version).

William Crashaw (1572–1626) was an English divine, a solid academic and eloquent preacher. After being ordained Crashaw became the minister, first at Bridlington and then at Beverley in Yorkshire. Crashaw was known as a scholar and a strong Protestant who was associated with the Puritan movement. His wife, Elizabeth Crashaw, died in child-birth, and James Ussher preached her funeral sermon, (at a funeral noted for its large attendance).

Henry Burton (1579–1648) was a great puritan sufferer for the gospel of Jesus Christ and for his views of nonconformity. He was a man who feared God and not men for the cause of Christ's Gospel. From what he has published in his day, he appears to have been furnished with considerable learning and skill, and was an eminent scholar. He was courageous in the cause of truth and a man of a warm but firm Christian spirit.

John Owen (1616-1683) was one of the greatest Puritan theologians, and preachers who ever lived. He is possibly the supreme Reformed theologian of all time writing in the English language. In his early twenties he was converted from sin into the Kingdom of Christ, and in 1637 he became a minister of the Gospel. In the 1640s he was chaplain to Oliver Cromwell, and in 1651 he was made Dean of Christ Church, Oxford. In 1652 he was given the additional post of Vice-Chancellor of the University. After 1660 he helped lead the Independents until his death in 1683.

Thomas Manton (1620-1677) was a powerful Reformed preacher, with an ease of understanding and a clear preaching style. He was one of the most prolific puritans of his day. He was best known for his skilled expository preaching, and his finest works are his exposition of James, his work on the temptation of Christ and his sermons on Psalm 119.

Thomas Draxe (1570-1618), was an English divine, who is said to be a pious man and an excellent preacher of the Gospel. Thomas Fuller states that Draxe translated the *Works of William Perkins* into Latin for the Geneva Edition in 1611. He was a capable and godly author and theologian.

A Sermon to be Read in the Time of Pestilence

by John Hooper

TO ALL PASTORS AND CURATES WITHIN THE KING'S MAJESTY'S DIOCESSE OF WORCESTER AND GLOUCESTER.

Even as we are blind and unthankful for God's favorable mercies, where with he follows us all in health, wealth and prosperity. So, we are blind, and insensible for his most just plagues, where all he persecutes and punishes us in sickness, scarcity and troubles. And now among other tokens of his displeasure and wrath, has sent us in diverse places one of the most extreme plagues (that he ever devised to punish man with in this life), the plague of pestilence. For as much as he means by it not only to kill and destroy the bodies of such, as by this plague he purposes to take out of this mortal life. But also, without repentance and turning to his mercy in Christ before death, the soul of such as depart from here, must necessarily perish by God's just judgment. And not only this to be the end of such as it pleases God to strike to death by this his servant and messenger the plague of pestilence. But also, the same danger of his displeasure remains to me, and to all others that have the cure, and charge of the people's souls in this the king's Majesty's most noble realm. Over these souls God has made us watchmen and overseers, to admonish and warn the people of all dangers, and plagues that God shall send for their punishment. In case we do not admonish in time the people committed to our charge of such plagues as for sin he purposes to punish us with, their loss and damnation shall be required at our hands.

For the discharge of myself, and also for the better instruction of such as have cures within this Diocese of Worcester and Gloucester (and yet not best able to discharge them), and further more for the profit and salvation of the people, among whom it may please God to send his fearful plague of pestilence. I have thought it my bound duty (seeing at all times I cannot comfort the sick myself) to collect or gather into some short sermon or homily a medicine and most present help for all men against the plague of pestilence. And in the same also to provide some present remedy for such as shall be infected with that disease. And for better understanding of the medicine, I will use this order, that all Physicians learned use in their practice of medicine.

First, I will show the chief cause of the pestilence. And then what remedy is best to be used against it, and to heal it when it has infected any man. And although I will speak in this something as other Physicians have done, yet because they have spoken already more than I can in the matter, though it is a great deal less than the matter of the disease requires, (for none of them have showed any ascertained remedy, even though their reason is never so good) I will briefly as by the way something speak of this disease, as they do. But as a preacher of God's word, and as a Physician for the soul, rather than for the body, entreat of its sickness and remedy, after the advice and counsel of God's word. God supplies all things omitted and not spoken of, concerning this most dangerous plague by such as have written, besides the scripture of God, their mind touching the same things. For indeed the chief causes of all plagues and sicknesses, is sin. This sin is that which remains within all men, works destruction, not only of the body, but also of the soul, if a remedy is not found. And whereas Galien says,[1] all pestilence comes by the corruption of the air, that both beast and man drawing their breathes in the air corrupt, draws its corruption into themselves, he says this well, yet not enough. He also says very naturally, that when the air is altered from his natural equality and temperature too much, and intemperate heat and moisture sets in, pestilence is likely then to reign. For as he says in the same place, that heat and moisture distempered is the most dangerous for the creatures of the world,[2] yet that is not enough. As Ezekiel says, whereas God sends all these distempers, and yet if Noah, Daniel and Job were in the midst of them, they shall be safe. Even too, David also says, though they die at the right hand ten thousand fold, and die at the left a thousand fold, *the plague shall not touch him that sits under the protection of the highest.* And where as reason has many good and probable arguments in this matter touching the cause of pestilence that it should come some time by reason of such diseases as are to be in the body disposed and apt to corrupt, then is the man quickly (by drawing and breathing as well the corruption of himself, as the infection of the air)

---

[1] Galen. De Differ. Febr. Lib 1. cap. 6.
[2] Galen. De Temper. Lib 1. c. 4.

infected. And that such diseases as are gross and inclined to corruption rises of an immoderate diet, and the infection takes his original and beginning from such beasts, carrion, and other loathsome bodies that rot on the face of the earth not buried, or else from moorish standing, and damp waters, stinks or other such unwholesome moistures, so that towards the fall of the leaf, both the air that man lies in, as also man's body itself is more apt and disposed to putrefaction more in that time than in any other time for diverse natural causes. These causes are to be considered as natural and consonant to reason. Yet there are reasons and causes of pestilence of more weight, and more worthy of deep and advised considerations and advertisements then this is. And the more, because they lie within man (and are marked but of very few) and hide themselves secretly until they have poisoned the whole man both body and soul. For indeed physicians that write, meddle with no causes that hurt man, but such as come into man from without, as the diseases (they say) take their infection from unwholesome meat and bad diet, or else from the corruption of the air with such like things. But our Savior Jesus Christ shows that our corruption and sickness rises from within us, as I will declare hereafter in the causes that the scripture teaches of pestilence and all other diseases. Requiring you diligently to look on the same, and to read it in your churches. That the people may understand both the cause of this plague from God, of pestilence, and how to use themselves in the time of this sickness or any other that shall happen to them by God's appointment, as God may be glorified in them, and you and I discharged of our bound duties. And they themselves that shall happen to be infected with the plague of pestilence, and by the same be brought to death may be assured through true and godly doctrine to die in the Lord, and so be eternally blessed straightway after their death, as Saint John says (Rev. 14). And in case God reserves them to longer life, they may live in truth and verity to him, with detestation and hatred of sin, the original cause of man's misery and wretchedness. And with the love of mercy and grace the original and only workers of man's quietness and everlasting salvation given to us form God the Father Almighty, through Jesus Christ his only Son our Lord. To whom with the Holy Ghost be all honor and praise, world without end. So be it.

"Repent, and believe the gospel," (Mark 1:15).

It is the desire of all sick men to know what medicine and remedy has been known most to prevail, best to remove, and soonest to cure and make whole the person diseased. And the greater and more dangerous the sickness is, the more circumspect and wise, the sick man must be in knowledge and choice of the medicine, lest he seek a remedy which is inferior and too weak for the greatness and strength of his disease.

The nature and condition therefore of pestilence being so dangerous (as it is indeed), that whosoever be infected or attainted with it, has need to be well instructed and thoroughly persuaded of a sufficient remedy, stronger than the sickness itself; or else the disease shall more hurt the sick patient than the medicine can do him good. For then, necessarily, will follow the death and the destruction of the diseased person. It behooves all men that are mortal, to know the most general and most dangerous diseases that mortality shall be troubled with; and then, as he sees his great and necessary adversaries and sickness, to know also the greatest and most necessary remedy and help against his diseases. And because sin has so prevailed in us, that truth, persuaded to us by the examples of others, sooner instructs and longer tarries than anything taught us by doctrine or testimony, I shall, before I enter into the causes of the pestilence, show the strength and nature of sickness from the examples of such godly people as in the word of God are mentioned of for our instruction.

King David, among other diseases, fell into the pestilence (Psalm 6:3); the greatness and danger of this passed all human and worldly helps, as it appears by his lamentable cry and complaint to the Lord, "My soul (he says) is sore troubled: but how long Lord, wilt thou defer thy help?" And the same cry and complaint he made to the Lord, when the plague of pestilence had infected his whole realm from Dan to Beersheba, and saw the remedy thereof to be only in God, praying him to command his angel to strike the people no more (Psalm 38).

Hezekiah the king saw that, besides God, all medicines and remedies were too weak and inferior for the strength and power of the pestilence and sickness. Therefore, he turned himself to the wall, and prayed God

to do that for him that no remedy nor medicine was able
to do (2 Kings 20:2).

In 1 Cor. 15, Paul, in his wonderful oration that
he makes concerning the resurrection of the dead,
weighs most deeply the nature and condition of man's
miserable estate in this life, burdening him with such
strong adversaries, sickness, and diseases, both of body
and soul, that every man may see how impossible it is for
man to find deliverance from the tyranny and strength of
sickness, except only the mercy of God in Christ Jesus;
numbering there six adversaries so strong, as the least of
them, except Christ help, is able to destroy both body
and soul. The first is corruption, the second mortality,
the third sin, the fourth the law condemning sin, the
fifth death, the sixth hell, which have necessary and
indivisible plagues and sickness of man in this life
against which he finds no remedy. No remedy can be
found neither by Galen nor Hippocrates,[3] neither yet by
the earth that men say cures all wounds. But with great
faith and confidence marks and weighs the strength of
diseases, though they are never so strong, to be yet
inferior to the medicine and remedy that God has
provided for us only in Christ. Therefore, he compares
the inferior strength of all those sicknesses to the
sufficient remedy of God through Christ, saying after
this manner, "Thanks be unto God, which hath given us
victory through our Lord Jesus Christ." By this it is
evident and plain that God is the only remedy for all

---

[3] Lib. l. c. 96. *In Taurorum peninsula in civitate Parasino terra est
qua sanantur omnia vulnera.* — C. Plin. Sec.
Hist. Nat. p. 40. Francof. 1599.

plagues and diseases. Howbeit, now I shall more specially open the causes of the plague, and the nature of the same, that our sickness and the causes of it may be more known, and the better avoided.

The principal cause of pestilence is opened by Paul by these words, "By sin came death into the world," (Romans 5), and for the cause of sin God sends the plague of pestilence and all other diseases that punish towards death. As king David says, "Thou dost punish the children of men for sin," (Psalm 39).

Moses also plainly shows that the principal and chief cause (Deut. 28) of pestilence is not in the corruption of the air, nor in the superfluous sicknesses within man; but that sin and the transgression of God's law is the very cause and chief occasion of pestilence and of all other diseases. And the experience of this was tried in the pestilence that reigned in king David's time (2 Sam. 24) for his sins, and the sins of the people. So that all the scripture of God manifestly declares, that the contempt and breach of God's laws is the chief and principal cause of pestilence, and of all other plagues that he sends for our punishment.

And from this cause proceeds those causes that physicians speak of, the corruption of the air, which is never corrupted, nor can corrupt man or beast, except man, for whose sake and comfort both air and all other beasts were made, be first corrupted by sin and transgression of God's laws. Neither could man take any surfeit by meats, nor any evil diseases could be engendered of any meats, were not the man that uses them in a corrupt manner and first infected with sin. But when the Lord sees that the people forget or condemn his blessed commandments, and that such as are appointed to rebuke and punish such transgressors of God's laws, suffer without punishment the glory of God and his holy commandments to be oppressed and set at nothing, as we see daily they are indeed. From these causes, our sin and abomination, the Lord takes occasion to turn his good creatures, made for our life, to be a means of our death; which never would be, if it were not from our heinous dishonoring and contempt of God. For the Lord's creatures are perfectly good, and made all one to comfort and rejoice in. Such creatures are wholesome, clean, and pure without all infection. But seeing that the contempt of God and the filthiness of sin is neither by ministers declared, opened, nor detected, neither by the heads of the country and officers appointed under God and the king punished, except, therefore, there should be nothing else live in this world than sin, abomination, and contempt of God, then God is forced, by taking away and destruction of filthy life and those living in a filthy manner, to appoint an extraordinary magistrate to reform and punish the mother of all mischief, which is sin and contempt of God's holy word. He alters, not by chance, nor by the influence of stars, the wholesomeness of the air into pestilent and contagious infection, and the meat and drink with their nutriment and food into poison and venom; that by their mean sin, sinners might be slain and taken out of this world, and no longer to blaspheme God.

In this way the word of God declares the effectual and principal cause of pestilence to be the

19

contempt of God's word, that should keep men in order both to God and man. The breaking of this word has always brought these plagues into realms, as profane writers also manifestly declare. Orosius[4] says that the great shortage and famine that came among the Romans in the time of Caesar Augustus, was because Caius, his nephew, condemned to honor the living God, as he was taught at Jerusalem, when he passed into Syria.

Therefore, it is expedient, and before all things necessary, forasmuch as the plague is come into sundry places about us, for everyone to try himself, what just causes of this pestilence each man has within himself. Every Christian man and woman must search whether their religion and Christianity are such as God by his word maintains to be good. For, there is no greater occasion of pestilence than superstition and false religion.

The bishop, parson, vicar, and curate, must examine themselves, what knowledge of God's word is in them, and what diligence they have taken to bring the people to a right knowledge and perfect honor of God. There is no greater danger of pestilence than whereas the clergy is either ignorant of God's word, or negligent in teaching of it.[5]

The justices and gentlemen must look how they keep themselves and the king's majesty's people in the true knowledge and obedience of God's laws and the king's. For, nothing provokes the pestilence more dangerously than where as such as sit and are appointed

---

[4] Lib. 7. cap 1. See Oros. *Hist.* Lib. vii. c. 3. p. 575. Colon, 1582.
[5] *Nota bene* -Editor.

to do justice, do their own affections with contempt and injuries both to God and man; and the plague of God will revenge it.

All we, therefore, that are subjects, and live under one God and one king, must (now that God has sent us this pestilence) see that we have true, loving, faithful, trusting and obedient hearts; with one whole mind altogether to obey, reverence, love, help, succor, defend, and uphold with all our minds, goods, riches, and strength, with this our only king, the magistrates and counsellors that are appointed under his highness. For, as Paul says, "He that disobeyeth and resisteth the higher powers appointed by God, resisteth God," (Rom. 13). They provoke the pestilence and vengeance of God against us. And we must take heed also that we do not hate one another (1 John 3). If we do, the plague will not cease, and the places that yet are not infected God shall infect, no matter what defense man makes against it. And although Galen, of all remedies, says, "To get away from the air that is infected is best," yet I know that Moses by the word of God says, "Flee whither thou wilt, in case thou take with thee the contempt of God and breach of his commandment, God shall find thee out," (Deut. 28). Yes, and although many medicines are devised, and assures the infected to be made whole, yet, notwithstanding, I know God's word says the contrary, that he will send to insensible, careless, and willful sinners such a plague and incurable a pestilence, that he shall not be delivered, but die and perish by it.

Therefore, forasmuch as sin is the occasion chiefly of pestilence, let every man shun and avoid it both speedily and penitently; and then shall ye be preserved from the plague sufficiently, as you shall perceive in the remedy of this dangerous plague that begins to reign among us. For no doubt, although we could fly to Locris or Crotone, where the pestilence is not raging, yet God says, if we do not fear him, we shall surely be infected.

THE REMEDY AGAINST THE PESTILENCE

As the scripture of God only shows the very cause of pestilence, so it shows the very true and only remedy against it. I do not dislike the remedies that natural medicine has prescribed, yet I do not hold them as *sufficient* remedies, for their imperfection's sake. I wish also they were used, and the remedies prescribed in God's book not omitted. For, I see all the remedies that ever was devised by man is not able to remove assuredly the pestilence from him that is infected with it, although they are never so excellent and good. And I find the same concerning the preservation from the pestilence devised by man, also insufficient for man's preservation, yet not to be condemned. For the reason of their chief preservation is very good and allowable, and yet not sufficient, which is of all things chiefly to be used against the pestilence, fleeing and departure from the place where as the air is corrupt.

Therefore, for such as may, nothing is better than to flee; and except he does, he offers himself to a present danger of death. But, the word of God says plainly that, "flee whither we will, if we forsake not sin, and serve the living God, the plague shall overtake us." And this fleeing cannot be a sufficient remedy; for there are certain people that cannot flee, although they would if they could. These are the poorer sort of people, that have no friends nor place to flee to, more than the poor house they dwell in. Likewise, there are such offices of trust as men for no cause may flee from it; as the bishop, parson, vicar, and curate, who has the charge of those that God pleases to infect with the pestilence; and if they forsake their people in this plague–time, (John 10) they are hirelings and not pastors. And they flee from God's people into God's high indignation.

Such also as have places and offices of trust for the commonwealth; as the captains of soldiers in the time of war, judges and justices in the time of peace; in case they should flee their countries, or leave their wars for the plague of pestilence, they shall never be good soldiers nor good justices for the commonwealth; and they shall be accountable to Almighty God for all the hurt and detriment that has happened to the people in their absence.

Therefore, seeing there is no certain remedy devised by man, neither for such as cannot flee, nor for them that may flee, we must seek another medicine and help at God's hand, who can and will preserve those that are whole, and make them whole that are sick, if it is expedient for man, and most for his own honor. The best preservative, therefore, to keep men from the pestilence is this that Moses speaks of, "Let us do sacrifice unto the Lord, lest we be stricken with pestilence or sword," (Exodus 5). And Joshua and Caleb told the people in

Numbers 14 that a faithful trust in the Lord was the best remedy for them. If they condemned this, they should find that God there threatened, speaking to Moses, "How long will this people be unfaithful? I will strike them with pestilence, and consume them." Also, David knew (2 Sam. 24) that the only remedy to keep Jerusalem from the plague was, that God should turn his wrath from the city for his sins and the sins of the people.

But now, to bring the remedy the better to the understanding of the people, I will show it by this place of Mark, "Repent ye, and believe the gospel," (Mark 1) in which the words demonstrate the only medicine against the pestilence, and also all other diseases. This text should be well and advisedly considered, in which Christ uses a very natural order to heal all diseases. For, as the remedy naturally of all diseases is taken from contrary conditions and qualities to that which work and maintains the sickness, so Christ in these words declares that the preservation and help from sin and wickedness, the cause of pestilence, proceeds from virtues and conditions contrary to the qualities and nature of such things as preserve and keep this wicked sin and sickness in man. As when a man is fallen into sickness by reason of too much cold and moisture, the remedy must be gathered naturally from the contrary, heat and drought; for this is a common and true principle, "Contraries be holpen by their opposites."[6] If nature waxes too cold, it must be helped with heat. If it

---

[6] Gal. De Temper. Lib. i. c. 3.

24

is too hot, it must be cooled. If it is too moist, it must be dried. If it is too dry, it must be moistened. If it is too cold and moist, it must be heated and dried. If it is cold and dry, it must be heated and moistened. If it is too hot and moist, it must be cooled and dried. If it is hot and dry, it must be cooled and moistened. These are very natural remedies, if they are well used with true proportion and convenient use after medicine.

And as these are good and natural for the body in which the pestilence dwells, even so is Christ's medicine in the first chapter of Mark a more present and certain remedy for the soul, that keeps the body in life, to remove or to remedy the sin of man, which is the cause of all plagues and pestilence. In the case to remove sin, the cause of sickness, this medicine of Christ is used, as the other is used to remove the effect of sin, which is sickness. As the body that is fallen into sickness by too much cold or moisture, either by nature, that originally was corrupted by Adam, either by our own accustomed working of sin, it must be made whole by the heat of repentance and true faith in the merits of Christ Jesus, who died for the sins of the world.

For this is a true and most certain principle of all religion, "One contrary must remedy the other." Seeing Adam by his fault began our death by sin, it must be cured by Christ, that is without sin. And where our own works are sin and filthiness, which with God is displeased, we must desire the works of Christ, to work the good will and favor of our heavenly Father again. And where by our own minds, wisdoms, religion, and learning we have committed idolatry and superstition, we must now by God's wisdom, God's word, and his most true religion amend our faults, and turn to true and godly honoring of him. Further, where our own inventions have brought us from the knowledge of God, the remedy is, that God's word must bring us to him again; for against all untruths brought in by man the word of God is the only remedy (Psalm 19, 119; 2 Tim. 3).[7]

The experience of this we may have plainly in the scripture. Where, for the salvation of the world, God appointed Christ his only Son to be born, and also to be opened to the world, that by him it might be healed of all sickness and sin, as it appears by Matthew, and other of the evangelists (Matthew 1, 2; Luke 2, John 1), yet the world was so blind and so corrupted with sin, that Christ was born and opened to them, and they of the world are nothing the better, as it appears in Matthew, where John the Baptist in few words, says, "Repent ye, for the kingdom of God is at hand." This shows the remedy of all sins and sickness, and the means how to receive and take the same remedy. The remedy was only Christ, as he says in John, and also in Matthew, and the means to come by the remedy was *to repent*, as you shall know further hereafter, when you know what repentance is.

The same may you also see in John, in the dialogue between Christ and Nicodemus (John 3), a man, after the judgment of the world, that knew life and death, sickness and health, the cause of the one, and also of the other, as well as any learned man among all the

---

[7] *Nota bene* -Editor.

congregation and church of the Jews. Yet, indeed, as ignorant of his own sickness, and also so far from the true knowledge how to come to health, as an ignorant man might be. And the cause was, that he did not understand the nature of sin, as it is esteemed by the word of God, neither its remedy that God has prescribed and appointed. Therefore, Christ told him by plain words, except he be helped and cured of his disease and sickness by contrary remedies, he could never understand nor come by his health. This is no wonder, for he knew the sickness of sin no otherwise than his forefathers and the worldly men knew sin, that is to say, knew such sins as were known to reason, and done by the body and outward actions of men. The same knowledge he had, and no more, of the remedy against the sickness of sin. And as his fathers and the world thought, so he did, that the merits of their sacrifices and the well-doing of themselves was a sufficient remedy to heal them both in body and in soul. Where Christ most mercifully pities the poor man, and with contrary knowledge both of sickness and its remedy show that the disease man is infected with goes further than reason and the outer action of the body. It occupies the soul of man with concupiscence, rebellion, frowardness, and contumacy against God. In this, Christ calls all that man has of himself but *flesh*; and shows that the remedy against this sickness does not come from the worthiness of any sacrifice or merits of man, or any sinful man's works; but that the remedy there depends only upon the merits of his blood and passion, and shows the same by the comparison of the brazen serpent appointed by

Moses. He argues this way: as the people that were stung with the serpents in the wilderness were not made whole by their own works, or for the dignity or service of any sacrifice that they offered, but by the sight of the serpent that represented Christ to come; even so Nicodemus, nor any other that is stung with the serpents of sin, is made whole by their own works, or any sacrifice they can offer. It is only by the merits of Christ. And even as the people could not come to the knowledge of this remedy by the serpent through their father's or their own wisdom, no more can Nicodemus, or any man living, come to the knowledge of the remedy for sickness and sin in our Savior Christ, except he learns it by the word of God through the instruction of the Holy Spirit.[8]

The same remedy Christ also uses in his words before in Mark 1, "Repent ye, and believe the gospel." In the words our Savior Christ shows all things to be considered in sin, and in its remedy. For in the first part of his words he declares how that men should know the causes of sickness; and in the second part the remedy and help for the same. The cause of sickness, as it appears by this word, "Repent," is, that men have by their own folly turned themselves from the truth of God to the error and fond opinion of man; from true faith to uncertain fables; from virtuous and godly works to uncleanliness and corruption of life. Christ, therefore, seeing the world how it is in danger, by reason it has forsaken the wisdom and rule of God's word, calling it

---

[8] *Nota bene* -Editor.

home again to a better way, bidding it repent. This is as though he had said, "Turn to a better mind, and leave the ways accustomed, and learn to be wise, and walk in the ways and wisdom appointed by God."

Here also appears, that the causes of all the dangers that Christ willed his audience to repent for, was their sin and iniquity. The cause of sin was infidelity and accustomed doing of evil. The cause of infidelity and accustomed doing of evil was ignorance or misunderstanding of God's word. The cause of ignorance or misunderstanding of God's word was Satan, God's and man's enemy, and man's willing consent to the devilish sophistry and false construing of God's word. And from these causes springs all diseases and sickness, death, and everlasting damnation; from the which Christ Jesus was sent, of God's inestimable love towards us, to redeem and save us (John 3:16). Notwithstanding, these effects of pestilence, sickness, death, and everlasting damnation cannot be removed, except first the causes of them are shunned.

Therefore you must learn, and teach others to know the causes above–mentioned, and also, how they may be removed; for as long as they work their proper nature in man, so long will they bring forth their natural effects, sickness, troubles, death, and damnation. The original cause of all evil was Satan, and the ungodly consent of our forefather Adam in paradise (Gen. 3), in crediting more the devil's sophistry and gloss than the plain and manifest word of God. And the remedy of this cause is God, that, of love against Satan's hatred, promised in the seed of a woman help again for man; and that every man that believes the devil in evil must repent and believe God and his word is good.

Ignorance and mistaking of God's word Is the second cause of evil; the remedy for this is knowledge and the right understanding of God's word.

Infidelity and being accustomed to doing evil is the third cause of evil; true faith and accustomed doing of good remedies them. Sin and iniquity are the causes of sickness, death, and damnation; virtue and godliness heals and removes them, that they shall not bring man to everlasting death. Although sin and sickness are not cleanly taken from man, yet God in Christ takes away the damnation of sin, and suffers death to destroy by sickness none other thing than the body of the sinner, so that he use this remedy, "Repent, and believe the gospel;" and shall at length call the body, dead by death, out of the earth, and place it alive with the soul in heaven.

But now, to use this help and remedy against the pestilence, which Christ calls, "Repent, and believe the gospel," the sick man must remember what the first word, "Repent," means, and how to come by it.

Repentance that God requires, is the return of the sinner from sin into a new life in Christ; which return is an innovation and renovation of the mind of man by God's Spirit in Christ, with denial of the former life, to begin a new and better life.[9] And this repentance springs from the knowledge of sin by the law of God. From the knowledge of sin comes the hatred of sin. From

---

[9] *Nota bene* -Editor.

the hatred of sin proceeds the leaving and departure from sin. From the departure from sin comes, by faith through Christ's blood, remission of sin. From remission of sin comes our acceptation into God's favor. From our acceptation into God's favor comes the gifts of the Holy Spirit to do and work by a virtuous life the will of God. From doing in Christ the will of God comes God's defense and favor, that takes from us all plagues and pestilence. From the deliverance of plagues and pestilence comes everlasting life, as Christ says, and as this medicine is called, "Repent ye, and believe the gospel," declares.

There are, also, many that are sick and in great danger and peril by reason of sin, and yet feel not the sore and grief of it. Therefore, they do not consider whether they seek for any remedy or not; and, for lack of taking heed, they fall daily to more wickedness than others. Therefore it is every minister's office of the church diligently (and especially in the time of pestilence and plagues) to call upon the people for amendment of life, and to show them truly, diligently, and plainly, this medicine of repentance, which consists of these parts: first, in knowledge of sin; then, in hatred of sin; thirdly, in forsaking of sin; fourthly, in believing the forgiveness of sins for Christ's sake; and fifthly, to live a virtuous and godly life, to honor God, and to show his obedience to God's law, that by sin is transgressed.

And these parts of penance, which are the very true and only medicines against sickness and sin, are known only by God's laws; for by the law of God sin is known, detested, and forsaken. If it is heard or read by men that pray to God, they *may* understand it. Faith also, that believes remission of sin, is showed, opened, and offered by the gospel, in which are contained God's merciful promises towards sinners; and those promises sinners receive by faith, that believe whatever God has promised in Christ he will perform it. Faith credits and receives forgiveness of sins by the operation of God's Holy Spirit in the poor sinner. The sinner studies and lives a virtuous life, being led by the Holy Spirit, and works to serve God with such works as God's holy commandment commands every true Christian man to work and do. And for a better assurance and further establishing of repentance and acceptation into the favor of God by believing the gospel, the poor sinner uses and receives the holy sacrament of Christ's precious body and blood, in remembrance that Christ died to be his medicine against sin, and its effect.

Therefore, now that it pleases God for our offences to show by plagues and sickness how he is offended, let us all, that are ministers of the church, and the watchmen of the people, call upon them diligently to "Repent, and believe the gospel," and to live a godly and virtuous life; that for Christ's sake he will turn mercifully his plagues from us, and give us his most gracious favor to preserve his universal church, our most godly sovereign lord and king, king Edward the Sixth, his majesty's most honorable council, and the whole realm. So be it.

FINIS

A Sermon of the Pestilence
by Lancelot Andrewes

"Thus they provoked him to anger with their inventions: and the plague brake in upon them. Then stood up Phinehas, and executed judgment: and so the plague was stayed," (Psa. 106:29–30).

Here is mention of a plague, of a great plague. For, there died from it twenty-four thousand. And we complain of a plague at this time. The same axe is laid to the root of our trees. Or rather, because an axe is long in cutting down of one tree, the razor is hired for us, and it sweeps away a great number of people at once. Isaiah calls it a scythe (Isaiah 7:20) that mows down grass, a great deal at once.

But here is not only mention of the breaking in of the plague, in the 29th verse, but of the staying or ceasing of the plague, in the 30th.

Now, whatever things were written aforetime, were written for our learning; and so was this text. Under one, to teach us how the plague comes, and how it may be sopped.

The plague is a disease. In every disease, we consider the cause and the cure. Both which are here set forth to us in these two verses. In the former, we find the cause as to how it comes. In the latter, we find the cure of how it may be stopped. To know the cause is expedient; for if we do not know it, our cure will be but palliative, as not being applied in the right way. And if knowing the cause, we must not fail to add the cure, when we are taught it. Who will pity us if we do that? For, none is then to blame, but ourselves.

I. Of the cause first: and then of the cure. The cause is set down to be twofold: 1) God's anger: and 2) their inventions. God's anger, by which, and their inventions, for which, the plague broke in among them.

II. The cure is likewise set down: and it is twofold, out of two significations of one word. The word *Palal* in the verse. Phinehas prayed (some read it), Phinehas executed judgement (some other), and the word bears both meanings. Two then, 1) Phinehas' prayer, and 2) Phinehas' executing judgement; by both of these the plague ceased. His prayer refers to God's anger. His executing judgement, to their inventions. God's wrath was appeased by his prayer. Prayer refers to that. Their inventions were removed by his executing of judgement. The execution of judgement refers to that. If his anger provoked sends the plague, his anger appeased will stop it. If our inventions provoke his anger, punishing of our inventions will appease it. The one works on God, and pacifies him. The other works on our soul, and cures it. For there is a cure of the soul, no less than of the body, as appears by the Psalm, "heal my soul, for I have sinned against thee."

We are to begin with the cause of the plague, in the first verse. And then to come to the cure in the second.

Of the cause. First, that there is a cause. And second, what that cause may be. That there is a cause (that is) that the plague is a thing causal, not casual; comes not merely by *chance*, but has something, some cause that procures it. Surely, if a sparrow does not fall to the ground without the providence of God, of which two are sold for a farthing, much less does any man, or woman, which are more worth than many sparrows fall. And if any one man does not come to his end (as we call it) by casualty, but it is God that delivers him so to die, how much more, then, when not one, but many *thousands* are swept away at once? The Philistines, in their plague, put the matter on trial in both of these ways. 1) Whether it was God's hand; 2) or whether it were but by some chance. And the event showed, it was no casualty, but the very handy work of God on them.

And indeed, the very name of the plague tells us as much. For *Deber* in Hebrew shows, there is a reason, there is a cause, why it comes. And the English word *plague*, comes from the Latin word *plaga*, which is properly *a stroke*, necessarily infers a cause. For where there is a stroke, there must be One that strikes. And in that both it, and other evil things (that come on us) are usually in Scripture called God's *judgements*. If they are judgements, it follows, there is a Judge from which they come. They do not come by adventure, by chance; no. Chance and judgement are utterly opposite. Not casually then, but judicially. We are judged, for when the church is chastened, we are judged of the Lord.

There is a cause. Now, what is that cause? Concerning which, if you ask the physician, he will say, the cause is in the air. The air is infected; the diseases are corrupted. The contagion of the sick, coming to and conversing with a sound person can corrupt them. And they bare all true causes.

The air. For so we see, by casting ashes of the furnace towards heaven in the air, the air became infected, and the plague of botches and blains, was so brought forth in Egypt.

The disease. King David ascribes the cause of his disease, that his moisture in him was corrupt, dried up, turned into the drought of Summer.

The contagion. Which is clear by the Law, where, the leprous person for fear of *contagion* from him, was ordered to cry out, that nobody should come near him. He was to dwell apart from other men. The clothing he had worn was to be washed, and in some cases to be burned. The house–walls he had dwelt in, were to be scraped; and in some cases, the house itself to be pulled down.

In all three respects, Solomon says a wise man fears the plague and departs from it, and fools run on and are careless. A wise man does it, and a good man too. For king David himself did not dare to go to the altar of God at Gibeon, to enquire of God there, because the Angel that struck the people with the plague, stood between him and it. That is, because he was to pass through infected places there.

We acknowledge this to be true, that in all diseases, and even in this also, there is a natural cause. Yet, we say, there is something more, something divine, and above nature in it as well. As some things which the physician must look to in the plague, so also there is something for Phinehas to do, and Phinehas was a priest. And so, there is some work for the priest, as well as for the doctor, and more, then (it may be).

It was King Asa's fault. He in his sickness, looked to all the doctors, and did not look after God at all. That is noted as *his fault.* It seems his conceit was that there was nothing in a disease but something natural, nothing but pertains to the body. But this is not so. For infirmity is not only a bodily thing, but there is a spirit of infirmity as we find in Luke 13:11.[10] And something spiritual is there in all infirmities; something in the soul to be healed. In all infirmities this is true, but especially in this, in which we might know it to be spiritual, that we find it oftentimes to be executed by *spirits.* We see an Angel, a destroying Angel, in the plague of Egypt. There is another in the plague in Sennacherib's camp (Isa. 37:36). There was a third in the plague at Jerusalem under David. There was a fourth, pouring his vial on earth, and there fell a noisome plague on man and beast in Revelation. So that no man looks deeply enough into the cause of his sickness, unless he acknowledges the finger of God in it, over and above any natural causes.

God then has his part. God is in it, but how is this affected? God is provoked to anger. So it is in my text. His anger, his wrath is in it, and it is that which brings the plague among us. The verse is plain, "They provoked him to anger, and the plague brake in among them."

Generally, there is no evil (Job says) but it is a spark of God's wrath. And of all evils, the plague is there by name. There is wrath gone out from the Lord, and the

---

[10] "And, behold, there was a woman which had a spirit of infirmity eighteen years, and was bowed together, and could in no wise lift up herself," (Luke 13:11).

plague is begun (Moses says in Numbers 16:46). It is said, God was displeased with David, and he struck Israel with the plague. So that if there is a plague, God is angry. And if there is a great plague, God is very angry. In this way we see much as to how this takes place. It is because of the anger of God, by which the plague is sent. Now let us consider for what reason.

There is a cause in God, that he is angry. And there is a cause, for which he is angry. For he is not angry without a cause. And what is that cause? For what is God angry? What, is God angry with the waters when he sends a tempest? This is Habakkuk's question. Or is God angry with the earth, when he sends barrenness? Or with the air, when he makes it contagious? No indeed, for his anger is not against the *elements*, because they do not provoke him. It is against those that provoke him to anger; it is against men, against their sins, and for them comes the wrath of God on the children of disobedience.

And this is the very cause indeed. There is the corruption of the soul, and then the corruption of our ways, more than the corrupting of the air. The plague of the heart, more than a plague of a sore, which is seen in the body. The cause of death, that is sin, the same is the cause of this kind of death, of the plague of mortality. And as the Balm of Gilead, and the physician there, may yield us help, when God's wrath is removed, so, if it is not a help, no balm, no medicine will serve us. Let us with the woman in the Gospel, spend all we have on doctors, and yet, we shall never be the better, until we come to Christ, and he cure us of our sins, who is the only Physician of the diseases of the soul.[11]

And with Christ, the cure begins always *within*. For, "Son thy sins be forgiven thee;" and then after, "take up thy bed and walk." His sins are first, and his limbs after. As likewise, when we are once well, Christ's counsel is, "sin no more, lest a worse thing come unto thee," as if sin would certainly bring a relapse into a sickness.

But shall we say, the wrath of God for sins resides indefinitely? That were something too general. May we not specify them, or set them down in particular? Yes, I will point you at three or four.

First, this plague here, as appears by the 28th verse, the verse next before, came for the sin of Peor (that is) for fornication (as you may read.) And not every fornication, but fornication and past shame; as was that of Zamri there, with a daughter of Moab. And indeed, if we mark it well, it fits well. For, that kind of sin (fornication) ends in ulcers and sores; and those as infectious as the plague itself, which is a proper punishment; such sores for such evil.

Secondly, David's plague of seventy thousand (which we mentioned in our prayer) that, came for pride, plainly. His heart was lifted up to number the people. And that seems something kindly too, and to agree with this disease. That pride, which swells itself, should end in a tumor, or swelling; as for the most part this disease does.

---

[11] *Nota bene* -Editor.

Thirdly, Sennacherib's plague (it is plain) came from Rabshake's blasphemy. Blasphemy is able to infect the air, and it was so foul. In this regard, Aaron's act might be justified, in putting odors into his censer, to purify the air from such corruption.

And last, the Apostle sets down the cause of the plague at Corinth. "For this cause," (he says) that is, for neglect of the sacrament. It was either in not caring to come to it, or in coming to it, we do not care how. For this cause, is there a mortality among you, and, "many are sick, and many are weak, and many are fallen asleep." And this is no new thing. Moses himself, his neglect of the sacrament, made him be stricken of God, that it was likely to have cost him his life (Exodus 4:24–25). And he says plainly to Pharaoh, if they neglected their sacrifice, God would fall on them with pestilence. This appears by this, that the sacrament of the Passover, and its blood, was the means to save them from the plague of the destroying Angel in Egypt.

A little now of the phrase that their sins are here called by the name of their inventions. And so sure they are that this was in no way taught to us by God, but of our own imagining or finding out. For indeed, our inventions are the cause of all sin. And if we look well into it we shall find our inventions are so. By God's injunction we should all live, and his injunction is, "You shall not do every man what seems good in his own eyes (*or finds out in his own mind*) but, whatsoever I command you, that only shall you do." But we, setting light by that charge of his, out of the old disease of our father Adam[12] think it a goodly matter to be witty, and to find out things ourselves to make to ourselves, to be authors, and inventors of something, so that we may seem to be as wise as God, if not wiser. And to know what is for our turn, as well as he, if not better. It was Saul's fault. God told him to destroy Amalek and everything, and he would invent a better way to save some for sacrifice, which God could not think of. And it was Peter's fault, when he persuaded Christ from his passion, and found out a better way (as he thought) than Christ could devise.

This is the proud invention, which will not be kept in, but makes men even not to forbear in things pertaining to God's worship; but there, to be still devising new tricks, opinions and fashions, fresh and newly taken up, which their fathers never knew of. And this is that, which makes men that have itching ears, to heap to themselves teachers, according to their own lusts, which may fill their heads full, with new inventions.

And this is that, that even out of religion, in the common life, spoils everything. The reckless invention, in finding out new meats in diet, in inventing new fashions in apparel, which men so love (as the Psalm says at the 39th verse) as they even go *a whoring* with them, with their own inventions, and do not care what they spend on them. They know no end of them. But as fast as they are weary of one, a new invention is found out; which whatsoever it costs, how much it takes from our

---

[12] Eritic sicut Dii, scientes bonum and malum.

alms, or good deeds, must be had, until all come to nothing. That the Psalmist has chosen a very fit word, that for our inventions, the plague breaks in among us, for them, as for the primary, or first moving cause of all. Indeed, for them, as much and more than for anything else.

We see then, 1. first, that there is a cause. 2. That that cause is not only natural, but that God himself having a hand in it. 3. God as being provoked to anger. 4. To anger for our sins in general (and for what sins especially.) For our sins proceeding from nothing, but our inventions. Which cause if it continues, and yet we do not turn to the Lord (as Amos 4 says) then will not his anger be turned away, but his hand will be stretched out still (Isaiah 9) and there is no way to avoid the one, but by appeasing the other.

For the cure now. One contrary is ever cured by another. If then it is anger; which is the cause in God, anger would be appeased. If it is inventions, which is the cause in us, of the anger of God, they would be punished and removed. So that, the cause being taken away, the effect may cease. Take away our inventions, God's anger will cease. Take away God's anger, the plague will cease.[13]

We said there were two readings in the text that are important, 1. Phinehas prayed, or 2. Phinehas executed judgement. *Palal*, the Hebrew word will bear both. And both are good. And so, we will take them both in.

---

[13] *Nota bene* -Editor.

Prayer is good against the plague, as appears not only in this plague in the text, in which all the congregation were weeping, and praying before the door of the tabernacle. But in King David's plague also; where we see what his prayer was, and their very words.

And in Hezekiah's plague, who turned his face to the wall, and prayed to God (and his prayer is set down). God heard his prayer, and healed him. And (for a general rule) if there is in the land any pestilent disease, whatever plague, whatever sickness it is, the prayer and supplication in the Temple made by the people, every man knowing the plague of his own heart, God in heaven will hear it, and remove his hand from afflicting them any further.

And it stands with good reason. For, as the air is infected with noisome scents or smells, so the infection is removed by sweet odors, or incense; which Aaron did in the plague (put sweet odors in his censer, and went between the living and the dead). Now there is a fit resemblance between incense and prayers. *Let my prayer come before your presence, as the incense.* And when the Priest was within, burning incense, the people were without at their prayers. And it is expressly said, that the sweet odors were nothing else but the prayers of the saints (Rev. 5:8).

Prayer is good, and that Phinehas' prayer was good indeed. Phinehas was a priest, the son of Eleazar, the nephew of Aaron. So as, there is virtue, as in the prayer, so also in the person that prayed; which was in Phinehas himself.

As we know the office of a policeman being able to arrest; the office of a notary to make acts; the act that is done by one of them, is much more authentic, then that which is done by any common person. So every priest being taken from among men, and ordained for men, in things pertaining to God, that he may offer prayers. The prayers he offers, he offers out of his office, and so even in that respect there is (*caeteris paribus*) a greater force, and energy in them, as coming from him whose calling it is to offer them. This is more than in those that come from another, whose calling it is not so to do.

To this end, God says to Abimelech, Abraham is a Prophet, and "he shall pray for thee, and thou shalt live." So that the prayer of a prophet, in that he is a prophet, is more effectual.

And in the Law, you shall find it all along, when men come to bring their sacrifice for their sins, it is said, the Priest shall make an atonement for them before the Lord, and their sins shall be forgiven them.

And in the prophets we see plainly, in time of distress, Hezekiah sent to the prophet Isaiah, to entreat him to lift up his prayer for the remnant that were left; and so he did, and was heard by God.

And in the new Testament, James' advice is, "In time of sickness to call for the elders," and they to pray over the party, and that prayer shall work his health; and if he "have committed sins, they shall be forgiven him." For where the grace of prayer is, and the calling both, they cannot but avail more, than where no calling is, but the grace alone.

The prayer of Phinehas, and of Phinehas' standing is to be considered. What need is there to have any mention of Phinehas' standing? Was it not enough to say "Phinehas prayed?" Does it matter whether he sat or stood; for praying itself was enough.

No, we must not think the Holy Spirit sets down anything that is superfluous. There is something there in that he *stood*. Of Moses it is said before in this Psalm, that he stood in the gap to turn away the wrath of God. In Jeremiah it is said, "Moses and Samuel stood before me." So, there is mention made of standing also. And the prophet himself puts God in mind, that he *stood* before him, to speak good for the people, and to turn away his wrath from them (that is) put God in mind of the very sight of his body.

For, though God is a spirit, and so in spirit to be worshipped, yet in as much as he has given us a body, with that also are we to worship him, and to glorify him in our body and spirit, which both are God's. We are to present (or offer) our bodies to God, as a holy and acceptable sacrifice, in the reasonable service of him (Rom. 12:1). And we are to present them decently. For that also is required in the service of God. Now judge in yourselves, is it comely to speak to our superiors, sitting? *Sedentem or are, extra disciplinam est* (Tertullian says) to pray sitting, or sit praying, is against the order of the church. The church of God never had, nor has any such fashion.

All tends to this, as Cyprian's advice is, *Etiam habitu corporis placere Deo*, even by our very gesture, and the carriage of our body, to behave ourselves so, as with it we may please God. Unreverent, careless, undevout behavior does not please him.

It is noted of the very angels, (Job 1:6; Isaiah 6:2; Dan. 7:10), that they were standing before God. If it becomes them to stand, if Phinehas, if Moses, if Samuel, and Jeremiah stand, it may well become us to learn our gesture from them.

Prayer is available to appease God's wrath, and so consequently to remove the plague, but not prayer alone. For though it abates the anger of God (which is the first) yet it does not go high enough, and does not take away the second cause (that is) our inventions, which are the cause of God's anger. We see it plainly in Num. 25:6, they were all at prayers, and Phinehas among them, he and the rest. But yet the plague did not cease for all that. It was not until (in the verse following) Phinehas took his javelin, by which in the very act of fornication, he thrust them both through, Zamri and his woman, and then the plague was stopped from the children of Israel. For, as prayer refers properly to anger, so executing judgement does to sin, or to our inventions as the cause of it.

Prayer then does well, but prayer and doing justice, both these together (jointly) will do it indeed. And if you disjoin or separate them, nothing will be done. If we draw near to God with our mouths, and honor him with our lips, it will not avail us, if judgement is turned back, or justice stands afar off.

There are two people. Both of them were in Phinehas. For, as he was a priest, so he was a prince of his tribe. So then, both of these must join together, as well the devotion of the priest in prayer, which is his office. This is as the zeal of the Magistrate in executing judgement, which is his. For, Phinehas the Priest, must not only stand up, and pray, but Moses (the Magistrate also) must stand in the gap to turn away the wrath of God, that he would not destroy the people. No less he, than Aaron with his golden censer, to run into the midst of the congregation, to make atonement for them when the plague is begun.

Moses gave a charge for executing them, that were joined to Baal–Peor, (Num. 25:4). Phinehas executed the charge. Moses stood in the gap, when he gave the sentence. Phinehas stood up, when he did the execution. And these two are a blessed conjunction. One of them without the other, may miss; but both together never fail. For when Zamri was slain, and so when Rabshaketh perished, and so when the incestuous Corinthian was excommunicated; in all three, the plague ceased.

But what if Moses gives no charge? What if Phinehas does not execute anything, as often as it falls out? What will happen then? In that case, every private man is to be Phinehas to himself; is not only to pray to God, but to be wrecked, do judgement, chasten his own body; and so judge himself, that he may not be judged of the Lord. For every one, for his part, is a cause of the judgements of God sent down; and so may be, and is to be, a cause of the removing them. David as king was in sin, by the pride of his heart. Other people, by their murmuring against Moses and Aaron, were in sin. So that, king and people *both*, must judge themselves, every private offender, himself.[14] Zamri, if he had judged himself, Phinehas should not have judged him. The incestuous Corinthian, if he had judged himself, Paul would had not judged him. For, either by ourselves, or by the Magistrate; or if by neither of both, by God himself. For, one way or other sin must be judged. Zamri, by his repentance; Phinehas, by his prayer, or doing justice; or *God by the plague sent among them.*

Now then, these two; 1. Phinehas stood up and prayed, 2. And Phinehas stood up and executed judgement, if they might be coupled together, I dare undertake, the conclusion would be, and the plague would be ceased. But if either of them are lacking, I dare promise nothing.

To conclude then. 1. The plague comes not by chance, but has a cause. 2. That cause is not altogether natural, and pertains to the physical; but has something supernatural in it, and pertains to divinity. 3. That supernatural cause is the wrath of God. 4. Which yet is not the first cause. For, the wrath of God, would not rise, but that he is provoked by our sins (and the certain sins, that provoke it, have been set down.) 5. And their cause, is our own inventions. So, our inventions beget sin; sin provokes the wrath of God; the wrath of God sends the plague among us. To stop the plague, God's wrath must be stopped. To stop it, there must be a ceasing from sin. That sin may cease, we must be out of love with our own inventions, and not go a–whoring after them. Prayer, that assuages anger. To execute justice, that abhors sin.

---

[14] *Nota bene* -Editor.

To execute justice, either publicly, as the Magistrate does; or privately, as every man does, or may do on himself, which joined with prayer, and prayer with it, will soon rid us of that which we complain about; and otherwise, his anger will not be turned away, but his hand stretched out still.

FINIS.

London's Lamentation for Her Sins and A Medicine Against the Plague

by William Crashaw

"O thou sword of the LORD, how long will it be ere thou be quiet? put up thyself into thy scabbard, rest, and be still. How can it be quiet, seeing the LORD hath given it a charge against Ashkelon, and against the sea shore? there hath he appointed it," (Jer. 47:6–7).

TO THE RIGHT HONORABLE, THE LORD MAYOR OF LONDON, THE RIGHT WORSHIPFUL THE SHERIFFS AND ALDERMEN, AND THE REST OF THE GODLY CITIZENS AND OFFIERS, WHO HAVE EITHER STAYED IN THEIR PLACES AND DUTIES DURING THIS VISITATION: OR SENT THEIR LARGE AND COMFORTABLE BENEVOLENCE FOR THE POOR. THE BLESSINGS OF THIS AND A BETTER LIFE.

RIGHT HONORABLE:

It was the ordinance and appointment of God's own wisdom in the Law, that all his sacrifices and burnt offerings should be seasoned with salt, the fire importing zeal, by which every sacrifice must be offered, and the salt signifying discretion with which it must be seasoned. If it lacked either of these, it could not be accepted. Now, as this literal fire and salt belonged to the Jews, so the Spiritual is both commended and commanded to us, that live under the sweet yoke of the Gospel even to the world's end. Namely, that all our sacrifices and service, if we mean to have them acceptable to God, or available to ourselves, must not only be offered with the fire of holy zeal, but tempered with holy wisdom, and seasoned with the salt of due discretion. Therefore, Christ says even in his Gospel, "every one shall be salted with fire, and every sacrifice shall be seasoned with salt," (Mark 9:49). Where Paul alluding to this exhorts all Christians to see that their service and sacrifice, are not only holy and lively, but also reasonable.

It is here right Honorable, and Worshipful, that as our gracious King, out of his humility and holy zeal, commanded public fasting and prayer, for the diverting of this public judgement. So now, out of holy and deep discretion has suspended for a time those public meetings within the city. This was done not out of any dislike of fasting and prayer, nor any weariness of those holy exercises, as some malignant spirits maliciously traduce him. But out of conscience to his God and care of his subjects lives, wisely considering (and in our knowledge most truly) that seeing the sick and sore (do what we ministers could to the contrary) mingled themselves confusedly, with the sound (by which means it's more than manifest, many thousands have perished in this city and suburbs). It therefore lays on him as Supreme Magistrate and God's lieutenant to look to the lives as well as to the souls of all his people, and to take order, that the fasts ordained for the bettering of the soul, should not so be used, as to tend to the destruction of the body. Leaving us therefore in this distressed city, the Lord's Day or Sunday for our souls, which being of divine institution, can admit no dispensation by human power, and still commending and commanding us that *day* to fast and pray in private, and all the kingdom to do this for us. And also for saving our lives, and to avoid the tempting and provoking of God. He has wisely forbidden all other public meetings of dangerous concourse in places infected, until order can be taken (which is no easy thing to do) to keep the sound and sick apart.

Now as all those that are well are notwithstanding to repair to the church, to be partakers of the public prayers and the holy service appointed for that day, so, for a help, of humiliation and holy devotion to them that stay at home, of which also many thousand families especially in our suburbs are not able to buy the Book of God, I have therefore been persuaded to make public this meditation, confession, and prayer, which in these days of public calamity, I walking hourly through the valley of the shadow of death, (burying forty, fifty, sometime sixty a day, and in the total, more than two thousand already) I poured out in the presence of my God. First, in private for myself, afterwards for the use of those many thousand sick souls that are or have been in my great poor church. And lastly, that by this I might offer some sacrifice and special piece of service in way of holy thankfulness to the Lord our God, who has here pleased to preserve me, and my brethren the pastors of this city by his own hand and power, beyond all human help and hope. This even while we walk continually, even in the midst of the fiery flames always in danger, and never in more peril than in the pulpit. In this the Lord has been so marvelous, and so magnified, his love and power on us, as if he should now take us away, yet he has so delivered us, in discharging our duties, and by his holy angels kept us, in this way being in our way, until he has literally made good that promise in the Psalm, yes, and much more. For, alas, we have not only seen a thousand fall at one side of us, and ten thousand at another, but (alas, alas, that our sins should so provoke our God) even more then ten thousand on the one, and more then twenty thousand on the other. Which mighty work of God, if we should sit still and swallow and superficially pass over, and not commend it to our brethren in the country, whose turns must follow, God knows how soon, as sure as God has begun with us. And if we did not preserve its memory, and represent it to posterity, for their instruction, and that the generations yet unborn may praise the Lord, all holy men would accuse us, God's church would censure us, our own consciences would condemn us, and God himself take vengeance on us, as most unthankful caitiffs, even monsters of mankind, and unworthy to breathe on the earth.

Being, therefore, in some sort touched with the sense of this hand of our God, both of his hand of justice and of mercy, and being every moment put in mind of our mortality, either by the sound in our ears, or sights in our eyes; can we but be moved (unless we were senseless stocks and Stoics) to take into our serious and continual consideration, the now most lamentable case, of this late so flourishing city, and of this whole kingdom into which this wild–fire of God's wrath begins so fast to fly, and can we but lay to heart so great a sorrow? Or do we dare for our souls but deal truly with our God, in seeking sincerely and carefully searching out the true cause in ourselves, in our people, and in the whole kingdom that should in this way provoke the Lord against us? Certainly some heavy judgement must fall on us if we do not, and will follow them whoever they are that double and dissemble with their God in this case.

And if any that are abroad and yet unvisited, think I deal too far and too freely in this confession, I ask no more but to forbear his judgment until they are under the hand of God, as we have been now three months and more, and then they will judge I am too short. While God in mercy pardons that, and in which I may be thought to go too far, I shall easily answer it to God or God's anointed. I shall sigh and sob in secret to consider the wrath and woes that wait for those wicked ones, who as they deeply have had their hand in pulling down this plague, so carelessly seek to pass it over, and do not look after the God that has struck them, and the whole land for their sakes. And if they will not turn in these times, he will strike them down to hell. What stony hearted Stoic can he be who sees more than forty thousand Christians, many as good, and some better then himself laid in the dust, in little more than twice forty days, and is not humbled under the hand that did it, and sensible of the sin that procured it? Can he be a good servant of God or subject to his sovereign, that besides ten thousand aged, weak, and poor, shall see an army of ten thousand more, brave and serviceable young men, and ten thousand more comely and marriageable young women, and ten thousand more young infants, whose proof and hope had been still before them, already taken out of one corner of this Kingdom, and then not sit down in dust and ashes mourning to that God that took them, for that King that lost them, with that land that lacks them. For that sin that plucked them from us? I dare pronounce on him from God whoever he is that can or dare in this way slightly and slyly pass by the works of God, and laughs in his sleeve at such a judgement as this. Such a person is marked up by God for some greater vengeance as sure as the fourteenth of Ezekiel is God's true word. For if he that mourns for sin is the man that is marked by God for blessing and deliverance, what's he that makes a *sport* of sin; and lays from his heart the judgements by it procured. He is one that is sealed up for confusion and destruction.[15]

O therefore that my heart were a fountain, and my eyes rivers of tears, that I might worthily bewail the sins of our Nation together with my own, and weep for the slain of the daughter of my people. So cried the holy prophet of the abundance of his holy zeal; and so I am sure in their several measures do all the ministers and men of God among us, that have but tasted of the same spirit, mourning for the desolations of this city; and more for the contagion that causes it, and most of all, for

---

[15] *Nota bene* -Editor.

the sins that procured them both. And who would not care to sacrifice themselves whatever way the Lord should please, so the wrath of God might be pacified towards this church and nation, and those plagues removed which are the cause of this plague? And until these are removed, we shall find the prophets tell us what is true, that either this plague shall still stay and creep like a canker over our whole body, or else only make way to some more fearful thing that shall follow after it.

That this may be prevented, he cannot be a Christian that will not both cry to God, and confess to him the public, and private, and personal sins that are the cause thereof. And as all that are enabled and taught by the Holy Spirit of God; to pour out their souls in humble prayer, and hearty confession, will in holy obedience to the holy prophet's counsel, take "unto themselves words, and return unto the Lord." So, for those that cannot open their mouths as they desire, and yet have hearts that groan after God, and souls that seek the Lord. For only their assistance have I been persuaded to publish this, which now I leave to them, and them and it together, with ourselves to the merciful acceptation and gracious blessing of our good God. May God grant us all in these days of danger (when sometimes almost a thousand a day are picked up, and plucked away before our faces), so to live and so to dye, as when we dye we may be sure to live forever. And so, we will part with one another here, as we may be sure to meet in heaven, and here so to confess our sins, as at the last day Christ may confess us to be his own. Let us pray here as we may praise God eternally in heaven.

A PRAYER,
LONDON'S LAMENTABLE COMPLAINT

Most high and holy Jehovah, you are the Being of beings, who gives life and being to every creature, give leave to us, the most unworthy ones of all your children, to come before you, and present our petitions at the Throne of Grace. We do not dare to rush so rudely into your holy presence, mighty Lord God, nor beg so boldly so great a Savior, were it not that you have graciously promised, not only to call and invite us, but even command us to come to you, and call on you in the day of our affliction. You have moreover mercifully promised, that you will hear us and deliver us, that we may glorify your great name.

In this confidence we take comfort, to come to You O Lord, in this day of our trouble, and common calamity of our church and kingdom. And first we do all, in the name one of another, and we for our parts, every one of us for himself, humbly and freely, we have all had our hands in this blood, and each one borne apart, in pulling down these heavy plagues on this city and our Nation. O Lord none of us excuse ourselves, but we do every one of us accuse, and arraign ourselves at the bar of your justice, and we all pronounce ourselves guilty in your sight. Nor are we only tainted with original sin in our natures, but Lord our lives are stained, with all actual pollutions, in our thoughts, words, and deeds, by sins of commission and omission, by sins not only of ignorance, but even of negligence, carelessness and presumption. Miserable sinners that we are, we have not only committed foul and fearful things, abominable to your pure and holy majesty, dishonorable to your holy religion, offensive to your holy Law, and therefore just provocations of your wrath. But alas, we have sometime totally omitted, and at the best always failed in all the good and holy duties required at our hands. We have not been humbled for your judgments, nor thankful for your mercies, as we ought to have been, therefore your mercies being abused, we have here made way for your judgments, but we are wicked wretches that have been bettered by neither of both. You have written to us the great things of your Law, but we have not regarded them. You have revealed to us your blessed Gospel, but we have not believed it. You have honored us with your love, but we have not walked worthy of it. You have afforded us blessed means and many opportunities to do good, and by well doing to come nearer to you, but we have, either so neglected them, or abused them, as by them we have done much evil instead of good. You have also given us time to turn and repent, but we have turned it the wrong way, and misspent it in vanities. You have showed us the way, and offered us the means to know and fear you, but we have willfully wandered in our own ways, and have not cared to come near you, and have put your fear far from us. Such sinful caitiffs are we O Lord, as the means of your honor, we have turned to your dishonor, our own helps into hinderances, our comforts into crosses, and our crosses into curses, your mercies into judgments, and your visitations into vengeance. And the gracious blessings that were given us, as helps to bring us nearer to you. We have perverted these things, to drive us further from you. Your heavenly word, and holy Sacraments, which you have graciously given us, (more then to many other Nations) to be the means of our conversion, and salvation, we have profaned and perverted, to our hardening in sin, and aggravating our condemnation.

These, O Lord, are the common and general sins of our times, of us, our city, and our Nation, which as an universal deluge running over our Land, we also have been carried away by the violence of these sinful streams, besides the personal sins prevailing in this age, as bane swearing, inordinate drinking, superfluous feastings, profuseness in gaming, vanity and pride in apparel, oppressions and frauds in bargaining, profaning your Sabbaths, neglect of your poor members, contempt of your word and holy ministers, formality in religion, dullness in devotion, and coldness in charity.

In all these O Lord and every one of them, we are not able to excuse, much less exempt ourselves, besides also the public sins of our state, in letting our laws be laid asleep against idolatry and superstition, by which much Popish impiety has not only been practiced in private, but so publicly professed, that even the idolatrous Dagon did stand in defiance with your holy ark, by which your religion has been vilified, your ordinances despised, your great name dishonored, and your sanctuary trodden under foot. Nor was this the sin alone of some set over us, who by their places, ought rather to have defended your truth and maintained the integrity of it with their lives and blood, and yet either wickedly, or weakly have given way to these enormities, by which Popery and idolatry, were in a sort invited and prepared for, before they came. But in this sin, like the sin of Jeroboam, all our Israel has sinned against the Lord of Hosts, for alas we have all either held our hands, or held our tongues, and not been zealous in the cause of you our God. And when for this our profaneness and presumptions against you, you have declared yourself angry against us, both at home, and abroad, we have been so far from fearing you, and seeking your face, in prayer, and fasting, and holy humiliation in true contrition, and hearty repentance. As contrariwise when other Nations were sighing, and sorrowing for our sin and security, we were lulled asleep, and cried *peace, peace*, when there was none. And when other churches were fasting and praying, we alas were masking, feasting and playing. And when as your Gospel had glutted us, so as holy lectures, begun to be now held, like meat out of season, and preaching in some places to be put down, yet even then O Lord, were the theaters magnified, and enlarged, where Satan is served and sin secretly instilled, if not openly professed.

In this way have you O mighty God been little better then forgotten among us these many years. And in this way has your glorious name been dishonored, your precious religion vilified, your gracious ordinances despised, your fearful judgments neglected, your bounteous mercies abused, your holy councils condemned, your Fatherly warnings not regarded, and your sacred Word thrown away, and ceremony advanced, but indeed and truth trodden under foot. It is true O Lord, we thought and spoke otherwise of ourselves while our plenty pleased us, our prosperity bewitched us, and worldly carnalities blinded us. Then we seemed to ourselves to be a glorious Nation, a beautiful church and outwardly appeared to be a people that did righteousness, and forsook not the ordinances of their God. But now that affliction has made us wiser, and your corrections have opened our eyes, now we see what we are, and are ashamed of ourselves. Now we cast the dust of contempt on our own heads, we go out of ourselves, and we cry to you in the hearing of your holy angels, and all your holy churches on earth, we are unclean, we are unclean. And like unclean and loathsome leapers deserve to be cut off from the blessed body of your church, may even to be rooted out of the land of the living, as being the Nation, next to the Jews, who having been honored, and blessed by you, above all the world, have most dishonored you of all others, playing with your mercies, dallying with your judgments, and profaning all your holy things, not considering we are no better than the fly playing with the candle, we in our sins being flax and stubble, and you our God in your fury a consuming fire.

Therefore, it is O Lord, that now your mercies are gone aside, and given place to your justice, and your justice provoked has kindled your wrath and the fire of your wrath being now broke out in the most fearful pestilence this Nation ever saw. Now our beauty is turned into ashes, our melody into mourning, our songs into howlings, our glory into confusion of face, our triumphs into tears, and our flourishing city into a wilderness, there being now at our doors nothing but death, destruction, and desolation, nothing but misery and mourning, crying and confusion in our streets. This is our present estate O Lord, and it is your doing, and only in this are we happy that we see your hand, and know, and believe it to be your doing. And we all confess O Lord, righteous are you in all your ways, and most just are all your judgments. For seeing we all offended you, therefore, now, you make us to one offend one another; And because we did not fear you, you have now justly made us afraid one of another. And because we wickedly and carelessly misspent our time, now you have made us weary of our time, and brought to pass that which you did threaten, that in the morning we wish it were evening, and in the evening that the morning would appear and as though we were either weary of our time, or afraid of the air, we breath in and we vainly wish, the long desired Summer, would now fly fast away, and turn us over, to the cold and careful winter. And because we poisoned all things by our sins now you justly make us fear poison, in our very meat, drink, and apparel. No, but for your special mercy, we are not safe in our pews, and pulpits in our church. And because we did not delight to come to your house, now you make us glad to fly from our own houses. And because we cared not to come to your house for the food of our souls, you have justly brought it to this, that we do not know where to go, nor to what house safely to send for the food of our bodies.

And because we have wickedly set our hearts, on the miserable mammon of this world, you have now in justice made a great number at their minds and, not knowing what to do with it, where to hide it, with whom to leave it, nor whom to trust with it, neither can they carry it with them, nor dare they tarry with it themselves, and because they would lend nothing in charity, they have now none left, to lend to at all. And now they that love it best, (by your wonderful judgment) are afraid to touch it, lest that which formerly poisoned their souls, should now infect their bodies. O Lord how wonderful are your works, and how just are all your judgments.

And now, O Lord, that we see our case, and are sensible of your hand that is on us, what shall we say, what shall we think might be the cause of this so fearful a plague? And that so merciful and pitiful a Father, is now become so severe and angry a Judge? Shall we be so foolish as to think it comes because our king is not crowned, as though former experience has not proclaimed the contrary? Or so profane as to ascribe it to the Summer, and season of the year, as though you were not God as well of the winter as the summer? Or so proud as to think that because we have here held up your religion, better than some other nations, and have in some measure maintained the preaching of your word, and have been a sanctuary and refuge, for some distressed Christians of other countries, we may therefore with the hypocritical Jews trust to our external profession, and cry, "The Temple of the Lord, The Temple of the Lord," as though you had need of any nation to keep up the credit of your cause? Or so presumptuous, as to think that because you have taken us to be your church, and some of your children are among us, you cannot therefore be angry with us? Or because we have done some good, we may be therefore more bold? Or because there are some holy lots among us, therefore our Sodom cannot be consumed? O, Lord, all these are the broken staves of Egypt, these cannot comfort us in this our calamity. These will not uphold us in this day of our distress, and this hour of temptation, that you have brought on us. No, Lord, all these and all other like to these, are either lies or vanities. And your holy Prophet has told us, and we believe it, that those who trust to lying vanities forsake their own mercies. Therefore, O Lord, we renounce, for those our idle and idol conceits have spoken vanity, our diviners have seen a lie, and have told false dreams. O, Lord, they comfort us in vain. For contrariwise your Word has taught us, your Spirit informs us, and now our own consciences tell us, that our own ways and doings have procured this on us, and none but ourselves, and nothing but our sins have pulled down this plague, and that we have forsaken you the Lord our God, who did lead us the right way, but with your people Israel, we have committed two evils, we have forsaken you, the Fountain of Living Waters, and have hewed ourselves broken cisterns that can hold no water. In this way have we requited you, the Lord our God, being a foolish people and unkind, therefore now our own wickedness both correct us, and our backslidings do reprove us, and have made us know, and see, and feel; how evil and bitter a thing it is that we have forsaken you the Lord our God, and that your fear was not in us.

And now, O Lord, that we see our case, and see also the cause of it, now what shall we do for remedy, where shall we seek relief, where shall we go, to whom shall we fly, but even from you to you, even from your deserved anger, to your undeserved mercy? For destruction is from ourselves, but salvation is of you, O Lord, and you are he that can both wound and heal, both kill and make alive. None but you could have laid this on us, none but you can remove it from us. To you therefore do we lift up our eyes, O you that dwell in the heavens, and do implore you to help us in this distress, for vain is the help of man, and though our sins plead against us, and make you for a time keep back your comfort from us, yet our eyes shall wait on the Lord our God until he has mercy on us. For whatever we are, you are *the Lord that does not change*, for else your children should be all consumed. We therefore take comfort, and say one to another, *Come let us return to the Lord, for he has torn us, he will heal us. He has smitten, and he will bind us up, after two days he will revive us, in the third day he will raise us up, and we shall live in his sight.* For are you not he in whom our Fathers trusted and were delivered? Are you not the God that brought your people through the raging sea, and through the barren wilderness into the land of peace and plenty? Are you not he that saved your servants in the fiery oven, in the lion's den, and in the whale's belly? And is there not mercy with you, else there should not be left a man on the earth to fear you? And is not your mercy everlasting, and endures to all generations? And though we are cast into the last ends of the world, and many fear that the store-house of your mercies is exhausted and spent, yet have not you taught us twenty times in one Psalm, that your *mercy endures forever?* And in that mercy, have you not made a *covenant of peace*, pardon, and reconciliation with the sons of men? And have you not sealed that covenant, and made it firm in the blood of your blessed Son? And have you not proclaimed yourself to be the God that keeps covenant and mercy to a thousand generations? Seeing then you have promised to take us and make us your people, and to receive us into your holy covenant, and have pleased to place your holy tabernacle among us, and honored us with your holy word and sacraments, and have among us hundreds and thousands whom you have separated from the sinful mass of mankind, and sanctified, and sealed for yourself, so as they run not riot with the wicked world, but wait on you in the holy ways of your ordinances, judgments, and mercies, and lay to heart your words and warnings, and mourn in Zion for the affliction of Joseph, and for their own, and the sins of others, and for the iniquities of the time.

Therefore, our faith bids us believe, and the truth and certainty of your covenant causes us to hope, that you will chastise us to our correction, but not plague us to destruction. And in this confidence we come to you, you Father of mercies, and are bold to implore you to call to mind your covenant, by which you have bound yourself, to be our God, and to take us to be your people, and never to forsake us (although by our sins we have forsaken you) as long as by faith we cleave to you, and in repentance and humility do seek your face. And in the virtue and merit of that blessed blood of your holy Son, which he has shed for us, and all believers, we take boldness to ourselves, to challenge at your hands the performance of those sweet promises, you have made to us, and sealed in his shed blood..

And first we beg at the hands of your holy Majesty (even rather than our lives, or deliverances from this dreadful plague) peace and pardon to our poor souls, and assurance of your love in Christ, for our eternal happiness, and then we implore you not so much to deliver our bodies from this plague, as to save our souls from sin which is the plague of all plagues, and the true cause of this plague, therefore we cry and pray with your holy prophet, Lord *have mercy on us, and heal our souls, which have sinned against you.* Then we implore you, you are a God of compassion, look in mercy on this land, do not make us like Sodom, Gomorrah, as we have deserved, we confess, we are under your hand, and all the world could not have laid this on us, but only you, O Lord. And it was time for You O Lord, to lay to your hand, for we had almost made void your Law. You have therefore justly taken us under your hand, and because your gentle warnings were despised, your holy counsels condemned, your judgments neglected, and your mercies abused, you have therefore justly given way to your wrath, and let loose your heavy judgments on our land. Yet this is our comfort, and man, nor devil can take it from us, that we are in your hand, O Lord, and with you is mercy. And as we bless your name, that you have not given us over into the cruel hands of merciless men, the wicked bloody Papists, so in this, our souls take comfort, that we are under the hand of our heavenly Father, whose mercies are great. And in the multitude of those your mercies, we look up to you, O Lord, and implore you, be merciful to this Land. You are our Father, and we have foully offended, therefore you must necessarily correct us, or else you would not love us, and punish us also, or else you would not be just. Correct therefore Lord, and do not spare, but yet in your judgment, not in your fury, lest we be all consumed. And forasmuch, as corrections are to work out not only humiliation, but reformation also, we do not beg the removing of your judgment, until it has wrought your work, and not only brought us down under your hand, but even purged our hearts, and renewed the face of our church and commonwealth. And seeing until then, O Lord, we neither may expect, nor dare desire you should remove it, we implore you to prepare us all to be both willing and ready to meet you our God, and now to be content, you glorify yourself in us, and on us by life or death, so you save our souls. But when it has accomplished your work, and finished that for which you did send it on us, then, O Lord, in mercy remove it from us. And prevent the other grievous plagues that must necessarily follow on, and after this.

And howsoever your just and long forborne decree is now gone out against us, so as yet our cries and tears do not move you, no, the prayers of our prophets do not prevail with you, insomuch as those Noah's, Daniel's and Job's, that are among us, are only able to deliver themselves (and scarcely at that, O Lord, so great is the contagion of our sins) yet we implore you give us leave to take comfort, in believing your own word, and trusting to that which no mortal creature, no human assurance, but your own holy self has told and taught us. Even that in wrath you remember mercy, and that you do not keep anger forever, but that your mercies endure forever. And that you have not only betrothed us to yourself in faithfulness and truth, but even married yourself to us, and though we wickedly, in our spiritual idolatries, and other sinful courses, cut off ourselves from you, and whorishly given ourselves to others. Yet most mercifully have you called on us, to return again to you, and you will receive us. But miserable contemptable people that we are, we cannot turn to you, we could of ourselves fall away from you, but of ourselves, we cannot return home to you. Cause us therefore to return, O Lord, and seeing you so love us, as you will not leave us, we implore you also to not loose us, nor suffer us good Lord to loose ourselves, but renew our hearts towards you, and cause us to cry and mourn after you, and say with Ephraim, *turn you us and we shall be turned, convert us, and we shall be converted,* you are the Lord our God. And bring us back again, O Lord, the right and holy way.

First, make our faces ashamed of our backslidings, and our souls more grieved for the same, then for the plague that is on us. Then make us seek you sincerely, and not slavishly, and out of love more than fear, and make us turn unfeignedly and with the whole heart. And let us not come, with sorrow only in our hearts, but holy words also in our mouths, and take to ourselves the words that you have taught us, and say to you, take away all iniquity, and receive us graciously, so will we render the fruit of our lips.

And that our preparations are not in vain, let us, whet and sharpen them by wisdom; nor let us bring the bare words, but let our humiliation be accompanied with works of mercy, piety, pity and compassion. And that the humiliation of us both prince and people, may be both more acceptable to them and available to us, stir up the holy heart of our holy Phineas, your servant and our Sovereign, that he may stand up in the zeal of his God, and execute your just judgment on the Zimries, and Cozbies, that be among us, even the great sins, and bold sinners of this nation, that then, as your word has told us, your plague may be stopped. To which end also make those who are like Moses among us, to stand in the gap, and those like Aaron, with their holy sweet incense, to stand between the living and the dead, and stir up our priests, the ministers of the Lord, to weep for us before your altar, and let them cry and say, "spare your people, O Lord, and do not give over your heritage to reproach." Let not the Papists and schismatics insult over us; let them not say at their idolatrous meetings, nor profane conventicles, "Where is now their God?" for you are our God, and you are in heaven, and you do what you please, and all your ways are right, and the just walk in them, but transgressors shall fall therein. Let them know, O Lord, that you being our Father, and we having justly provoked you, you will take your children in hand, and that they ought not to have rejoiced over us, in the day of our destruction. O suffer them not good Lord, to make your correction, their advantage. O let them not lay their hands on our substance, in this day of our calamity, suffer them not to stand in the crossways, to cut off those whom you shall spare, and make a prey of those that shall remain. We shall ever acknowledge, no matter how great this plague is, yet your mercies are greater, in that you took us into your own hand to correct us, and gave us not over into the hands, of these men the Jesuited Papists, whose mercies are cruel, and their cruelties insatiable. Therefore good Lord, when you have removed your hand, let us not fall into their hand, but save us for yourself, and let us live to call on your name, and let us desire rather now to die under the hand of our Father, and in your fear and love, then to live to heap sin on sin, and to be reserved for further vengeance, or to be exposed to the cruel Papists the wicked enemies of religion. O look on us in mercy Lord, who lie down in the dust of desolation, and are covered with confusion of our faces, O look down on us, who look up to you, and who desire to rend our hearts though not our garments, and to turn to you the Lord our God, O look on this desolate, and distressed city, who now may cry to all her stately sisters the cities of Europe, and to all her beautiful daughters, the cities of England, and with ashes now on her head, instead of her stately and costly crown calls on them all and says, "Come and behold the works of the Lord what desolations he has made in the midst of my most wealthy and populous streets, learn by me, and seek the Lord while he may be found," lest he pull down your pride. And rejoice not over me, O you mine enemy, you daughter of Babylon, lest the Lord turn his wrath from me to you, and hasten the vengeance, so long now deserved by you, and pronounced on you; trust you in your horses and in your chariots, your idols and your idle superstitions. We will remember the Lord our God, for your name, O Lord, is a strong tower, and the righteous flying to it, are always helped. You have spoken it Lord, and we believe it, and in that belief are we bold to press to you, no, to press you with performance of your promise. Therefore, O you that are the helper of the friendless, help us in this city, who are forsaken by so many friends, and left destitute by them, that should have stood to us in this day of our desolation, but have not you told us, that if our fathers and mothers should forsake us, yet you Lord will take us up. You therefore who sees our friends fail us and our acquaintances to stand afar off, stand you so much the nearer us, O Lord our God. And now that human helps fall short, help you us O God of our salvation for the glory of your name. O you in whom the fatherless finds mercy, in you let the comfortless find comfort, in you let this desolate city find consolation.

Look mercifully on us who come to you, with tears in our eyes, sorrow in our souls, lamentations in our mouths, heaviness in our hearts, works of mercy in our hands, and humiliation of the whole man. And you that do not loose a tear, do not forget one desire, but hear every groan, and counts the very sighs and sobs of all your saints, give us comfort, and fill our hearts with hopes, that this humiliation of our king and his people shall not be fruitless, but after it is not barely performed but accomplished, and perfected, as you appoint it shall then prevail with you our God, not only to make an end of our miseries, but to remember and renew your covenant with us, and to bring us and this city, and our whole land, both court and kingdom nearer to you, and having in this fire of affliction consumed our corruption, and purged away our dross both in church and common–wealth, will make us come out new creatures, both high and low, both public and private persons, pure as silver, and as gold most precious before you. And by this work out that inward renovation, and that outward reformation, in our church and state, in our court and kingdom, and all that see it shall say, "this has God done," for they shall all perceive it is your work. Then we that which did sow in tears, shall reap in joy. Then the long night of our sorrow being ended, the long-desired morning of our joys shall shine forth. *The voice of the turtle shall be heard in our land,* blessed shall then they all be that come to us in the name of the Lord. And beautiful are the feet of those, that bring us the glad tidings of the Gospel, whose faces formerly have been condemned, old things shall then be done away, and all things shall be made new. Truth shall flourish, and heresy find no footing, justice shall reign, oppression shall be oppressed. The hand of bribery shall be broken. The arm of injustice cut off, and the mouth of iniquity shall be stopped. Then shall our sons grow as plants, and our daughters be like polished precious stones, our garners shall be full, and our cattle shall increase, we shall fear no breaking of enemies to invade us, nor hear any news or noises to affright us, no cries, nor clamors, nor complainings in our streets; our poor shall eat and be satisfied, and our rich shall rejoice in the blessings of their God. Our priests shall be clothed with salvation, and Zion's saints shall sing aloud for joy. Our princes shall be wiser, and our judges better instructed, and instead of serving themselves and the time, will then learn to serve the Lord with fear, and rejoice to him with reverence. Then shall our king and queen joy in your strength, O Lord, and exceedingly rejoice in your salvation. Then all our friends shall rejoice with us, and all our enemies be covered with confusion, and the world shall say, "Blessed are the people that be in such a case, yes, a thousand times blessed the people, that have such a Lord for their God, who has purged them, from their old pollution, and purified them for himself, that now he may dwell among them for evermore."

Hear us O God of mercy for your names sake, But Lord we implore you, begin with the better part first, even the spiritual sores of our souls and of our land, remove those plagues first which has pulled down this plague, therefore begin we implore you at the right end, and make us not healthful and sound in body, and leave us sick in soul, and miserable in our spiritual state. Turn us therefore O God of our salvation cause your loving countenance to shine on us, and we shall be safe. Bring us again into your temples with joy, and into your courts with praise, satisfy us early with your mercies, and comfort us according to the days wherein you have afflicted us. Now let your work appear to your servants, and your glory to their children. Then we will get into your house with true burnt offerings, and with cheerfulness of heart will pay you our vows, which our lips have uttered, and our mouths have spoken in the days of our affliction. And we that are your people and sheep of your pasture will give you thanks forever, and show forth your praises to the generations that shall follow after us, to the world's end.

And this our poor prayer which here we have presented, and this our weak thanksgiving which we have here rendered to your holy majesty, we humbly beg may be accepted, not for ourselves alone, but for your whole church, even the blessed body of your dear Son. Nor for our friends alone, but even our enemies, for whom we implore rather your mercy to convert them, then your justice to confound them, yet if they will not be reclaimed, restrain their rage, good Lord, and frustrate all their fury, make the malice of man turn to your praise, and if our prayers can do them no good, at least, let their causeless curses and cursed plots do us no hurt. Stand by all the armies and forces of your church both by sea and land, and by all them that stand up for your holy cause, especially that chief champion of your church, your devoted servant our Sovereign Lord, rouse up his royal heart, inflame him more and more with zeal and love to you, that your church may find him and your foes may feel him to be the Great Defender of your Christian faith, and the man of men whom you have marked for yourself, even a second Cyrus raised up anointed and sanctified by yourself to perform all your pleasure, and to execute your great and glorious designs, not only for the building up of our Jerusalem, in the reformation and restoration of our church, but to subdue the nations before you, and to weaken and loose the loins of such kings as will not open their hearts to thee. The promise you were pleased to make to Cyrus, who did not know you, make good we implore you much more to him who knows you, and fears you, and submits his soul to you, and casts his crown down at your feet. That is, make him your great shepherd, hold up his right hand, subdue your enemies before him, open to him all doors of difficulties, break in pieces the gates of brass, and cut in sunder the bar of iron, and go before him when he goes to make the crooked places of the world straight. To which end give him good Lord beside all your other blessings, the treasures of darkness, and hidden riches of secret places, that even by this also he may know that you the Lord who has called him and set him on work, are able to pay his armies, and provide for him; do this O Lord for Jacob your servant's sake and Israel your elect.

Bless the queen. You that have made her his, make her also yours, so that she may be a help to him, a blessing to us, a comfort to the distressed churches of France and a joy to the Christian world. Bless therefore good Lord, and make powerful all means of her conversion public and private, and for the settling of her soul in your holy truth, and in the ways of righteousness. And besides the prayers of us, and your whole church over the world, daily made for her, we implore you graciously to regard the serious supplications which we are sure his majesty daily pours out before you, for her happy and speedy conversion, so that she may be a nursing mother, as he is a nursing father to your church shine from heaven with the beams of love and mercy on those glorious servants of yours, the king and queen of

Bohemia, and their royal branches, and as you have honored them not only to believe in you, but to suffer for you, so give them in your good time; a blessed issue of all their unjust sufferings, and in the meantime arm them with faith and patience to wait on you. Look down in mercy, and bless with your special blessing the high court of parliament, be with them at their meetings, consultations and conclusions, set your fear before their eyes, and let your glory be their greatest aim, knit the hearts of prince and people one to another, and all to thee; confound all private plots any way tending to the hinderance of the comfortable continuance of that blessed meeting, until they have first discovered, and then found means to cure the corruptions, plagues, and great diseases of this church and state. Bless this whole land, make his majesty's council faithful to you, lest otherwise they prove false to him, purge the tribe of Levi, that their lips may preserve pure knowledge, and their lives may express the life of true religion. Refine our nobility, from the filthy dregs of popery, and all ignoble baseness, cleanse the hearts and hands of our judges and magistrates, and purify our people in this furnace of affliction, and humble us all from the king to the captive, so that we may be a people prepared for the Lord. And look down in mercy as you are a God of mercy on those many hundreds, no, yet, alas, alas, thousands of our dear brethren in this land, and especially in this city, who still lie groaning under the burden of your wrath, and the sword of your destroying angel.

Alas O Lord these sheep, what have they done? Or are we better than our brethren? Or are these thousands that fall before our faces any greater sinners then the rest? Or rather have not we sinned more then they, and yet they are smitten, rather then we? O how wonderful are your works, how unsearchable are your judgments, and your ways past finding out. Again, how infinite and unmeasurable are your mercies to all them that fear you, and seek your face? Therefore, we implore you let the sorrowful sighing of these your prisoners come before you, and according to the greatness of your power, preserve you those that are appointed to die. At least, we implore you as you empty the earth, fill the heavens, and whom you take from us, Lord take to yourself and fill your heavenly mansions with their souls, whose bodies have left so many houses desolate in our streets. And for so many of us whom you please to preserve, Lord, let us not live, but to honor you; therefore mark us with your holy stamp, and seal us for yourself; that when the angel of justice sees us sorrowing for our sins, and for the iniquity of the time, and mourning for the miseries and sighing for the sufferings of your saints, and laying to our hearts the affliction of Joseph, he may then not only pass by us, but even in the midst of this common calamity leave us some badge of your blessing, and some better testimony of your love, in the holy use of this your judgment, then the more secure times of our lives past have formerly afforded us.

In this way Lord, have we poured out our souls into the bosom of your mercy. You are he that hears the prayer, to thee shall all flesh come, and if all flesh may come shall not then your children be bold to press to you? And seeing we have poured out our hearts to you,

O do not pour out the vials of your wrath on us, but pour down on us the newness of your favor, the showers of sweet compassion.

Hear us you blessed Father, plead for us you blessed Son, help our infirmities you blessed spirit of grace, and make you intercession for us, with those holy groans that cannot by us be expressed. Hear us and answer us you glorious Trinity in holy unity, not for any merits of ours, for we lay our hands on our mouths, nay, we abhorred ourselves in dust and ashes, but only for the precious blood–shedding, and all sufficient satisfaction of Jesus Christ, the Surety and Savior of our souls, the Mediator of our peace, and the eternal high priest of the New Testament. In whose blessed name and holy words, we shut up this our weak prayer, offer this our poor sacrifice, and tender this pitiful complaint of our poor souls to the hands of your heavenly majesty, as he has taught us, and left us in his holy gospel the charter of our peace. *"Our Father which art in heaven, Hallowed be thy name. Thy kingdom come. Thy will be done in earth, as it is in heaven. Give us this day our daily bread. And forgive us our debts, as we forgive our debtors. And lead us not into temptation, but deliver us from evil: For thine is the kingdom, and the power, and the glory, for ever. Amen,"* (Matthew 6:9-13).

Exhortation: A Medicine Against the Plague

A sovereign medicine for and against the plague. Being an ancient and approved antidote, and the sure and infallible way how to escape the plague, or at least the plague of the plague.

Take your heart (for that is the place the plague begins) and every morning, wash it, in the tears of true repentance and hearty sorrow for your sins. But that it may be thoroughly washed, see first you stretch it out on the rack of a strict examination, so that it may pour itself out, and make a free and full confession. Then mollify it in the precious oil, and bathe it in the blood of Jesus Christ the true Balm of Gilead, by a true and lively faith. Being in this way cleansed, then strengthen it by cordial comforts confected of nothing else, but the pure and sweet promises of the Gospel. And this remedy is only to be made by the skillful hand of the holy physician and spiritual apothecary, the minister of God, whom you shall always find at the sign of the bible, or the holy Lamb, and there you are sure of true and wholesome remedies. But take heed of them at the Crosskeys, or the sign of Agnus Dei, for though the shops are gorgeous, and all things gloriously painted, you are sure to be made sleepy with counterfeit drugs, and with the corrupt balsam of Egypt, instead of the true Balm of Gilead.

Your heart in this way rectified, let it then command your tongue and lips, to acknowledge that you for your part by your sins of commission and omission have had your hand, and born your part in pulling down this pestilence and all other plagues of God. Let it then command itself to promise and vow, that if you for your part, may by the power and mercy of God be preserved, you will perform some special service to him, his church or children, more than before. And let it command the said tongue and lips to utter and publish the same promise, the better to bind itself to obedience. Let it then command the eyes, to turn away from beholding, and the ears from hearkening after vanity, and yield themselves, the instruments of holy observation, to mark and consider the works of the Lord. It must then command the hands, to keep themselves free from corruption, and that they are painfully, and faithfully employed in the honest labor of your lawful calling, and your feet to walk in those ways, and tread only in those steps, which God has appointed you.

This done, then take for your breakfast, in the name of the Lord, a chapter of the blessed Bible, and so set yourself to your work, and faithful labor of your lawful calling. Then after your day's labor is done bodily take for your spiritual dinner and supper your heartful holy observations of those mighty works of God, both of his justice and mercy towards you and others. Which all that day long, either your eyes have seen, or your ears have heard of. Then the day being done, see that you and yours for your banquet, or supper, close up your stomachs, with those true sweet-meats, certain selected chapters of the blessed Bible. Then after a holy commemoration, of what everyone has heard or seen, or observed that day touching the wondrous works of God, and application of the same one to another. And each one to himself, let then the heart command the tongue with comfort and boldness, to recommend the souls and bodies of you and yours into the blessed training, powerful protection and safe keeping of the keeper of Israel.

But do not forget nothing as you would have all this profitable, and to do you any good, namely, to learn (which you may do, of that excellent apothecary Saint Paul) what it is to live the life of faith, when natural reason and human helps not only fail you, but may be all against you. This faith I tell you afore–hand is not easily found, but I deal truly with you who have it, and can teach you how to get it, for though himself cannot give it you, yet he will both direct and lead you, and bring you acquainted with that Holy Spirit, who gave it to him, and will not deny if your tongue begs for it, and your soul seeks it. Even a little of this faith is precious, therefore you must get it and have it right, and do not care for the quantity; for it is a holy elixir, a true quintessence which will presently and perpetually multiply, beyond ordinary belief, to the infinite enriching of the soul that enjoys it.

But this faith has one strange property, that although it will be content to be gathered up by grains of young and weak Christians, and treasured up by drams and ounces of such as are rich and strong men in Christ, yet can it not abide to be measured or mixed with scruples. For these scruples are of a contrary nature to true faith. But otherwise, if it is more, if it is less, so let it be true. Let it perfect you, and you shall find yourself happy if you have it. For the least quantity of this faith will afford you every morning and evening a proportion of that true treacle, or mithridate, which yet was never made at Venice (except closely in some corners) by reason of that great juggler the pope, who conveys in corrupt drugs and false ingredients. This mithridate is made of more strange ingredients, then is the blood of scorpions, or the flesh of vipers. For it is and must be confected of the flesh and body, and blood of a man, but such a man as the world never had a second, for he must be the child of Adam, and yet the son of no man, and a true man, and yet no man to be his father. Now his blood taken from him while he is alive, and yet so taken from him as he must necessarily die, is of that sovereign excellency, and that infinite virtue and merit, as the quintessence that may be extracted out of it, (which only this fore-named faith can do,) is that superexcellent, no, super-celestial elixir of that high infallible and invaluable virtue, as the soul that out tastes of it morning and evening, will never perish, nor shall to the world's end. Therefore, I say again, as you would have this medicine work, and become powerful for your preservation, do not forget to take a taste of this continually, the first thing in the morning, and the last at night.

Then lie the down in peace, and securely take you rest, for you are free from the fear of all that are able to hurt you. But be sure, for a sign by which to know this medicine works well, that instantly when you wake up your heart, fix it immediately on God, and on him bestow your first thoughts. And so when your body has received so much sleep and rest as may make it serviceable for the soul, then be up with it in the name of the Lord, so that both body and soul may set themselves to serve their God. Then taking this medicine, and following all the former directions, you may safely enter on your business, and adventure on the dangers of that day both you and yours. Provided first, that you always set together (as occasion is) with the duties of your calling, such works of piety towards God, justice and equity towards man, mercy and charity towards the poor, as the divine providence shall lay before you, or cast in your way. For take it for a rule, that these four must always go together, and God himself has so joined them all together, as *cursed be the man that puts them asunder*, for he carries such a heart about him, as this medicine can never do him any good. But where these four are conscionably conjoined, this medicine never failed to work this work. But where any of the four are wanting, and totally neglected, there the other three will do no good, but contrariwise, if they cannot get the company of their companion, they mourn and pine away, and in a short time will be gone, and they stay no longer there, where they cannot be complete.

Provided also that man, nor God do ever find you out of thy way, but always either walking faithfully in your lawful calling, or else doing some good in the performance of some of the foresaid duties of piety, justice, or mercy. For these are the ways of a Christian, and he that is found outside all these is utterly out of his way, and consequently out of that protection which God has granted to them that wait on him, which runs in these words, "that he has given his angels charge over them, to keep them in all their ways," *etc.* And the power of this protection no creature can infringe. So as by virtue of it, the servants of God have walked in safety in the midst of such dangers as has been an amazement to the world, and a wonder to themselves. And for the lack of this, many thousands have miscarried, not only of God's enemies, who walk in wrong and wicked ways, but even such of his friends and followers, who being misled by the world or their own presumptions, took to themselves the boldness to step aside, out of their own ways, and so have shifted themselves out of that shelter or safety, which otherwise they might have challenged as their own.

And lastly, provided that in all times of danger you take heed of tempting God, for otherwise you may justly provoke him to deny his blessing to this medicine, without which, as sovereign and powerful as it is, it can do no good. Now if you will avoid this fearful and dangerous sin of tempting God, you must take heed in the following ways.

First, of putting yourself into any needless danger. And it is then needless, when without necessary cause or lawful calling, either for gain or pleasure, or any private respect you put yourself into places, or among persons infected.

Secondly, you must also at your utmost peril, carefully use all good helps of nature and art, which God's good providence affords you, whether they are commended to you by a learned physician, or approved by true and real experience, and whether they are a means of preservative, curative, or restorative.

Thirdly, you must be wary of all willful distemper, and be diligent in keeping a careful and orderly diet, not only for moderation and sobriety, in respect of the quantity both of meat, and drink especially, but also for wisdom in the choice of the quality and condition of that little which you may feed on.

And lastly, abhor more than poison or the plague itself all these wicked opinions, and all that hold them.

First, that the pestilence is not infectious in itself, and of its own nature, but so immediately, and only the hand of God, as none become infected, but only by his stroke.

Secondly, that every man's days are so numbered, as do or not do what he will, he cannot live longer, nor die sooner than his day and hour appointed.

Thirdly, do not believe that all careful avoiding of persons or places infected, and diligent using of means appointed for prescription are needless and to no purpose.

The foulness and falseness of all these three appears:

First, in that the leaper must be shut up, and all men avoid him, yes, though he were a king, which being nothing so deadly as is the pestilence, (seeing some lived with it many years) it is manifest it was so commanded, only in respect of the contagion.

Secondly, that Job's friends being loving, wise, and religious, and coming to comfort him, having the pestilence, leprosy, or some such contagious sickness, stood afar off, and refused to come near him.

Thirdly, Hezekiah having (that which never man had else) a lease of his life for fifteen years, from him that was able to make it good, yet used all ordinary means and human helps, for preserving his health, and prolonging his life.

Fourthly, Saint Paul having an express grant from God, of the lives of everyone in the ship with him. Yet the next day, when the mariners, who are the means under God to command and rule, and save a ship, would have craftily conveyed themselves out, to have saved their own lives, leaving Paul and the rest to be saved by that promise and power of God. Saint Paul plainly told the captain, if these men go out of the ship we cannot be saved. For howsoever that condition of using means was not expressed, yet he knew it to be implied, which was all the same thing.

Lastly, our Lord Jesus himself, whose deity could delivered him from all danger, yet to teach us to be careful in use of all good means, and to let us see how it made these men, when such as had plagues pressed too near upon him, called for a little ship to wait upon him, because (the text says) of the multitude, lest they should throng him. Yet he that refused the throng, he did not refuse his duty, he that fled from the danger, did not flee from his calling, but preached God's word to them, himself in the ship, and the people on the shore.

The last wicked opinion to be avoided, is, that none who love, fear and serve God, and believe in him can die of the plague, and all that do, lack faith. The wickedness of this doctrine appears in this, that diverse of the dearest of God's saints have tasted, no, even drunk as deeply the cup of all external crosses, and bodily afflictions whatever they have been, as any unbelievers or enemies of God have done. Again, in that many of God's children, who in common calamities turn to the Lord in faith and true repentance, however by this they saved their souls, yet for their bodily lives were swept away with the rest, by the general judgment. As a great number of them that perished in the flood, and diverse of those that die by the hand of justice, and all histories and ages afford frequent examples.

And lastly, if you would take heed of tempting God, stand in your station, make conscience to do your duty, do not fly with Jonah from the presence of the Lord, for he can follow you, and find you wherever you are, and reach you afar off as well as at home. He made Jonah feel his hand (being fled from his duty) even when he thought he was most safe, and slept securely. You, therefore, that may boldly beg God's blessing in your place and duty, how dare you tempt and try the power of God, by flying from it. Use this medicine and observe these rules, and as sure as God is true and just, you may boldly believe the plague shall either not touch you, or not hurt you; but instead of a plague shall be a blessing to you. And where many of God's good children have taken and died of this infection, as it is manifest on the one side they did not lack grace, nor faith for salvation, so it is as clear on the other, that they someway failed in the use of this medicine either, in not believing what in this case ought to be believed, or in not doing something to be done for their deliverance in this danger. In all which cases, the rule of Christ is certain. According to your faith, and consequently your obedience, which always waits on true faith, so be it done to you.

This medicine is so ancient and so approved, that since the world began it was never found to fail in one particular, saving only such as either seem to use it but did not, or using it in part; yet failed in some particulars which in the use of medicines may not be allowed. And by the virtue of this medicine alone, many about this city have been preserved to this day, whose callings and duties inevitably bound them within the reach of such dangers, from which all the human helps in the world could not have delivered them. And still if they do not fail in faith, nor discharge of their duties. God who is the author of this medicine will not fail in performance of his promise.

FINIS.

Self–Denial and Humiliation in a Time of Plague

by Henry Burton[16]

"Let him deny himself ..." (Luke 9:23).

The first lesson is the A.B.C. that Christ teaches us in his school which is this, for a man to deny himself, and so is it also the highest task that is set to any.

These words were spoken to them all, a great many professed Christ, and thronged upon him. Therefore, Christ taught them a lesson, that most of them never thought of. "If anyone will follow me, let him deny himself." The *condition* is, "let him deny himself," the terms are "self–denial.

Self–denial consists, 1. In denying ourselves in all good things. 2. In denying ourselves in all evil things.

1. In all good things, self–denial ought to be in all good things. 1. Internal. 2. External. Internal as the understanding, will, and affection. So, in moral habits, as temperance, fortitude, wisdom, *etc.* 3. In labor of knowledge, even of such as are gotten by study. 2. Self–denial ought to be in external good things.

1. In matters of duty. 2. In Objects.

1. In matters of duty, that is toward God, where is discovered a main duty between true exercise of piety,

---

[16] A most godly sermon preached at St. Albons in Woodstreet on the Lord's Day October 10, 1641. Showing the necessity of self-denial and humiliation, by prayer and fasting before the Lord; in regard of the present plague we now lie under; which God, in his good time, may remove from among us.

and counterfeit. Those are true, which are set down in Scripture, and nowhere else; for God will be served of himself, he does not command as man prescribes. 2. Here appears the vainness of that duty which is prescribed of men.

Those of men may be known like trees by their fruits.

That of human invention, set on the conscience, those who maintain it, cannot but confess the superstition which they maintain.

The next thing, is the duty we owe to our neighbor, as of charity, of equity, of mercy. When we have done all that is commanded, we must confess we are unprofitable servants. Here is self–denial. Yet, there may be duties of piety, where there is a lack of it, as 1 Cor. 13:3.[17] There may be seeming charity, yet false. There may be a giving up of the body to be burned, yet lack of charity because it is not proceeding from faith. Even in these works a Christian must deny himself.

Use 1. To condemn all Popish charity, and many which they call good works, instead of denying themselves in those works, they deny Christ; for in those works, they say they deserve the kingdom of heaven. For there is salvation in none other but in Christ Jesus only.

Use 2. To condemn another sort of carnal, profane men that build their salvation on common duties, works of morality; who say that they do all men right (though perhaps they are compelled so to do) this

---

[17] "And though I bestow all my goods to feed the poor, and though I give my body to be burned, and have not charity, it profiteth me nothing," (1 Cor. 13:3).

overthrows the doctrine of Christ, this is not to deny themselves, but to deny Christ.

Use 3. To put a difference between true charity and false, some men are naturally given to be upright, to do justice, to deal uprightly. This is not to deny oneself, to build in these; for this is not of grace. For works of grace humble a man. This may be a trial of our grace; if they are of grace, you will deny yourself in them. In the next place, we are to consider certain objects, of a threefold relation. 1. A natural. 2. A civil. And, 3. A sensitive relation.

And first, a natural relation, as to father, mother, wife, children, kindred, *etc.*, we must deny ourselves in all relations, where they stand in opposition to Christ. For proof of this, Luke 14:26, "If father, mother, wife, children," *etc.* call us to stand in opposition to Christ, in that respect we must hate them, (Matthew 10:35).[18] It is no wonder, then, if the world cries out against Christ, and calls him a seditious person. For a man to hate his parents, as he is a father; but to deny obedience to his father, so far as he is hindered from coming to Christ. A notable example is in Deut. 13:6.[19] The son must not conceal the father, if he seeks to bring him to idolatry. We must not acknowledge father and mother in bidding

---

[18] "For I am come to set a man at variance against his father, and the daughter against her mother, and the daughter in law against her mother in law," (Matt. 10:35).

[19] "If thy brother, the son of thy mother, or thy son, or thy daughter, or the wife of thy bosom, or thy friend, which is as thine own soul, entice thee secretly, saying, Let us go and serve other gods, which thou hast not known, thou, nor thy fathers," (Deut. 13:6).

us to do that which Christ forbids.[20] So there is also a notable proverb, "Who said unto his father and to his mother, I have not seen him; neither did he acknowledge his brethren, nor knew his own children: for they have observed thy word, and kept thy covenant," (Deut. 33:9). This denial brought a blessing on them, and it is a type of the Gospel. For every true believer is a priest, and must not in that respect look on outward relations in competition with Christ. We must deny ourselves in those things, which otherwise we are bound to love by the law of nature. Trample on your father, cast off your wife and children, Christ directs, if they seek to draw you away from Christ.

Use. To condemn the Papist who hangs all their faith and religion on their ancestors because they lived and died in this religion. This is to set up the parents against Christ.

Use 2. To reprove too many Papists in this land, that do propagate their children and children's children in that religion. Many among us send our children to monasteries in Rome, to make them bond–slaves in darkness forever. God be thanked we have good laws, and I hope we shall have them increased by the happy parliament; but happy would it be if there were good Magistrates to put those laws into practice.

Use 3. For parents that profess true religion. When the Spirit of Christ touches the heart, then they see the true way whose heart is so touched. Yet how many parents cannot endure that their children do

---

[20] "And call no man your father upon the earth: for one is your Father, which is in heaven," (Matt. 23:9).

outstrip their parents in purity, even for this they abhor their own children, and sometimes dispossess them; and cannot endure them. This is lamentable. Kings in their own thrones, are not above Christ, much less parents in their families. If God comes into their families, into the hearts of their children, shall parents lift their hands up against Christ to abhor and hate their own children, because of this? The body is received from the parents, but the soul from God. Parents may instruct their children, but not to keep them from Christ.

Use 4. For children that have received a greater measure of light from Christ, then the Parents they must be modest and humble, and bear their reproaches patiently for Christ. But if the Parents will keep them from Christ, we must hate and deny our parents. But in the meantime, to be patient to convince them, and (if possible) to persuade them.

Use 5. To persuade these children, that they follow this light, and not let their parents, nor any friend in the world draw them from Christ.

The second point, 2. Relation is civil. A Christian must deny himself in all civil relation, if Princes or States make laws against the Law of Christ, against his religion, and his pure ordinances, threatening punishment to those that will not observe them.

In this a true Christian must deny himself, both in matter of terror, and in matter of favor. 1. In matter of terror, whatever is threatened against a man, a Christian may say, I am lower than all the terrors of the world

which could hurt me.[21] We should deny ourselves with
Paul, and be ready, not only to be bound, but to die for
Christ. Theodorus (a heathen man) was told, that he
should rot above ground, "I care not," (he says) "it is all
one to me, to rot above, or underground." In this way a
Christian should resolve against all fears, and terror no
matter what they are *and all for Christ.* So, for the matter
of having favor, as Polycarp had great promotion
promised in the time of persecution, answered, "I have
served Christ," he says, "forty years and he has always
been a good Master to me, and I will not deny him now."
This is self-denial. How many have been overcome with
these things for lack of self-denial. Those that are
compelled to Popery and Popish ways, are not Christ's
followers, but the followers of Antichrist.

Objection. Some may say, what need do we have
for such a doctrine as this of self-denial, in respect of
civil relation to be taught now?

Answer. God be thanked, it is true, the storm is
over of this oppression. Yet, this doctrine may be very
useful for this very season. We are in the expectation of
a true Reformation, and in the very Reformation, self-
denial is to be used.

2. If some by Reformation are reformed, and not
others, will they be quiet? No, the nearer we come to
Christ, the more we must look for persecution. "Yea, and
all that will live godly in Christ Jesus shall suffer

---

[21] "And fear not them which kill the body, but are not able to kill the
soul: but rather fear him which is able to destroy both soul and body
in hell," (Matt. 10:28).

persecution," (2 Tim. 3:12). Let us not look for a true powerful Reformation of religion without persecution.

3. The next thing is the consideration of such things as are part of sense to a man.

The sensitive part of man, which has three heads, 1. Pleasure, 2. Profit, and 3. Honor, must be denied. They were in great esteem among the heathen. These three were all represented to Eve, in the forbidden fruit, (Gen. 3:6), and it took such an impression then, that every mother's child of us, have the print of it remaining on us. I heard a story of a kind of fish in Garnasie, when I was there, by some of the best people there. There is a fish in their area that being stuck by the fisherman, her young, if she has any in her belly, are all wounded in the very same place. This is a direct emblem of mankind[22] and with these three weapons the devil assailed Christ, tempting him, (Luke 4). These three are often set together in the Scripture (Phil. 3).

A Christian must deny himself in pleasure and delight, even the delights of meat and drink, and lawful recreation, which are in themselves lawful meat and drink in a continual moderation, keeping himself from excess, and sometimes in a total abstinence for a time.

1. To avoid excesses at all times, "Settle it therefore in your hearts," (Luke 21:14). There are many reasons why we should deny ourselves in the immoderate use of things in the world. 1. It is an enemy to the soul, an enemy to all Christian duties, (1 Peter

---

[22] "For all that is in the world, the lust of the flesh, and the lust of the eyes, and the pride of life, is not of the Father, but is of the world," (1 John 2:16).

2:11). 2. They hinder us in the Christian race, (1 Cor. 9:2). When a soul is over-charged, he is more fit to lie down then to run. 3. It brings many evils on a state, (Luke 20). Swilling in drink brought a deluge. So, in Lot's time Sodom and Gomorrah ate and drank, and swilled, until fire came down from heaven, and burned them all to ashes, (Psa. 76:4). It brings a man in the way to hell, (Luke 16). Dives in Luke 16 was so full that he forgot poor Lazarus, and now he must suffer for it in hell-flames, burning in torments forever. A Christian may have great occasion of mirth. But then we must have the most care of all. As the wise man said, *when you come to a full table, if you have an appetite, put a knife to your throat.* This duty is requisite for all true Christians.

1. Sometime we should wholly abstain from things in the world, for the removal of some calamity we lie under, or to prevent a calamity coming on us, or to procure a blessing to be more fit for some good duties. We have many examples of this in Scripture. 2 Sam. 12, Jonah 3, Ezra 8, 1 Cor. 7, for fasting keeps the spirit of prayer awake.

Use. Here is a heavy charge that lies on many professors, it is to be wished, that the whole kingdom were not to be blamed in this, like the children of Israel. "All thy rulers are fled together, they are bound by the archers: all that are found in thee are bound together, which have fled from far," (Isa. 22:3). They are cramming themselves with a desperate saying due to the plague, "let us eat and drink, for tomorrow we must die." Is this a time of eating and drinking, *etc.* when the plague is so hot among us? Is this a time to be so desperate? It is true, perhaps tomorrow we shall die, but is this a time to drink and swill, and feast? No, it is rather a time to deny ourselves; for we may be shut up in our houses before tomorrow night, and perhaps die tomorrow, and be swept away with the plague. Is this a time to gorge ourselves with eating and drinking?

What issue may we expect from here. We had indeed a day of thanksgiving, but we had need, that the next day should have been a day of humiliation; for then was the plague among us.

Indeed, when the motion of humiliation was made, one in the city (and that of great note too) made an answer, that Winter was coming on, and then the plague would be stopped.

FINIS

Perilous Times
by John Owen

"This know also, that in the last days perilous times shall come," (2 Timothy 3:1)

The words contain a warning of imminent dangers. And there are four things in them. First, the manner of the warning. "This know also," Secondly, the evil itself that they are warned of, "perilous times." Thirdly, the way of their introduction, "they shall come." Fourthly, the time and season of it, "they shall come in the last days."

First. The manner of the warning. "This know also," "Thou Timothy, unto the other instructions which I have given the how to behave thyself in the house of God, whereby thou mayest be set forth as a pattern unto all gospel ministers in future ages, I must also add this, 'This know also.' It belongs to thy duty and office to know and consider the impending judgments that are coming upon churches." And so, as a justification of my present design, if God enables me to it, I shall here premise that it is the duty of the ministers of the gospel to foresee and take notice of the dangers which the churches are falling into. And the Lord help us, and all other ministers, to be awakened to this part of our duty! You know how God sets it forth (Ezekiel 33) in the parable of the *watchman*, to warn men of approaching dangers. And truly God has given us this law. If we warn the churches of their approaching dangers, we discharge our duty; if we do not, their blood will be required at our hands. The Spirit of God foresaw negligence apt to grow on us in this matter; and therefore, the Scripture only proposes duty on the one hand and on the other requires the people's blood at the hands of the watchmen, if they do not perform their duty. So speaks the prophet Isaiah, 21:8, "He cried, A lion. My Lord, I stand continually upon the watch–tower." A lion is an emblem of approaching judgment. "The lion hath roared; who can but tremble?" the prophet Amos says. It is the duty of ministers of the gospel to give warning of impending dangers.

Again. the apostle, in speaking to Timothy, speaks to us also, to us all, "This know ye also." It is the great concern of all Christian professors and believers, of all churches, to have their hearts very much fixed on present and approaching dangers. We have inquired so long about signs, tokens, and evidences of deliverance, and I know not what, that we have almost lost the benefit of all our trials, afflictions, and persecutions. The duty of all believers is, to be intent on present and imminent dangers. "O Lord," say the disciples, (Matt. 24), "what shall be the sign of thy coming?" They were fixed upon His coming. Our Savior answers, "I will tell you.

1. There shall be an abounding of errors and false teachers. Many shall say, 'Lo here is Christ,' and, 'Lo, there is Christ.'

2. There shall be an apostasy from holiness. "iniquity shall abound, and the love of many shall wax cold."

3. There shall be great distress of nations. "Nation shall rise against nation, and kingdom against kingdom."

4. There shall be great persecutions. "And they shall persecute you, and bring you before rulers; and you shall be hated of all men for my name's sake."

5. There shall be great tokens of God's wrath from heaven. "Signs in the heavens, the sun, moon, and stars."

The Lord Christ would acquaint believers how they should look for his coming. He tells them of all the dangers. Be intent on these things. I know you are apt to overlook them; but these are the things that you are to be intent on.

Not to be sensible of a present perilous season, is that security which the Scripture so condemns; and I will leave it with you, in short, under these three things.

1. It is that frame of heart which, of all others, God does most detest and abhor. Nothing is more hateful to God than a secure frame in perilous days.

2. I will not fear to say this, and go with it, as to my sense, to the day of judgment. A secure person, in perilous seasons, is assuredly under the power of some predominant lust, whether it appears or not.

3. This secure, senseless frame is the certain presage of approaching ruin. This know, brethren, pray to know this, I beg of you, for yours and my own soul, that you will be sensible of, and affected with, the perils of the season into which we are cast. What they are, if God help me, and give me a little strength, I shall show you by-and-by.

Secondly. There is the evil and danger itself in this way forewarned of, and that is hard times, perilous times, times of great difficulty, like those of *public plagues*, when death lies at every door; times that I am sure we shall not all escape, let it fall where it will. I will say no more of it now, because it is that which I shall principally speak to afterward.

Thirdly. The manner of their introduction, "shall come." We have no word in our language that will express the force of the original. The Latins express it by "immineno, incido," *the coming down of a fowl to his prey.* Now, our translators have given it the greatest force they could. They do not say, "Perilous times will come," as though they prognosticated future events; but, "Perilous times shall come." Here is a hand of God in this business; they shall so come, be so instant in their coming, that nothing shall keep them out; they shall instantly press themselves in, and prevail. Our great wisdom, then, will be to eye the displeasure of God in perilous seasons; since there is a judicial hand of God in them, and we see in ourselves reason enough why they should come. But when shall they come?

Fourthly. They "shall come in the last days." The words "latter" or "last days" are taken three ways in Scripture. Sometimes for the times of the gospel, in opposition to the Judaical church–state; as in Heb. 1:2, "Hath in these last days spoken unto us by his Son"; and elsewhere it may be taken (though I remember not the place) for days towards the consummation of all things and the end of the world; and it is taken often for the latter days of churches. 1 Tim. 4:1, "The Spirit of vile lusts, and the practice of horrible sins." This rendered the seasons perilous. Whether this is such a season or not, you judge. And I must say, by the way, we may and ought to witness against it, and mourn for the public sins of the days wherein we live. It is as glorious a thing to be a martyr for bearing testimony against the public sins of an age, as in bearing testimony unto any truth of the gospel whatsoever.

Now, where these things are, a season is perilous.

1. Because of the infection churches and professors are apt to be infected with it. The historians tell us of a plague at Athens, in the second and third years of the Peloponnesian war, of which multitudes died; and of those that lived, few escaped but they lost a limb, or part of a limb – some an eye, others an arm, and others a finger – the infection was so great and terrible. And truly, brethren, where this plague comes – of the visible practice of unclean lusts under an outward profession – though men do not die, yet one loses an arm, another an eye, another a leg by it. The infection diffuses itself to the best of professors, more or less. This makes it a dangerous and perilous time.

2. It is dangerous, because of the effects; for when predominant lusts have broken all bounds of divine light and rule, how long do you think that human rules will keep them in order? They break through all in such a season as the apostle describes. And if they come to break through all human restraints as they have broken through divine, they will fill all things with ruin and confusion.

3. They are perilous in the consequence which is, the judgments of God. When men do not receive the truth in the love of it, but have pleasure in unrighteousness, God will send them strong delusion, to believe a lie. So, 2 Thess. 2:10–11 is a description how the Papacy came on the world. Men professed the truth of religion, but did not love it, they loved unrighteousness and ungodliness; and *God sent them Popery.* That is the interpretation of the place, according to the best divines. Will you profess the truth, and at the same time love unrighteousness? The consequence is, security under superstition and ungodliness. This is the end of such a perilous season; and the like may be said as to temporal judgments, which I need not mention.

Let us now consider what is our duty in such a perilous season:

1. We ought greatly to mourn for the public abominations of the world, and of the land of our nativity in which we live. I would only observe that place in Ezekiel 9, God sends out His judgments, and destroys the city; but before, he sets a mark on the foreheads of the men that sigh for all the abominations that are done in the midst of it. You will find this passage referred in your books to Revelation 7:3, "Hurt not the earth, neither the sea, nor the trees, till we have sealed the servants of our God in their foreheads." I would only observe this, that such only are the servants of God, let men profess what they will, "who mourn for the abominations that are done in the land." The mourners in the one place are the servants of God in the other. And truly, brethren, we are certainly to blame in this matter.

We have been almost well contented that men should be as wicked as they would themselves, and we sit still and see what would come of it. Christ has been dishonored, the Spirit of God blasphemed, and God provoked against the land of our nativity; and yet we have not been affected with these things. I can truly say in sincerity, I bless God, I have sometimes labored with my own heart about it. But I am afraid we, all of us, come exceedingly short of our duty in this matter. "Rivers of waters," the Psalmist says, "run down mine eyes, because men keep not thy law." Horrible profanation of the name of God, horrible abominations, which our eyes have seen, and our ears heard, and yet our hearts have been unaffected with them! Do you think this is a frame of heart God requires of us in such a season – to be regardless of all, and not to mourn for the public abominations of the land? The servants of God will mourn. I could speak, but am not free to speak, to those prejudices which keep us from mourning for public abominations; but they may be easily suggested to all your thoughts, and particularly what they are that have kept us from attending more unto this duty of mourning for public abominations. And give me leave to say, that, according to the Scripture rule, there is not one of us that can have any evidence that we shall escape outward judgments that God will bring for these abominations, if we have not been mourners for them; but that as smart a revenge, as to outward dispensations, may fall on us as on those that are most guilty of them; no Scripture evidence have we to the contrary. How God may deal with us, I do not know.

This, then, is one part of the duty of this day – that we should humble our souls for all the abominations that are committed in the land of our nativity; and, in particular, that we have no more mourned under them.

2. Our second duty, in reference to this perilous season is, to take care that we are not infected with the evils and sins of it. A man would think it were quite contrary; but really, to the best of my observation, this is, and has been, the frame of things, unless on some extraordinary dispensation of God's Spirit, as some men's sins grow very high, other men's graces grow very low. Our Savior has told us, Matthew 24:12, "Because iniquity shall abound, the love of many shall wax cold." A man would think the abounding of iniquity in the world should give great provocation to love one another. "No," our Savior says, "the contrary will be found true. as some men's sins grow high, other men's graces will grow low."

And there are these reasons for it.

(a) In such a season, we are apt to have light thoughts of great sins. The prophet looked on it as a dreadful thing, that upon Jehoiakin's throwing the roll of Jeremiah's prophecy into the fire, "until it was consumed, yet they were not afraid, nor rent their garments, neither the king, nor any of his servants that heard all these words," (Jer. 36:24). They were grown senseless, both of sin and judgment. And where men (even if they are in other respects ever so wise) can grow senseless of sin, they will quickly grow senseless of judgment too. And I am afraid the great reason why many of us have no impression on our spirits of danger and perils in the days in which we live, is because we are not sensible of sin.

(b) Men are apt to countenance themselves in lesser evils, having their eyes fixed on greater abominations of other men, that they behold every day; there are those who pay their tribute to the devil – walk in such and such abominations, and so countenance themselves in lesser evils. This is part of the public infection, that they "do not run out into the same excess of riot that others do," though they live in the omission of duty, conformity to the world, and in many foolish, hurtful, and noisome lusts. They countenance themselves with this, that others are guilty of greater abominations.

(c) Pray let such remember this, who have occasion for it (you may know it better than I, but yet I know it by rule, as much as you do by practice), that general converse in the world, in such a season, is full of danger and peril. Most professors are grown of the color and complexion of those with whom they converse.

This is the first thing that makes a season perilous. I do not know whether these things may be of concern and use to you; they seem so to me, and I cannot but acquaint you with them.

II. A second perilous season, and that we shall hardly come off in, is when men are prone to forsake the truth, and seducers abound to gather them up that are so; and you will have always these things go together. Do you see seducers abound? You may be sure there is a proneness in the minds of men to forsake the truth; and when there is such a proneness, they will never lack seducers – those that will lead off the minds of men from the truth; for there is both the hand of God and Satan in this business. God judicially leaves men, when He sees them grow weary of the truth, and prone to leave it; and Satan strikes in with the occasion, and stirs up seducers. This makes a season perilous. The apostle describes it, 1 Tim. 4:1, "Now the Spirit speaketh expressly, that in the latter times" (these perilous days) "some shall depart from the faith, giving heed to seducing spirits, and doctrines of devils." And so Peter warns them to whom he writes, 2 Peter 2:1-2, that "there shall come false teachers among them, who privily shall bring in damnable heresies, even denying the Lord that bought them, and bring upon themselves swift destruction; and many shall follow their pernicious ways." There shall come times full of peril, which shall draw men from the truth into destruction.

If it be asked, how may we know whether there be a proneness in the minds of men in any season to depart from the truth? There are three ways by which we may judge it.

1. The first is that mentioned, 2 Tim. 4:3, "The time will come when they will not endure sound doctrine; but after their own lusts shall they heap to themselves teachers, having itching ears." When men grow weary of sound doctrine – when it is too plain, too heavy, too dull, too common, too high, too mysterious, one thing or other that displeases them, and they would hear something new, something that may please – it is a

sign that there are in such an age many who are prone to forsake sound doctrine. and many such we know.

2. When men have lost the power of truth in their conversation, and are as prone and ready to part with the profession of it in their minds. Do you see a man retaining the profession of the truth under a worldly conversation? He desires baits from temptation, or a seducer, to take away his faith from him. It is an inclination to hearken after novelties. And a loss of the power of truth in the conversation is a sign of proneness to this declension from the truth. Such a season, you see, is *perilous*. And why is it perilous? Because the souls of many are destroyed in it. The apostle tells us directly, 2 Peter 2:1, of "false prophets among the people, who privily bring in damnable heresies, even denying the Lord that bought them, and bring upon themselves swift destructions." Will it abide there? No. "And many shall follow their pernicious ways, by reason of whom the way of truth shall be evil spoken of." Brethren, while it is well with us, through the grace of God, and our own houses are not in flames, pray, do not let us think the times are not perilous, when so many turn into pernicious errors, and fall into swift destruction. Will you say the time of the public plague was not perilous, because you were alive? No. Was the fire not dreadful, because your houses were not burned? No, you will, notwithstanding, say it was a dreadful plague, and a dreadful fire. And I pray you, consider, is not this a perilous season, when multitudes have an inclination to depart from the truth, and God, in just judgment, has

permitted Satan to stir up seducers to draw them into pernicious ways, and their poor souls perish forever?

Besides, there is a great aptness in such a season to work indifference in the minds of those who do not intend utterly to forsake the truth. Little did I think I should ever have lived in this world to find the minds of professors grown altogether indifferent as to the doctrines of God's eternal election, the sovereign efficacy of grace in the conversion of sinners, justification by the imputation of the righteousness of Christ; but many are, as to all these things, grown to an indifferency; they know not whether they are so or not. I bless God I know something of the former generation, when professors would not hear of these things without the highest detestation; and now high professors begin to be leaders in it. And it is too much among the best of us. We are not so much concerned for the truth as our forefathers; I wish I could say we were as holy.

3. This proneness to depart from the truth is a perilous season, because it is the greatest evidence of the withdrawing of the Spirit of God from his church. For the Spirit of God is promised to this end, "to lead us into all truth"; and when the efficacy of truth begins to decay, it is the greatest evidence of the departing and withdrawing of the Spirit of God. And I think that this is a dangerous thing; for if the Spirit of God departs, then our glory and our life depart.

What, now, is our duty in reference to this perilous season? Forewarnings of perils are given us to instruct us in our duty.

1. The first, is, not to be content with what you judge a sincere profession of truth; but to labor to be found in the exercise of all those graces which peculiarly respect the truth. There are graces that peculiarly respect the truth that we are to exercise; and if these are not found in our hearts, all our profession will issue in nothing.

And these *are:*

(a) Love. "Because they loved not the truth." They made profession of the gospel; but they did not receive the truth in its love. There was lack of love of the truth. Truth will do no man good where there is no love of it. "Speaking the truth in love," is the substance of our Christian profession. I pray, brethren, let us labor to love the truth; and to take off all prejudices from our minds, that we may do so.

(b) It is the great and only rule to preserve us in perilous times, to labor to have the experience of the power of every truth in our hearts. If so you have learned the Lord Jesus in this way ... how? So as to "put off the old man, which is corrupt according to the deceitful lusts," and to, "put on the new man, which after God is created in righteousness and true holiness," (Eph. 4:22–24). This is to learn the truth. The great grace that is to be exercised with reference to truth in such a season as this, is to exemplify it in our hearts in its power. Labor for the experience of the power of every truth in your own hearts and lives.

(c) Zeal for the truth. Truth is the most proper object for zeal. We ought to "contend earnestly for the truth once delivered to the saints," to be willing, as God shall help us, to part with name and reputation, and to undergo scorn and contempt, all that this world can cast on us, in giving testimony to the truth. Everything that this world counts dear and valuable is to be forsaken, rather than the truth. This was the great end for which Christ came into the world.

2. Cleave to the means that God has appointed and ordained for your preservation in the truth. I see some are ready to go to sleep, and they think they are not concerned in these things. The Lord awaken their hearts! Keep to the means of preservation in the truth – the present ministry. Bless God for the remainder of a ministry valuing the truth, knowing the truth, sound in the faith – cleave to them. There is little influence upon the minds of men from this ordinance and institution of God, in the great business of the ministry. But know there is something more in it than that they seem to have better abilities to dispute than you. They have more knowledge, more light, better understandings than you. If you know no more in the ministry than this, you will never have benefit by it. They are God's ordinance; the name of God is on them and God will be sanctified in them. They are God's ordinance for the preservation of the truth.

3. Let us carefully remember the faith of those who went before us in the profession of the last age. I am apt to think there was not a more glorious profession for a thousand years upon the face of the earth, than was among the professors of the last age. And pray, what faith were they of? Were they half Arminian and half Socinian? Half Papist and half I know not what?

Remember how zealous they were for the truth? how little their holy souls would have borne with those public defections from the doctrine of truth which we see, and do not mourn over, but make nothing of, in the days in which we live. God was with them; and they lived to his glory, and died in peace, "whose faith follow," and example pursue. And remember the faith they lived and died in. Look round about, and see whether any of the new creeds have produced a new holiness to exceed theirs.

III. A third thing that makes a perilous season is, professors mixing themselves with the world, and learning their manners. And if the other perilous seasons are come on us, this is come on us also. This was the foundation and spring of the first perilous season that was in the world, that first brought in a deluge of sin and then a deluge of misery. It was the beginning of the first public apostasy of the church, which issued in the severest mark of God's displeasure. Gen. 6:2, "The sons of God saw the daughters of men that they were fair; and they took them wives of all which they chose." This is but one instance of the church of God, the sons of God, professors, *mixing themselves with the world.* This was not all, that they took to themselves wives; but this was an instance the Holy Spirit gives that the church in those days did degenerate, and mix itself with the world. What is the end of mixing themselves in this manner with the world? Psa. 106:35, "They mingled themselves with the nations." And what then. "And learned their manners." If anything under heaven will make a season perilous, this will do it – when we mingle with the world and learn their manners.

There are two things I shall speak of on this head. 1. In which professors mingle themselves with the world. 2. The danger of it.

1. Professors mingle themselves with the world in that in which it is the world, which is proper to the world. That which is more eminently and visibly of the devil, professors do not so soon mingle themselves with that; but in that in which it is the world, in its own colors – as in corrupt communication, which is the spirit of the world, the extract and fruit of vanity of mind – that where the world is corrupted with it, and corrupts people. An evil, rotten kind of communication, by which the manners of the world are corrupted – this comes from the spirit of the world. The devil has his hand in all these things; but it is the world and the spirit of the world that is in corrupt communication. And how has this spread itself among professors! Light, vain, foolish communication! – to spend a man's whole life in that; not on this or that occasion, but almost always, and on all occasions everywhere. Vain habits and attire of the world is another instance. The habits and attire of the world are the things in which the world designs to show itself what it is. Men may read what the world is by evident characters, in the habits and attire that it wears. They are blind that cannot read vanity, folly, uncleanness, luxury, in the attire the world puts on itself. The declension of professors in imitating the ways of the world in their habits and garb, makes a season perilous; it is a mixture in which we learn their manners;

and the judgments of God will ensue upon it. In this, likewise, we are grown like the world, that upon all occasions we are as regardless of the sins of the world, and as little troubled with them, as others are. Lot lived in Sodom, but "his righteous soul was vexed with their ungodly deeds and speeches." Should we live where we wish, when are our souls vexed, so that we do not pass through the things of the world, the greatest abominations, with the frame of spirit that the world itself does? Not to speak of voluptuousness of living, and other things that attend this woeful mixture with the world that professors have made in the days in which we live – corrupt communication, gaiety of attire, senselessness of the sins and abominations of the world round about us, are almost as much on professors as on the world. We have mixed ourselves with the people, and have learned their manners. But –

2. Such a season is dangerous, because the sins of professors are in it. God directly works contrary to the whole design the mediation of Christ in this world. Christ gave himself for us, that he might purge us from dead works, and purify us to himself a peculiar people (Titus 2:14). "Ye are a royal nation, a peculiar people." Christ has brought the hatred of the devil and all the world on him and against him, for taking a people out of the world, and making them a peculiar people to himself; and their throwing themselves upon the world again is the greatest contempt that can be put upon Jesus Christ.[23] He gave his life and shed his blood to recover us

---

[23] *Nota bene* -Editor.

from the world, and we throw ourselves in again. How easy were it to show that this is an inlet to all other sins and abominations, and that for which I verily think the indignation and displeasure of God will soon discover itself against professors and churches in this day! If we will not be differenced from the world in our ways, we shall not long be differenced from them in our privileges. If we are the same in the way we walk, we shall be so in our worship, or have none at all.

As to our duty in such a perilous season, let me leave three cautions with you, and the Lord fix them on your hearts.

1. The profession of religion, and the performance of duties, under a world–like conversation, are nothing but a sophistical means to lead men blindfold into hell. We must not speak little things in such a great cause.

2. If you will be like the world, you must take the world's lot. It will go with you as it goes with the world. Inquire and see, in the whole book of God, how it will go with the world, what God's thoughts are of the world, whether it saith not, "If it lies in wickedness, it shall come to judgment," and that "the curse of God is upon it." If, therefore, you will be like the world, you must have the world's lot; God will not separate.

3. Lastly, consider we have by this means lost the most glorious cause of truth that ever was in the world. We do not know that there has been a more glorious cause of truth since the apostle's days, than what God has committed to his church and people in this nation, for the purity of the doctrine of the truth and ordinances; but we have lost all the beauty and glory of it by this

mixture in the world. I verily think it is high time that the congregations in this city, by their elders and messengers, should consult together how to stop this evil, that has lost all the glory of our profession. It is a perilous time, when professors mix themselves so with the world.

There are other perilous seasons that I thought to have insisted on, but I will but name them.

IV. When there is great attendance on outward duties, but inward, spiritual decays. Now in this, my brethren, you know how long I have been treating of the causes and reasons of inward decays, and the means to be used for our recovery; I shall not, therefore, again insist upon them.

V. Times of persecution are also times of peril.

Now, I do not need to tell you whether these seasons are on us or not; it is your duty to inquire into that. Whether there is not an outward retaining of the truth under a visible prevalence of abominable lusts in the world; whether there is to a proneness to forsake the truth, and seducers at work to draw men off, whether there is not a mingling ourselves with the world, and in this learning their manners; whether there is not inward decays, under the outward performance of duties; and whether many are not suffering under persecution and trouble, judge ye, and act accordingly.

One word of use, and I will complete this.

Use 1. Let us all be exhorted to endeavor to get our hearts affected with the perils of the day in which we live. You have heard a poor, weak discourse concerning it, and perhaps it will be quickly forgotten.

Oh, that God would be pleased to give us this grace – that we may find it our duty to endeavor to have our hearts affected with the perils of these seasons! It is not time to be asleep on the top of a mast in a rough sea, when there are so many devouring dangers round about us. And the better to effect this, consider the following:

(a) Consider the present things, and bring them to rule, and see what God's word says of them. We hear this and that story of horrible, prodigious wickedness; and bring it in the next opportunity of talk, and there slightly pass it over. We hear of the judgments of God abroad in the world; and bring them to the same standard of our own imaginations, and there is an end. But, brethren, when you observe any of these things, how it is with the world, if you would have your hearts affected, bring it to the word, and see what God says of it. Speak with God about it; ask and inquire at the mouth of God what God says unto these prodigious wickednesses and judgments – this coldness that is on professors, and there mixtures with, and learning the manners of the world. You will never have your hearts affected with it, until you come and speak with God about it; and then you will find them represented in a glass that will make your hearts ache and tremble. And *then:*

(b) If you would be sensible of present perilous times, take heed of centering in self. While your greatest concern is self, or the world, all the angels in heaven cannot make you sensible of the peril of the days in which you live. Whether you pursue riches or honors, while you center there, nothing can make you sensible of the perils of the day. Therefore, do not center in self.

(c) Pray that God would give us grace to be sensible of the perils of the day wherein we live. It may be that we have had confidence, that though thousands fall at our right hand and at our left, yet we shall be able to carry it through. Believe me, it is great grace. Point your private, closet prayers, and your family prayers this way; and the Lord help us to point our public prayers to this thing, that God would make our hearts sensible of the perils of the time into which we are fallen in these last days!

Use 2. The next thing is this, that there are two things in a perilous season, the sin of it, and the misery of it. Labor to be sensible of the former, or you will never be sensible of the latter. Though judgments lie at the door, though the heavens be dark over us, and the earth shake under us at this day, and no wise man can see where he can build himself an abiding habitation – we can talk of these things; and hear of other nations soaking in blood; and have tokens of God's displeasure, warnings from heaven above and the earth beneath; and no man sensible of them! Why? Because they are not sensible of sin; nor ever will be, unless God make them so.

I shall range the sins that we should be sensible of under three heads – the sins of the poor, wretched, perishing world, in the first place; the sins of professors in general, in the second place; and our own particular sins and decays, in the third place. And let us labor to have our hearts affected with these. It is to no purpose to tell you this and that judgment is approaching; – for your leaders, and those that are upon the watchtower, to cry, "A lion; my Lord, we see a lion." Unless God makes our hearts sensible of sin, we shall not be sensible of judgments.

Use 3. Remember there is a special frame of spirit required in us all in such perilous seasons as these are. And what is that? It is a mourning frame of spirit. O! that frame, that jolly frame of spirit that is on us! The Lord forgive it, the Lord pardon it unto us; and keep us in a humble, broken, mournful frame of spirit; for it is a peculiar grace God looks for at such a time as this is. When he will pour out his Spirit, there will be great mourning, together and apart; but now we may say there is no mourning. The Lord help us, we have hard hearts and dry eyes under the consideration of all these perils that he has given before us.

Use 4. Keep up church watch with diligence, and by the rule. When I say rule, I mean its life. I have no greater jealousy on my heart, than that God should withdraw himself from his own institutions because of the sins of the people, and leave us only the carcass of outward rule and order. What does God give them for? For their own sakes? No; but that they may be clothing for faith and love, meekness of spirit and bowels of compassion, watchfulness and diligence. Take away these, and farewell to all outward rule and order, whatever they are. Keep up a spirit that may live affected with it. Get a spirit of *church watch*, which is not to lie at catch for faults, but diligently, out of pure love and compassion to the souls of men, to watch over them, – to wait to do them good, all we can. As it was with a poor man, who took a dead body and set it up, and it fell; and he set it up again, and it fell; upon which he cried out, "There lacks something within," to enliven and quicken it; – so is it with church order and rule; set them up as often as you will, they will all fall, if there is not a love to one another, a delighting in the good of one another, "exhorting one another while it is called today, lest any be hardened through the deceitfulness of sin."

Use 5. Reckon on it, that in such times as these are, all of us will not go free. You find no mention of a perilous season in Scripture, but it follows that some shall have their faith overthrown, others shall follow pernicious ways, and others shall turn aside. Brethren and sisters, how do you know but you or I may fall? Let us double our watch, every one; for the season is come on us in which some of us may fall, and fall so as to be pained for it. I do not say we shall perish eternally; God deliver us from going into the pit! But some of us may so fall as to lose a limb, some member or other; and our works will be committed to the fire that shall burn them all. God has kindled a fire in Zion that will try all our works; and we shall see in a short time what will become of us.

Use 6. Lastly, take that great rule which the apostle gives in such times as those in which we are concerned, "Nevertheless the foundation of God stands sure," – Oh blessed be God for it! – "God knows who are his."

What, then, is required on our part? "Let him that nameth the name of Christ depart from evil." Your

121

profession, your privileges, your light, will not secure you; you are gone, unless every one that names the name of Christ departs from all iniquity. What multitudes perish under a profession every day! Oh, that our hearts could bleed to see poor souls in danger of perishing under the greatest profession!

Will you hear the conclusion of all this? Perilous times and seasons have come on us; many are wounded already; many have failed. The Lord help us! The crown is fallen from our head, the glory of our profession is gone, the time is short, the Judge stands before the door. Take but this one word of counsel, my brethren. "Watch, therefore, that none of these things may come upon you, but that you may escape, and be accounted worthy to stand before the Son of God." Amen.

FINIS

The Good of Adversity
by Thomas Manton

"Before I was afflicted I went astray; but now have I kept thy word," (Psalm 119:67).

In this verse you may observe two things.

1. The evil of prosperity, before I was afflicted I went astray.

2. The good of adversity, but now have I kept thy word. Before wandering, but now attentive to his duty. Or, if you will, here is the necessity of afflictions and the utility of them.

1. The necessity, "Before I was afflicted I went astray." Some think that David in his own person represents the debauchery and stubbornness of all mankind. If it should be so, yet the person in whom the instance is given is notable. If this was the disposition of the prophet and man of God, and he needed this discipline, we need it much more. If he could say it in truth of heart that he was made worse by his prosperity, we need always to be jealous of ourselves; and were it not for the scourge, we should forget our duty and the obedience we owe to God.

2. The utility and benefit of afflictions. But now have I kept thy word." *Keeping the law* is a general word. The use of God's rod is to bring us home to God, and the affliction drives us to make better use of his word. It changes us from vanity to seriousness, from error to truth, from stubbornness to teachfulness, from pride to modesty. It is commonly said, as the apostle tells us that

Jesus Christ himself "learned obedience by the things which he suffered," (Heb. 5:8); and here David was better for the cross given to him; and so should we. Or rather, you may in the words observe three things.

1. A confession of his wandering, "I went astray."

2. The course God took to reduce him to his duty, "I was afflicted."

3. The success or effect of that course, "I have kept thy word." Theodoret expresses this in three words, "I was sick; I was cut, or let out blood; I was well, or recovered my health again."

1. The one gives us the cause of afflictions; they are for sin, "I went astray;" in which there is a secret acknowledgment of his guilt, that his sin was the cause of the chastisement God brought upon him.

2. The true notion and nature of affliction to the people of God. The cross changes its nature, and is not a destructive punishment, but *remedium delinquentium*, a medicinal dispensation, and a means of our cure.

3. The end of them is obedience, or keeping God's word. The sum of the whole is, "I was out of the way, but thy rod hath reduced me, and brought me into it again." Aben Ezra thinks that in this last clause he intimates a desire of deliverance, because the rod had done its work; rather, I think he expresses his frame and temper when he was delivered; and accordingly I shall make use of it int his way.

I might observe many points, but the doctrine from the whole verse is this:

DOCTRINE: That the end of God's afflicting, is to reduce his afflicted and straying people into the right way.

I shall explain the point by these considerations.

1. That man is of a straying nature, apt to turn out of the way that leads to God and to true happiness. We are all so by nature. Isa. 53:6, "All we like sheep have gone astray." Sheep, of all creatures, are exceedingly subject to stray, if not tended and kept better, unable to keep out of error, and having erred, unable to return. This is the emblem by which the Holy Spirit would set forth the nature of mankind. But is it better with us after grace received? No; we are in part still the same in many ways. The best of us, if left to ourselves, how soon are we out of the right way? Into what sad errors do we run ourselves? Psa. 19:12, "Who can understand his errors? cleanse thou me from secret sins." Since we have grace, we all have our deviations; though our hearts are set to walk with God mainly, yet ever and forever we are swerving from our rule, transgressing our bounds, and neglecting our duty. Good David had cause to say, Psa. 119:176, "I have gone astray like a lost sheep. Oh, seek thy servant!" We go astray not only out of ignorance, but out of perverseness of inclination. Jer. 14:10, "Thus have they loved to wander; they have not restrained their feet." We have hearts that love to wander; we love shift and change, though it is for the worse; and so will be making excursions into the ways of sin.

2. This straying malady is greatly increased and encouraged by prosperity, which, though it is good in itself, yet, we are so perverse by nature, that we are the

worse for it. That the wicked are the worse for it, is clear. Isa. 26:10, "Let favour be showed to the wicked, yet will they not learn righteousness." The sunshine on the dung hill will produce nothing but stench, and the salt sea will turn all that falls into it into salt water; the sweet dews of heaven, and the tribute of the rivers all becomes salt when it falls into the sea. So wicked men convert all into their malady; neither God's mercies nor judgments will have any gracious and kindly work upon them. But, if it is well with them, they take more liberty to live loosely and profanely. The fear of God, which is the great holdback from all wickedness, is lessened and quite lost in them when they see no change. Psa. 55:19, "Because they have no changes, therefore they fear not God." That little slavish fear which they have, which should keep them back from wandering, is then lost, and the more gently God deals with them, the more godless and secure they are. When they go on prosperously and undisturbedly, the more obdurate they are. But is it not so with the people of God also? Yes, truly. David, whose heart struck him when he cut off the lap of Saul's garment when he was wandering in the wilderness, could plot the death of Uriah, his faithful servant, when he was at ease in his palace. We lose much tenderness of conscience, watchfulness against sin, much of that lively diligence that we should otherwise show forth in carrying in the spiritual life, when we are at ease, and all things go well with us. We are apt to indulge the flesh when we have so many baits to feed it; and to learn how to abound is the harder lesson of the two than to learn how to be abased, (Phil. 4:12); and therefore, if God did not correct us, we should grow careless and negligent. The beginning of all obedience is the mortification of the flesh, which naturally we cannot endure. After we have submitted and subjected ourselves to God, the flesh will be seeking its prey, and be rebelling and waxing malicious against the spirit, until God snatches its allurements from us. Therefore, the Lord by diverse afflictions is glad to break us and bring us into order. We force him to humble us by poverty, or disgrace, or diseases, or by domestic crosses, or some inconveniency of the natural and animal life, which we value too much. Besides, our affections to heavenly things languish when all things succeed with us in this world according to our heart's desire; and this coldness and remissness is not easily shaken off. Many are like the children of Reuben and Gad, (Num. 23), who, when they found convenient pastures on this side Jordan, were content with it for their portion, without seeking anything in the land of promise. So their desires insensibly settle here, and have less respect to the good of the world to come.

3. When it is thus with us, God sees fit to send afflictions. Much of the wisdom of God's providence is to be observed; partly in the season of affliction, in what state and posture of soul it surprises us, when we are wandering, when we most need it, when our abuse of prosperity calls aloud for it; when the sheep wander, the dog is let loose to fetch them in again. God suits his providence to our necessities. 1 Peter 1:6, "For a season ye are in heaviness, if need be." Alas! we often see that afflictions are highly necessary and seasonable, either to prevent a distemper that is growing upon us, or to

reclaim us from some evil course in which we have wandered from God. Paul was in danger to be lifted up, and then God sends a thorn in the flesh. This discipline is very proper and necessary before the disease run on too far. Partly in the kind of affliction. All medicine does not work on the same maladies; diverse lusts must have diverse remedies. Pride, envy, covetousness, wantonness, emulation, have all their proper cures. All sins are referred to three impure fountains. 1 John 2:16, "For all that is in the world, the lust of the flesh, the lust of the eyes, and the pride of life, is not of the Father, but is of the world." From the lusts of the flesh do arise not only the gross acts of depravity, fornication, adultery, gluttony, drunkenness, which the more brutish and base part of mankind are taken with, but an inordinate love of pleasures, vain company, and vain delights, carnal complacency, or flesh–pleasing, with which the refined part of the world are too often captivated and bewitched. The lust of the eyes, covetousness and worldly–mindedness, produce wretchedness, rapines, contentions, strife, or that immoderate desire of having or joining house to house, field to field, and building up ourselves one story higher in the world. From pride of life comes ambition, lofty conceit of ourselves, scorn and contempt of others, affectation of credit and repute in the world, pomp of having multitudes of servants, or greatness of train, fineness of apparel, and innumerable vanities! Now God, that he may meet with his servants when they are tripping in any kind, he sends out afflictions as his faithful messengers to stop them in their career, that the flesh may not sail and carry it away with a full and clear gale. Against the lusts of the flesh he sends sicknesses and diseases; against the lusts of the eyes, poverty and disappointments in our relations; against pride, disgraces and shame. And sometimes he varies the dispensation, for his providence keeps one tenor, and every cure will not fit every malady; all will not work alike on all. He sends that affliction which is sure to work; he knows how to strike in the right vein. In this way, he cures Paul's pride by a troublesome disease. None that study providence but may observe the wisdom of God in the kind of affliction, and how suitable it is to the work it is to do; for God does all things in number, weight, and measure. Partly by the manner how it comes on us, by what instruments, and in what sort. How many make themselves miserable by an imagined cross! And so, when all things without are well, their own maladies and passions make them a burden to themselves, and when they are not wounded in point of honor, nor lessened and cut short in estate, nor assaulted in their health, nor their relations diminished and cut off, but are hedged roundabout with all temporal happiness, there seems to be no room or place for any affliction or trouble in their hearts, yet, "in the fulness of their sufficiency, God makes them a terror and burden to themselves. He does this either by their own fears or misconceit, or the false imagination of some loss or disgrace. God makes them uncomfortable and full of disquiet; and though they lack nothing, yet they are not at ease, yes, more troubled than those that are called out to conflict with real, yes, the greatest evils. Haman is an instance of this. He was one of the princes of the kingdom of Persia, flowing in wealth and all manner of delights, in degree of dignity and honor next to the king himself, and flourishing in the hope of a numerous and fair issue; yet because Mordecai, a poor Jew, did not do him expected reverence, "All this availeth me nothing," (Esther 5:19). So soon can God send a worm into the fairest gourd, and a dissatisfaction into the most flourishing estate in the world, that men shall have no rest night and day, especially if a spark of his wrath light into the conscience. Psa. 39:11, "When thou with rebukes dost correct man for his iniquity, thou makest his beauty to consume away like a moth. surely every man is vanity, Selah." There is a secret moth that eats up all their contentment; they are under terror, discouragement, and lack of peace. God teaches them that nothing can be satisfactorily enjoyed apart from his blessed self. "A fire not blown shall consume them," (Job 20:26). Partly in the continuance of afflictions. God orders, takes off, and lays on afflictions at his own pleasure, and as he sees it conducible to our profit. Variety of afflictions may meet together on the best and dearest of God's children, there being in the best many corruptions both to be discovered and subdued, and many graces to be tried. 1 Peter 1:6, "Wherein ye greatly rejoice, though now for a season, if need be, ye are in heaviness, through manifold temptations;" and James 1:2, "My brethren, count it all joy when ye fall into divers temptations." One trouble works into the hands of another, and their succession is as necessary as the first stroke. We often force God to renew his corrections, *ab assuetis nulla fit passio* things to which we are accustomed do not affect us; therefore, under a general affliction there come in many special ones to rub up our sense and make it work the better. Under public calamities we have a private one, and they come one in the neck of another like waves. When God has begun he will make an end, and bring his discipline to some more comfortable and perfect issue. In all these things the wisdom of God is to be observed.

4. The affliction so sent has a notable use to reduce us to a sense and care of our duty. This is often pressed in the scripture. "The fruit of all shall be to take away their sin." Afflictions are compared in scripture to fire that purges away our dross. 1 Peter 1:7, "Now for a season, if need be, ye are in manifold temptations, that the trial of your faith, being much more precious than of gold that perisheth, though it be tried with fire, might be found unto praise, and honour, and glory at the appearing of Jesus Christ." To the fan that drives away the chaff, (Mark 3:12), "Whose fan is in his hand, and he will thoroughly purge his floor, and gather his wheat into the garner; but he will burn up the chaff with unquenchable fire." To a pruninghook, that cuts off the luxuriant branches, and makes the others that remain more fruitful. John 15:2, "Every branch in me that beareth not fruit he taketh away, and every branch that beareth fruit he purgeth it that it may bring forth more fruit." To medicine, that purges away the sick matter. Isa. 27:9, "By this therefore shall the iniquity of Jacob be purged, and this is all the fruit to take away his sin." To ploughing and harrowing of the ground, that destroys the ill weeds, and fits it to receive the good seed. Jer. 4:3, "Break up your fallow ground, and sow not among thorns." To the

file that works off our rust, and the flail that makes our husk fly off. So Heb. 12:11, "No affliction for the present seemeth joyous, but grievous; nevertheless afterward it yieldeth the peaceable fruit of righteousness to them that are exercised therewith." The affliction has a necessary tendency to lead us to such a comfortable effect. But because *things in general* do but beat the air, and do not so well fit themselves in the mind, I shall show you it is either the means of our first conversion, or subservient to the reformation of those that are converted.

[1.] It is a means of our first conversion. How many begin with God on the occasion of afflictions! The time of sorrows is a time of loves. The hot furnace is Christ's workhouse, where he forms the most excellent vessels of honor and praise for his own use. Manasseh, Paul, and the jailer in the Acts, were all chosen in the fire; as the Lord says, Isa. 48:10, "I have chosen thee in the furnace of affliction," where God began to discover his choice by his working on their affections. All men are vessels capable of any form, therefore God puts them into the furnace. Most of us are taken in our month, as the ram that Abraham offered was caught in the thickets. When stout and stubborn sinners are broken with want and distress, then they come to themselves, and think of returning to their Father. Luke 15:17-18, "And when he came to himself, he said, How many hired servants of my father's have bread enough and to spare, and I perish with hunger! I will arise and go to my father," *etc.* Afflictions make us more serious; conscience is then apt to work. Before, we were guided by the wisdom of the flesh, and governed by our carnal appetite, never minded heavenly things, until God gets us under, and then we think about ourselves. Have you never known any instance in this kind? That while they were young, rich, strong, noble, all their humor was for vain pleasure, today hunting, tomorrow hawking, another day feasting, and then brawling, fighting, drinking, carousing, dancing; all the warnings of parents, the good counsel of tutors and governors, the grave exhortations of ministers and preachers, will do no good on them; they are always wandering up and down from God and from themselves, cannot endure a thought of God, of death, of heaven, of hell, of judgment to come; but when God casts them once into some grievous disease, or some great trouble, they begin to come to themselves, and then they that would hear nothing, understand nothing, despised all grave and gracious counsel given, as if it did not belong to them, scoffed at admonitions, thought the day lost in which they had not acted some sin or other, when the cross preaches to them, and some grievous calamity is on them, then conscience begins to work, and this brings to remembrance all that they have heard before, then they come to themselves, and would be glad if they could come to Christ. Sharp affliction is a sound, powerful, rousing teacher. Job 36:8-9, "And if they be bound in fetters, and be holden in cords of affliction, then he showeth them their work, and their transgressions that they have exceeded." Grace works in a powerful but yet in a moral way, congruously but forcibly, and by a fit accommodation of circumstances.

I'll give you one more place. Jer. 31:18, "Truly I have heard Ephraim bemoaning himself thus, Thou hast chastised me, and I was chastised, as a bullock unaccustomed to the yoke. Turn thou me, and I shall be turned; for thou art the Lord my God." Affliction awakens serious reflections on our ways; therefore take heed what ye do with the convictions that arise on afflictions; to slight them is dangerous. Nothing breeds hardness of heart so much as the smothering of convictions. Iron often heated grows the harder. On the other side, see they do not degenerate into despair, either the raging despair which terrifies, or the sottish despair which stupefies. Jer. 18:12, "They said, There is no hope, but we will walk after our own devices, and we will every one do the imagination of his evil heart." The middle between both is a holy sensibleness of our condition, which is a good preparation for the great duties of the gospel. The work of conversion is at first difficult and troublesome, but pass over this brunt, and all things will be sweet and easy. The bullock at first yoking is most unruly, and fire at the first kindling casts forth most smoke; so when sin is revived it brings forth death. Rom. 7:9, "For I was alive without the law once, but when the commandment came, sin revived, and I died." But yet cherish the work until God speaks peace on sound terms.

[2.] It is a great help to those that are converted already. How many are reduced to a more serious, lively practice of godliness by their troubles! We are rash, inconsiderate, inattentive to our duty, but the rod makes us cautious and diligent. We follow the world, not the word of God; the vanities of it take us off from minding the promises or precepts of the word, until the affliction comes. In short, there are none of us so tamed and subdued to God but that we need to be tamed more. We are all for carnal liberty; there is a wantonness in us. We are high-minded, earthly-minded, until God comes with his scourge to reclaim us. He chastens us for our profit, that we may be partakers of his holiness, (Heb. 12:10); some lust still needs mortifying, or some grace needs exercising; our pride needs to be mortified, or our affections to be weaned from the world. The almond-tree is made more fruitful by driving nails into it, because that lets out a noxious gum that hinders its fruitfulness; so when God would have you thrive more, he makes you feel the sharpness of affliction. You have heard Plutarch's story of Jason of Chasrea, that had his ailment helped by cutting him open and letting out the sickness by a casual wound. There is some corruption God would let out. We are apt to set up our rest here, and therefore, we need to be disturbed, to have the world crucified to us, (Gal. 6:14), that the encumbrance of the world may drive us to seek for rest where it is only to be found, and to humble us by outward defects. We must look after inward abundance, that, by being poor in this world, we may be rich in faith, (James 2:5), and having nothing in the creature, we may possess all things in God, (2 Cor. 6:10). We are to be enlarged inwardly as we are straitened outwardly; in short, that we may be oftener with God. God sent a tempest after Jonah. Absalom set Joab's barley-field on fire, and then he came to him, (2 Sam. 14:30). Isa. 26:16, "Lord, in trouble have they visited thee; they poured out a prayer when thy chastening was upon them." Hosea 5:15, "In their affliction they will seek me early." It would be endless to run out in discourses of this nature.

5. The affliction of itself does not work in this way, but as sanctified and accompanied with the Spirit of God. If the affliction of itself and by itself would do it, it would do so always, but that we see by experience it does not. In itself it is an evil and a pain that is the consequent and the fruit of sin, and so breeds impatience, despair, murmuring, and blasphemy against God. As it is a legal curse, other fruit cannot be expected of it but reviving terrors of heart and repinings against the sovereignty of God. We see often the same affliction that makes one humble, makes another raging; the same poverty that makes one full of dependence on God, makes another full of shifts and evil courses by which to supply his lack. No, it is understood of sanctified crosses, when grace goes along with them to bless them to us. Jer. 31:19, "Surely after that I was turned, I repented; and after that I was instructed, I smote upon my thigh. I was ashamed, yea, even confounded, because I did bear the reproach of my youth." This shows that God worked a gracious change in him by his afflicting hand and Spirit working together afterwards. So, Psa. 114:12, "Blessed is he whom thou chastenest, and instructest out of thy law." The rod must be expounded by the word, and both must be effectually applied by the Spirit. Grace is God's immediate creature and production; he uses subservient means and helps,

sometimes the word, sometimes the rod, sometimes both; but neither does anything without his Spirit.

6. This benefit, though gotten by sharp afflictions, should be owned, and thankfully acknowledged as a great testimony and expression of God's love to us. So, David does this to the praise of God. It is a branch that belongs to the thanksgiving mentioned in verse 65, "Thou hast done well with thy servant, according to thy word." We are prejudiced against the cross out of a self–love, a mistaken self–love; we love ourselves more than we love God, and the ease of the body more than the welfare of the soul. We love the world more than heaven, and our temporal pleasure and contentment more than our spiritual and eternal benefit; and therefore, we cannot endure to hear of the cross, much more to bear it. O! this does not become men; surely it does not become Christians! Would you have your consolation here? Luke 16. Your portion here? Psa. 7. Would you value yourselves by the flourishing of the outward man, or the renewing of the inward man? 2 Cor. 4:16. Should we be so impatient of the cross? Afflictions are bitter to present sense, but yet they are healthful to the soul. They are not so bitter in present feeling as they will be sweet in the after–fruits.

Now, we are greatly unthankful to God, if the bitterness is not lessened and tempered by this fruit and profit. Consider, when are we most miserable? When we go astray, or when we are reduced into the right way? When we are engaged in a rebellion against God, or when brought into a sense of our duty? Hosea 4:17, "Ephraim is joined to idols. let him alone." Let him alone is the heaviest judgment that can be laid upon a poor creature. Providence, conscience, ministry ... let him alone; the case is desperate, and we are incorrigible when we are left to our own ways. There is no more necessary to make our case miserable and sad than to be suffered to go on in sin without let and restraint; there is no hope of such. God seems to cast them off, and to desert and leave them to their own lusts. It is evident he does not mind their salvation, but leaves them to the world, to be condemned with the world. Well, then, does God do the elect any harm when he casts them into great troubles? If we use violence to a man that is ready to be drowned, and, in pulling him out of the waters, should break an arm or a leg, would he not be thankful? *Yes,* he says, *I can dispense with that, for you have saved my life.* So may God's children bless his name. Blessed providence! I had been a witless fool, and gone on in a course of sin, if God had not awakened me. A philosopher could say that he never made better voyage than when he suffered shipwreck, because then he began to apply himself to the study of wisdom. Surely a Christian should say, *Blessed be God that he laid his chastenings on me, and brought me to a serious heavenly mind. I should otherwise have been a carnal fool, as others are.* Wicked men are left to their own swing. When the case of the sick is desperate, physicians let them alone, give them leave to take anything they have a mind unto. The apostle speaks much to this purpose. Heb. 12:6, "Whom the Lord loveth he chasteneth, and scourgeth every son whom he receiveth." Sharp afflictions, which in their visible appearance seem tokens of God's hatred, are rather tokens of his love. There is a twofold love of God *Amor benevolentice et complacentice* the love of good–will, by which the Lord out of the purposes of his own free grace regenerates us, and adopts us into his family; and having loved us, and made us amiable, he then delights in us. The text alleged may be expounded of either. O! then, why do not we more own God in our afflictions? If he uses us a little, hardly, it is not an argument of his hatred, but his love. You do not dare to pray, *Lord, let me have my worldly comforts, though they damn me; let me not be afflicted, though it will do me good.* And if you do not dare to pray that way, will you repine when God sees this course necessary for us, and takes away the fuel of our lusts? Is it not a good exchange to part with outward comforts for inward holiness? If he takes away our riotous spirit, and gives us peace of conscience, our worldly goods, and gives us true riches, have we cause to complain? If outward needs are recompensed with an abundance of inward grace, if we have less of the world, that we may have more of God, a healthy soul in a sickly body, it is a just matter of thanksgiving. 3 John 2, "I wish, above all things, that thou mayest prosper and be in health, even as thy soul prospereth." We can subscribe to this in general: all will affirm that afflictions are profitable, and that it is a good thing to be patient and submissive under them, but when any cross comes to knock at our door, we are loath to give it entrance; and if it thrusts in on us, we fret and fume, and our souls sit uneasy, and all because we are addicted so unreasonably to the ease of the flesh, the quiet, happiness, and welfare of the carnal life, and have so little regard to life spiritual.

7. At the first coming of the affliction we do not see this benefit so well as in the review of the whole dispensation. "Before I was afflicted I went astray; but now I have kept thy word." So Heb. 12:11, "Now no chastening for the present seemeth to be joyous, but grievous; nevertheless afterward it yieldeth the peaceable fruit of righteousness to them which are exercised thereby." There is a perfect opposition; the root and the fruit are opposed in affliction and fruit of righteousness, the quality of the root, and the quality of the fruit. God's medicine must have time to work. At first it may not be so, or at least not appear; for things are *before* they appear or can be observed for the present. We must tarry God's leisure, and be content with his blows, until we feel their benefit. It is first a matter of faith, and then of feeling; though we do not presently understand why everything is done, we must wait. The hand on the dial does not seem to stir, yet it keeps its course; while it is paving we do not see it, but that it has passed from one hour to another is evident. So is God's work with the soul; and spiritual renovation and increase is not so sensible at the first though it is on day by day, (2 Cor. 4:16), but in view of the whole it will appear. What, are we better? Does sin decay us? And what sin? Do we find it otherwise with us than it was before?

8. This profit is not only when the affliction is on us, but after it is over the fruit of it must remain. Their qualms and pangs most have. Psa. 78:34–37, "When he

slew them, then they sought him, and returned and inquired early after God. and they remembered that God was their rock, and the high God their redeemer. Nevertheless, they did flatter him with their mouth, and they lied unto him with their tongues; for their heart was not right with him, neither were they steadfast in his covenant." Many have a little forced religion in their extremities, but it wears off with their trouble. Sin is but suspended for a while, and the devil chained up; they are very good under the rod, they are frightened to it; but after the deliverance comes, they are more profane. It is true many may begin with God in their troubles, and their necessities drive them to the throne of grace; and Christ had never heard of many, if fevers and palsies, and possessions and blindness, deafness and dumbness, had not brought them to him; thanks to the disease. But if a course of godliness begins on these occasions, and continues afterwards, God will accept it; he is willing to receive us on any terms. Men will say, *You come to me in your extremity*, but he does not upbraid us, provided we will come so as to abide with him, and will not turn the back upon him when our turn is served. If you do so, take heed; God has other judgments to reach you. As John said, Matt. 3:11-12, "He that cometh after me is mightier than I, whose shoes I am not worthy to bear; he shall baptize you with the Holy Ghost and with fire. whose fan is in his hand, and he will thoroughly purge his floor, and gather his wheat into the garner, but he will burn up the chaff with unquenchable fire." So that which comes after is mightier than that which went before; the last judgment is the heaviest. "The axe is laid to the root of the tree; therefore every tree that bringeth not forth good fruit is hewn down, and cast into the fire," (Matt. 3:10). He will not only lop off the branches, but strike at the root; as the Sodomites that escaped the sword of Chedorlaomer perished by fire from heaven. The Israelites that were not drowned in the Red Sea, were stung to death by fiery serpents. "As if a man did flee from a lion, and a bear met him; or went into the house and leaned his hand on the wall, and a serpent bit him," (Amos 5:19). When you avoid one judgment, you may meet another, and find a stroke where you think yourselves most secure.

Use 1. Let us consider these things, that we may profit by all the chastenings of the Lord. It is now a time of affliction, both as to public judgments and as to the private condition of many of the people of God. We have been long straying from God, from our duty, from one another; it was high time for the Lord to take his rod in his hand, and to scourge us home again. On these three nations there is something of God's three great judgments war, pestilence, and famine; they are all dreadful. The pestilence is such a judgment as turns populous cities into deserts and solitudes in a short time; then one cannot help another. Riches and honors profit nothing then, and friends and kinsfolks stand afar off. Many die without any spiritual helps. In war, what destructions and slaughters, expense of blood and treasure! In famine, you feel yourselves to die without a disease, and do not know where to have fuel to allay and feed the fire which nature has kindled in your bodies. But, blessed be God, all these are in moderation.

Pestilence does not ragingly spread, the war is at a distance, the famine only a scarcity. Before God stirs up all his wrath, he observes what we do with these beginnings. Besides, the people of God are involved in a heap of miseries on all hands; the oppressed, dejected party burdened with jealousies, and ready to be hauled to prison and put under restraint. Holy men sometimes have personal afflictions added to the public calamities. Jeremiah was cast into the dungeon when the city was besieged. The chaff and grain both are threshed together, but the grain is, besides, ground in the mill and baked in the oven. Besides, who thinks of his strayings, and re turning with a more serious resolution to his duty? If we would profit by afflictions we must avoid both the faulty extremes. Heb. 12:5, "My son, despise not thou the chastening of the Lord, nor faint when thou art rebuked of him." Slighting and fainting must be avoided.

1. Let us not slight them. When we bear them with a stupid senseless mind, surely that hinders all profit. None can endure to have their anger despised, no more than their love. A father is displeased when his child slights his correction. That we may not slight it, let us consider.

[1.] Their author, God. We think them fortuitous, from chance, but they "do not rise out of the dust," (Job 5:6). Whoever are the instruments, or whatever are the means, the wise God has its whole ordering. He is the first cause; he is to be sought to, he is to be appeased, if we would stop evil at the fountain-head; for all creatures willingly or unwillingly obey him, and are subject to his empire and government. Amos 3:6,

"Is there any evil in the city, and I have not done it, saith the Lord?" Isa. 45:7, "I form the light, and create darkness; I make peace and create evil; I the Lord do all these things." Job 1:21, "The Lord giveth, and the Lord taketh away."

[2.] The meritorious cause is sin. Lam. 3:39, "Wherefore doth a living man complain, a man for the punishment of his sin?" That first brought mischief into the world, and still continues it. God never afflicts without a cause; either we need it, or we deserve it. Micah 7:9, "I will bear the indignation of the Lord, because I have sinned against him, until he plead my cause, and execute judgment for me. he will bring me forth to the light, and I shall behold his righteousness." We should search for the particular sins that provoke God to afflict us; for while we only speak of sin in general, we do but inveigh against a notion, and personate mourning; but those we can charge on ourselves are most proper and powerful to break the heart.

[3.] The end is our repentance and amendment, to correct sin past, or prevent sin to come.

(1.) For correction, to make us more penitent for sins past. We being in a lower sphere of understanding, know things better by their effects than their nature. Jer. 2:19, "Thine own wickedness shall correct thee, and thy backslidings shall reprove thee. know, therefore, and see that it is an evil and bitter thing that thou hast forsaken the Lord thy God, and that my fear is not in thee, saith the Lord of hosts." Moral evil is represented to us by natural evil; pain shows what sin is.

(2.) For prevention of sin for time to come. The pain should make us cautious and watchful against sin. Joshua 22:17-18, "Is the iniquity of Peor too little for us, from which we are not cleansed to this day, although there was a plague in the congregation of the Lord, but that ye must turn away this day from following the Lord? And it will be, seeing ye rebel today against the Lord, that tomorrow he will be wroth with the whole congregation of Israel." Afflictions also should stir up in us heavenly thoughts, heavenly desires, and more lively diligence in the exercise of those graces which before lay dormant in us through our neglect. Only I must tell you, that sometimes the affliction may be merely for prevention, and may go before sin. God has always a cause, but he does not always suppose a fault in act, but sometimes in possibility; looking into your actions or your temper, what you have done, or would do, to cure or prevent a distemper in your spirit, as well as a disorder in your conversation.

2. Let us not faint. When the afflictions sit close and near, then we are apt to fall into the other extreme, to be dejected out of measure. An *over-sense* works on our anger, and then it is fretting; or on our sorrow, and then it is fainting. The former is the worse of the two, for that is to set up an anti-providence, or a being displeased with God's government, a practical disowning of his greatness and justice.

All men will acknowledge God is great, yet what worm is there that will submit to him any further than they please? We say we deserve nothing but evil from his hands, but yet are maddened like wild bulls in a net when the goad is in our sides. We say, *Any other cross but this.* We do not dislike trial, but this trial that is upon us. God thought this fittest for us; our murmuring will not ease our trouble, but increase and continue it. Certainly, without submission troubles will do us no good. "Patience worketh experience," (Rom. 5:4). Fainting, properly so taken, is when we look on God's work through a false glass, and mis-expound his dispensation. God puts forth his hand, not to thrust us off, but pull us to himself. Hosea 5:15, "I will go and return to my place, until they acknowledge their offence, and seek my face: in their affliction they will seek me early." The very affliction gives us hope that he will not let us go on securely in our sins. It is not our being afflicted and made miserable by trouble which God aims at. Lam. 3:33, "He doth not afflict willingly, nor grieve the children of men." Nor is it that which we should chiefly be affected with under affliction. We should mind another lesson taught by it, which if we neglect, our sense of trouble will be but perplexing. It is to subdue sin, to make us more mindful of heavenly things, to have our hearts humbled. No affliction should be counted intolerable which helps to purge our sin. We evidence our love to sin if we are overmuch troubled at it, or peevishly quarrel with God. Fainting shows our weakness. Prov. 24:10, "If thou faint in the day of adversity, thy strength is small."

Use 2. Something concerning the profit of it. value it, observe it.

1. Value it. What do you count a profit or benefit, to flow in wealth, or excel in grace; to live in ease, or to be kept in a holy, heavenly, and humble frame? Heb. 12:10, "For they verily for a few days chastened us after their own pleasure, but he for our profit, that we might be partakers of his holiness." Not that we might have the health of this world, but that we might be partakers of his holiness. It is better to have holiness than to have health, wealth, and honor; the sanctification of an affliction is better than to have deliverance out of it. Deliverance takes away *malum naturale* some penal evil which God brings on us; sanctification, *malum morale* the greatest evil, which is sin. I am sure this is that which we should look after. Deliverance is God's work, the improvement of the trouble is our duty. Do you mind your work, and God will not be wanting to do his part?

2. Observe it, and see how the rod works, what thoughts it begets in you, what resolutions it stirs up, what solaces you run to, and seek after to this end.

[1.] In what temper and frame of heart you were when the affliction surprised you. Usually affliction treads upon the heels of some sin. If it is open, and in our practice, it discovers itself; if secret, and in the frame of our hearts, it must be searched after. Usually it is born out of slightness and carelessness of spiritual and heavenly things; your hearts were grown in love with the world, you began to neglect your souls, grew more cold in the love of God, more formal in prayer, and indifferent as to your spiritual estate; you did not watch over your hearts; therefore the holy and jealous God comes and awakens you by his painful scourge. The foregoing distemper observed, will help you to state your profit.

[2.] How that is cured by God's discipline, or what benefit you have gotten by it? You are more diligent in your duty, careful in your preparations for a better state. A Christian should be able to give an account of the methods by which God brings him to heaven. David could give an account, as here, "Before I was afflicted I went astray; but now have I kept thy word;" and verse 71, "It is good for me that I have been afflicted, that I might learn thy statutes;" not good that I should be, as accepting the punishment, but that I have been, as owning the profit.

FINIS.

Of the Plague or Pestilence
by Thomas Draxe

"And David spake unto the LORD when he saw the angel that smote the people, and said, Lo, I have sinned, and I have done wickedly: but these sheep, what have they done? let thine hand, I pray thee, be against me, and against my father's house," (2 Sam. 24:17).

Question: is the plague and pestilence of our time, contagious and infectious? Yes, without a doubt. For first, as the leprosy among the Jews infected not only men's persons, but also their garments, and their very habitations, so does the plague, as experience proves it.

Secondly, although the plague is God's special hand (2 Sam. 24:17), and his destroying angel, yet it does not come immediately by the sensible touch of an heavenly angel; for if it did come in that way, it would be extreme vanity, and madness itself, to shun the infected people and places; but ordinarily by outward means and occasions. This is true, experience teaches, that very many by declining the infected places and people, have been saved and preserved.

Thirdly, various people are not infected, have been so kept by medical preservatives; and many infected people have been cured by medicines and remedies. But if God had immediately struck them from heaven, (2 Sam. 24:15) (as he did 70000 of David's people) they would have all died without recovery.

Question. But why are not all people tainted and infected that live among the visited parties and people?

Answer. First, all people are not (by reason of their natural constitution) apt to take the infection. Secondly, God so rules and restrains the plague, that it shall touch none, nor in any further degree then God has appointed. Lastly, the execution of charitable duties about those visited, preserves many, and fervent prayer delivers various people.

Question. Is it lawful for any man to flee the infection?

Answer. Yes: for albeit Magistrates, necessary officers, and they that are pastors of the visited congregations may not flee, yet they that are either fearful, or freed from their ordinary calling, (for they are not bound, being in no public, and necessary office) may lawfully flee. For, first, a man may preserve himself by fleeing, so that he may not hurt another. A man may shun dangers of the same nature as war, famine, waters, fires, and why not then this judgement?

Consider, there is less danger of infection, when the concourse of people is abated and diminished.

1. Objection. They that flee cannot but distrust God's watchful providence.

Answer. The fault is not in the action, but in the person, because he distrusts.

2. Objection and Observation. But it is offensive for a man to flee.

Answer. The offence is taken and not given.

3. Objection and Observation. Whatever is against the rule of charity is unlawful. But to flee, and so forsake our neighbor, is against the rule of charity, *ergo*.

Answer. Our neighbor is not forsaken so long as he does not lack the help neither of Magistrate, nor of kinsfolk, and other friends.

4. Objection and Observation. But we are to visit the sick, and that by God's commandment.

Answer. Leprous people were excepted among the Jews, and why not then people with the plague in our days, seeing that this disease is no less contagious?

Question. What is the duty of them that flee?

Answer. First, they must seriously repent of their sins, otherwise God will correct them in some other kind (if not in this).

Secondly, they must earnestly entreat the Lord by prayer to stop his heavy hand, and to be merciful to the visited.

Lastly, they must willingly contribute money to the visited.

Question. What is the duty of them that abide at home?

Answer. They must not be secure and desperate (for oftentimes, God's most excellent servants are not only tainted and infected with, but also die of the plague) but humble themselves under God's hand, and endeavor by prayer and repentance to pacify and put away God's displeasure.

Secondly, they ought not censoriously to condemn, but charitably to judge of them that flee from infected places and people. For, many of them are not tied to be resident by any special calling, and many (especially those that live by their labors and by their trades) have no sufficient means at home to maintain themselves and their families in this way.

Question. Why does God sometimes in one country, or other, cut down and destroy so many thousands of men, by the sword of plague and pestilence?

Answer. First, if God, now and then should not take this strict course, the number of men, (especially amongst Turks, Papists, pagans,) would exceed. For ordinarily, men are faster born then they die, and on this God thrusts in his reaping hook, and cuts down certain thousands, when the places where they live and are resident, could not otherwise well contain, much less maintain them.

Secondly, to cut off and control the pride and presumption of such, who (with David when he numbered the people) glory and rest in their multitudes and millions. On this he represses their vain confidence, and to cure general and desperate sin, abates and lessens those numbers and multitudes.

Question. What meditations are necessary to comfort God's children in the time of a general infection by the plague or pestilence?

Answer. First, the plague is not casual and contingent, but is from God and in his disposition, so that none die and depart this life, sooner or later, in greater or smaller number then God permits and has pre-ordained.

Secondly, in the time of the Old Testament, in the time of the Apostles, and in every age since, (in one place, part, province or other) God's dearest servants have felt the contagion and noisiness of it, and various of them have died of this visitation.

Thirdly, it is a more mild, gentle, and sufferable chastisement, then either war or famine. For, in the beginning, progress and disposition of it, God rather works by himself then uses the ministry of men, and who in judgment remembers mercy. But men, when they are made the instruments to chastise us, so follow the violent stream of their own corrupt affections, that they show themselves destitute and deprived of all mercy and moderation.

Fourthly, when God by the plague corrects us, he will try and prove our faith in his powerful and gracious providence. He tries our tender compassion towards our distressed brethren, and our thankfulness towards them that either by public authority, or, of their charitable disposition attend on us, and that minister to our necessities.

Fifthly, God in the greatest infection when the plague most rages, preserves very many, and especially those that are employed about charitable offices which concern the visited.

Lastly, God's children that die by this visitation are as blessed as they that die by the common course of nature. For, the angels carry their souls into Abraham's bosom.

Question. What duties are the visited persons to perform?

Answer. First, they must commend themselves to God, who will for Christ's sake, be merciful to them.

Secondly, they must (while there is any hope of life, and while they have opportunity) use preservatives, medicines, remedies, restoratives, (for so did Hezekiah). But if they perceive the fatal hour has come, they must willingly, and confidently commend their spirits into God's hands.

Thirdly, if they are parents and masters of families, they must exhort their children, kinsfolk and servants, to the profession and practice of godliness and virtue. For, the last words that such people utter, do (commonly) leave the deepest impression in the hearts and minds of their children, friends and servants.

Lastly, if they recover from the plague, they must be thankful to God, (Psalm 66:14) pay to him the vows which their lips have promised and their mouth has spoken in affliction. And for the time to come they must fear an unexpected, and unpleasant sequel to a matter that had been considered closed, and beware lest a worse thing afterwards befall them.

FINIS

Other Helpful Works from Puritan Publications

The Nature, Danger and Cure of Temptation
by Richard Capel (1586–1656)

The Love of the World Cured
by Nathaniel Vincent (1639-1697)

The Cure of the Fear of Death
by Nicholas Byfield (1579–1622)

The Glorious Name of God the Lord of Hosts
by Jeremiah Burroughs (1599-1646)

Christ Inviting Sinners to Come to Him for Rest
by Jeremiah Burroughs (1599-1646)

The Excellency of Holy Courage in Evil Times
by Jeremiah Burroughs (1599-1646)

The Soul's Conflict Within Itself
by Richard Sibbes (1577-1635)

The Good Which Comes Out of the Evil of Affliction
by Nathaniel Vincent (1639-1697)

A Comfort for the Afflicted Christian
by William Plumer (1802-1880)

God's Sovereignty Displayed
by William Gearing (1625-1690)

www.ingramcontent.com/pod-product-compliance
Lightning Source LLC
Chambersburg PA
CBHW030838090426
42737CB00009B/1020

**"You can preach a better sermon with your life than
with your lips."**
-Oliver Goldsmith (1728-1774)

There's another saying that talk is cheap. Sure, it's easy to say something, but it takes time and effort to take action on it. Live life by example. We can't just say that we're "into the environment" and then go around driving SUVs and eating out of non-recyclable Styrofoam. Our actions give our words their meaning, and make them carry more weight. *-Lissa Coffey*

Excellence

**"The secret of joy in work is contained in one word –
excellence. To know how to do something well is to enjoy it."**
-Pearl S. Buck (1964)

When we enjoy doing something, we put our heart into it, and it shows. What we enjoy doing, we do well, we can't help it. And by the same token, what we do well brings us joy! We are rewarded for a job well done by feeling good about it. *-Lissa Coffey*

**"Excellence is not an act but a habit. The things you
do the most are the things you will do best."**
-Marva Collins (1987)

It would be easy if talent was all it took for us to achieve excellence. But it doesn't work that way. On "American Idol" there are many singers with talent. But the ones who have the most experience really stand out. The experience of singing for people over and over again hones their skills, and when the competition day comes, their excellence shows. We even see how week after week, each of the singers seems to get better. They're in an environment where they are focusing their energies and spending their time to cultivating excellence. *-Lissa Coffey*

**"When we do the best that we can, we never know what
miracle is wrought in our life, or in the life of another."**
-Helen Keller (1914)

Excellence is difficult to measure. In the Olympics there is a judging system of points and scores to compare the athlete's performances. But when it comes to our day to day lives, excellence for each one of us is doing the best that we can do. We know when we're slacking off. We know when we can do better. We're the only ones who can make that judgment accurately. And when we do strive for excellence, when we put ourselves out there and really give it our all, we know it, we can feel it. *-Lissa Coffey*

"When nobody around you seems to measure up, it's time to check your yardstick."
-Bill Lemley

Too often we have expectations of people that they just can't live up to. Where did these expectations come from? We need to remember that we're all doing the best that we can at any given moment in time. Rather than impose our own expectations on someone else, we can instead choose to be loving and accepting and see how it all works out cooperatively. *-Lissa Coffey*

"Hope for a miracle. But don't depend on one."
-Talmud

Of course we can work towards a goal with the best in mind. We can put every effort into making a project turn out just the way we want it to. But at a certain point we have to turn it over to the universe and just accept that we can't control everything, and we wouldn't want to! There are so many factors that can influence any situation. A project might not go well, but could it just as easily turn out better than we had planned. *-Lissa Coffey*

"I long to accomplish a great and noble task, but it is my chief duty to accomplish small tasks as if they were great and noble."
-Helen Keller

The expectations we set for ourselves are often higher, and more unrealistic, than the expectations we have for anything else. Why are we so hard on ourselves? We are here for a purpose, and there are no small purposes. We are learning and growing every day. We are doing the best we can. Good job! *-Lissa Coffey*

Experience

"We learn geology the morning after the earthquake."
-Ralph Waldo Emerson (1803-1882)

Aren't we funny? This is so true! Sometimes it takes something to "shake us up" so that we can learn. And then we do – we learn from our experiences, both positive and negative. All of life is our classroom; every day there are lessons for us. It's up to us if we want to do our homework and be prepared – and a lot of that is basically keeping up our spiritual practices. Or, we could goof off and take our chances that we won't get hit with a "pop quiz!" Whatever happens, we will eventually figure it out. *-Lissa Coffey*

"A moment's insight is sometimes worth a life's experience."
-Oliver Wendell Holmes, Sr. (1809-1894)

So where do these insights come from if not from experience? They come from the infinite wisdom of the Universe. We can tap into it at any time through meditation. Everything we need to know is right there for us. Meditation gives us direct experience of the spirit. *-Lissa Coffey*

"If it be knowledge or wisdom one is seeking, then one had better go direct to the source. And the source is not the scholar or philosopher, not the master, saint, or teacher, but life itself- direct experience of life."
-Henry Miller (1891-1980)

There are all different ways of learning and growing. There are amazing works by brilliant people available to us at any time. And we can gain so much from the words of our fellow man. But where did they get these insights? At some point, the knowledge has to be experienced to be understood. And when it is understood, then it can be expressed. We all know what lessons we have learned from our experiences. And this is a big part of why we're here – to experience life, to learn and to grow. *-Lissa Coffey*

"Experience is what you get looking for something else."
-Mary Pettibone Poole, 1938

And many years later, John Lennon said: "Life is what happens when you're busy making other plans." This is why "going with the flow" is such an important concept for our spiritual growth. We never know what we are going to encounter along the way! Our experiences help to shape our perceptions; they help us to discover more of who we really are. What are we looking for? It doesn't matter... what we find, through our experiences, is ourselves. *-Lissa Coffey*

"What is it which is bought dearly, offered for nothing, and then most often refused? Experience, old people's experience."
-Isak Dinesen, 1934

We learn from our experiences. And it is our privilege to share those experiences with other people. We're here to help each other. Whether or not we learn from each other is an individual choice. The gems of experiences that are collected over the years form a treasure chest of wisdom that longs to be distributed. Why not tap into that wealth? And in turn, we're giving someone the gift of being recognized and valued. *-Lissa Coffey*

Eyes

"The eye of the beholder may govern what is seen."
-James MacGregor Burns

We have heard the saying that beauty is in the eyes of the beholder, but this takes it one step further. Whatever it is that we see is interpreted through our eyes and our brain and we give it meaning. Whether it's beauty or anything else. What values are we putting on things? What are we reading into anything we see? It's interesting that when two or more people witness the exact same event, and then they describe it, it can seem like totally different experiences! *-Lissa Coffey*

"Eyes can speak and eyes can understand."
-George Chapman (1559?-1634)

We can say so much without speaking a word. Emotions show on our face. Our eyes can't lie. Experts who read body language say that so much is given away with the eyes. They have been called "the mirrors of the soul." We can communicate with our loved ones with merely a look. Sometimes a look can speak volumes! *-Lissa Coffey*

"So shall we come to look at the world with new eyes."
-Ralph Waldo Emerson (1803-1882)

New eyes, a fresh perspective, an improved outlook. Think of all of the ways that we describe clarity. Clarity is used here as in seeing more clearly, or understanding more deeply. Seeing with that inner vision, the mind's eye, is important for our learning and growth. *-Lissa Coffey*

"Close your eyes, and you will see."
-Joseph Joubert (1754-1824)

In many meditations, we close our eyes because we want to block out external distractions. The idea is to go within, to look within. In the silence, in the stillness, we gain great insight. We can see things more clearly. *-Lissa Coffey*

"In a dark time, the eye begins to see."
-Theodore Roethke (1908-1963)

When we go from a bright room to a dark room at first we can't see. But once our eyes adjust to the light, we start to see better, until we become comfortable making our way around. In a dark time, when things aren't going the best for us, and we feel as if we're struggling, it's difficult to find our way. But we learn, and we grow, and we begin to understand and benefit from the experiences we go through. *-Lissa Coffey*

Failure

"Failure is just another way to learn how to do something right."
-Marian Wright Edelman, 1987

We tend to think of failure as such a negative. But it's only a negative if we let it stop us. The other way of looking at failure is seeing it as one step closer to success! We learn from our trials and tribulations. And we take what we learn and grow from the experience – which makes us more prepared for success. It's part of the process.
-Lissa Coffey

"People fail forward to success."
-Mary Kay Ash, 1984

It's a matter of attitude. Some baseball players say that after they strike out they feel relieved, because it just means that the odds are better for them the next time they go up to bat. The important thing is that they do get back up there and have another go at it. Failure doesn't have to be an obstacle, it can be a stepping stone. *-Lissa Coffey*

"Apparent failure may hold in its rough shell the germs of a success that will blossom in time, and bear fruit throughout eternity."
-Frances Ellen Watkins Harper, 1875

We're learning and growing every day. We're building on our experiences. When things happen differently than we had planned, or expected, or wanted them to, we might see it as a failure. But it's not! There is a reason for everything, and sometimes what is an "apparent failure" is actually the beginning of something really beautiful.
-Lissa Coffey

"If you have made mistakes, even serious ones, there is always another chance for you. What we call failure is not the falling down, but the staying down."
-Mary Pickford, (in Reader's Digest, 1979)

Things happen. That's just the way it is. But at every point in time we have choices to make. We can choose to learn from our mistakes. We can choose to try again. If we were perfect, and never made mistakes, then how could we possibly learn? Our wisdom comes from our own experiences. Like the song says: "pick yourself up, brush yourself off, and start all over again!" *-Lissa Coffey*

"To think of losing is to lose already."
-Sylvia Townsend Warner, 1951

The mind is a very powerful tool. With it we create our reality. The surest way to fail is to focus on failure. Instead, we can picture ourselves doing well, achieving, succeeding, and being happy. When we drive, we look ahead to where we are going. We can't drive by looking in the rear view mirror. We can't drive by looking over at the ditch on the side of the road. We need to pay attention to where we want to go, and head in that direction. *-Lissa Coffey*

Faith

"Faith is a mental attitude that is so convinced of its own idea - which so completely accepts it - that any contradiction is unthinkable and impossible."
-Ernest Holmes

There is nothing stronger, or more powerful, than faith. Faith gets us further than anything else. With faith, we can accomplish anything. *-Lissa Coffey*

"There is no chance, no destiny, no fate, Can circumvent or hinder or control The firm resolve of a determined soul."
-Ella Wheeler Wilcox

Sometimes we want something so badly, yet we're afraid to really go for it. That's when we're told to take a leap of faith. Wow. That leap can be a pretty big one, too. But it is good for us to do this! It is only when we embrace the unknown and venture out into the field of infinite possibilities that we discover what is out there for us. *-Lissa Coffey*

"Any anxious thought as to the means to be employed in the accomplishment of our purposes is quite unnecessary. If the end is already secured, then if follows that all the steps leading to it are secured also."
-Thomas Troward.

Faith is knowing. It's not believing or guessing or hoping, it is KNOWING. It is complete trust in the Divine. There is an organizing power in the Universe. That power is also within each one of us! When we set our goals, the Universe - through us - orchestrates the avenues by which we reach those goals. We don't need to question, or fret, we just need to have faith and know that it is already done. *-Lissa Coffey*

> **"Faith is the centerpiece of a connected life. It allows us to live by the grace of invisible strands. It is a belief in a wisdom superior to our own. Faith becomes a teacher in the absence of fact."**
> -Terry Tempest Williams, Refuge (1991)

"Connected" and aware of our connection, is how we all want to live. Faith is all the evidence we need of that connection. When we turn to faith, we feel it. It is calming, comforting and all-knowing. We can't always see it with our eyes, but we can feel it with our hearts. *-Lissa Coffey*

> **"Faith makes the discords of the present the harmonies of the future."**
> -Robert Collyer (1823-1912) American Unitarian clergy

Just as we have faith that the sun is behind the clouds on a rainy day, we can have faith that whatever problems seems to be presenting themselves at the moment will be resolved. And they will. When we don't know what to do – we can always have faith. *-Lissa Coffey*

Family

> **"The happiest moments of my life have been the few which I have passed at home in the bosom of my family."**
> -Thomas Jefferson (1743-1826)

We know that not everyone is fortunate enough to have a happy, idyllic family life. But if we look at the broader definition of family, and choose to spend our time this holiday season with people who love us and whose company we enjoy, then we can share some happy moments. There is a joy we get from being with family that we can't get anywhere else. *-Lissa Coffey*

> **"The whole world is my family."**
> -Pope John XXIII (1881-1963)

There is so much truth, and so much simplicity in this statement. The whole world really is our family. We are each connected to the other. When we can all see this, feel this, understand it and accept it in our hearts, then there will truly be peace on earth. For how then could there be anything less? *-Lissa Coffey*

> **"The family. We were a strange little band of characters trudging through life sharing diseases and toothpaste, coveting one another's desserts, hiding shampoo, borrowing money, locking each other out of our rooms, inflicting pain and kissing to heal it in the same instant, loving, laughing, defending, and trying to figure out the common thread that bound us all together."**
> -Erma Bombeck, 1987

This is a good week to talk about family. I grew up reading Erma Bombeck's columns - my mother could really relate to her. Erma had a great way of seeing the humor and light in the most absurd situations. This family, this group of people we're somehow thrown together with, and with whom we share our tragedies and triumphs, is ultimately one of our greatest tools for learning in this lifetime. They challenge us, in ways no one else can, to grow. *-Lissa Coffey*

> **"Family life! The United Nations is child's play compared to the tugs and splits and need to understand and forgive in any family."**
> -May Sarton, 1970

I'm sure we all have our stories! What would we do without our families? Good or bad or indifferent, the families we have somehow have helped us to become the people we are today. Through our family we can see our connection to the world. And as our family grows, with children and grandchildren, cousins and in-laws, we are presented with more opportunities for learning and growth. It's interesting that there has been a rise in the popularity of genealogy and family tree research lately. Through these studies our connections throughout time become apparent. The world becomes smaller, and we don't feel as isolated when we start looking at our roots. *-Lissa Coffey*

> **"To us, family means putting your arms around each other and being there."**
> -Barbara Bush

What makes a family? By now we know it's more than merely bloodlines. A family is a support system - it's a group of people connected in some way. It's people who love each other and are there for each other in good times and bad. I feel so lucky to have my family, and to me that includes not only my relatives, but friends who have seen me through a lot of my own growth and changes. And it works both ways. We feel closer to people when we go through experiences together. There are some bonds that develop that just can't be broken. *-Lissa Coffey*

Fate

> **"One life is all we have and we live it as we believe in living it. But to sacrifice what you are and to live without belief, that is a fate more terrible than dying."**
> -Joan of Arc

How much of life is determined by fate, and how much by free will? For most of us, it's some combination, so we consult our horoscopes, just for added information! But as we grow wiser, and stronger, we understand that we are creating our own future, with very step, with every thought. Know who you are, be who you are, and live the life you were meant to lead. *-Lissa Coffey*

"Through kindness, you can change your fate."
-Nguyen T. Nguyen (1992)

It's amazing how far a good attitude will get us. It's the lemons into lemonade theory. Just add a little sugar and look what happens! There is always a better way. Use your power, your intellect, your creativity. Be kind. Be loving. And you'll soon taste the sweetness of life. -*Lissa Coffey*

**"Every human being is the artificer of his own fate –
Events, circumstances, etc., have their origin in ourselves.
They spring from seeds which we have sown."**
-Henry David Thoreau (1817-1862)

We are more powerful, and more creative, than we realize. And our power doesn't come from outside of us – it's not from our position at work, or our wealth, or our supply of weapons. Those are just symbols, and they come and go. Our real power comes from within, from our faith, our determination, the inner strength that we have developed from our experiences. When we summon up this power we can achieve anything. -*Lissa Coffey*

"Fate keeps on happening."
-Anita Loos, Gentlemen Prefer Blondes (1925)

Life keeps on happening. I am hearing that song from Journey in my head right now: "Wheel in the sky keeps on turning, don't know where I'll be tomorrow." I guess that's what keeps life interesting for us. We can't control everything that happens in the world, because everyone has free will. So, yes, some things are uncertain – and that is really wonderful! We can have happy surprises at any time. -*Lissa Coffey*

"If you believe in fate, believe in it, at least, for your good."
-Ralph Waldo Emerson (1803-1882)

Our thoughts are powerful. So, think good thoughts! It's that simple. Look forward to good things. Be positive; be optimistic. Create your own destiny as you would like it to be. Set your course, as the captain of your own ship. -*Lissa Coffey*

Feelings

**"The wide discrepancy between reason and feeling
may be unreal; it is not improbable that intellect is a
high form of feeling – a specialized, intensive feeling
about intuitions."**
-Susanne K. Langer, 1967

A lot of time we hear about the difference between the heart and the head, or between feelings and reason. But even if there is a difference between them, there is a connection between them. We can assimilate the two, and use the power as one, to make the important choices in our lives. It's that merger that empowers us to overcome any challenges we come across. *-Lissa Coffey*

"Our feelings are our most genuine paths to knowledge."
-Audre Lorde, 1983

Our feelings are what guide us. Our natural attraction to certain areas of study leads us to higher learning. When we follow our instincts we find opportunities for ourselves that help us to achieve our goals, and to make our visions a reality. *-Lissa Coffey*

"Human relations are built on feeling, not on reason or knowledge. And feeling is not an exact science; like all spiritual qualities, it has the vagueness of greatness about it."
-Amelia E. Barr, 1904

We all have some friends who we love and we're happy to have in our lives. It doesn't matter that we might have nothing in common, or live thousands of miles away, or communicate quite rarely. The minute we see that friend it's like no time has gone by at all. There's a spiritual connection between people that is beyond definition. We can't explain it, but we can certainly feel it when it is there. *-Lissa Coffey*

"One of the quickest ways to become exhausted is by suppressing your feelings."
-Sue Patton Thoele, 1988

Feelings need to be recognized, and expressed. Suppressing feelings not only can lead to exhaustion, but to depression and all kinds of dis-ease. We need to be self-aware, and work on understanding our feelings. It's all a part of taking care of ourselves. *-Lissa Coffey*

"The thoughts they had were the parents of the actions they did; their feelings were parents of their thoughts."
-Thomas Carlyle (1795-1881)

Why do we do some of the things we do? We had an idea! But where did that idea come from? At some level it came from a feeling, an intuition, an affinity that drew us toward the idea, or that created the idea. When we are in touch with our feelings, we can come up with some great ideas! *-Lissa Coffey*

Films

"Other than life experience, nothing left a deeper imprint on my formative self than the movies."
-Letty Cottin Pogrebin, 1991

Some movies just stick with us. There are certain phrases, certain scenes, we always remember. And we can learn from the effect that the movies have on us. Remember how Dorothy, in "The Wizard of Oz," just wanted to go home? And she was really there all the time. What a powerful message. And the Tin-Man wanted a heart so badly, and yet, it was there all along, he just didn't recognize it. We can relate to these characters on their journey as we follow our own yellow-brick road. -*Lissa Coffey*

"Perhaps making movies is a step toward being able to move backward and forward and in and out of linear time."
-Eleanor Coppola, 1979

There's a quote that Yoda says in one of the Star Wars films that I use on my boys all the time: "Do or do not, there is no try." They even gave me a Yoda action figure one year as a present because they said I love Yoda so much! It's funny because it doesn't matter where or when a story takes place, there are certain basic truths that resonate, certain experiences that are universal. Sometimes a movie can act as a mirror for us, and show us what our options are. -*Lissa Coffey*

"In my films I always wanted to make people see deeply. I don't want to show things, but to give people the desire to see."
-Agnes Varda, in John Robert Columbo, "Popcorn in Paradise" 1979

I quote Gandhi quite a bit in WisdomNews. We can learn a lot from what this very wise man had to say. And we can also learn from how he lived his life. Fortunately, there is a beautiful movie, called "Gandhi," which gives us some insight into his character. It's amazing that in basically 3 hours we can see the kinds of things that Gandhi experienced. It gives us insight into our own nature, and our own potential for growth. -*Lissa Coffey*

"Good movies make you care, make you believe in possibilities again."
-Pauline Kael, 1968

Some movies are so big, so fabulous, so rich with story and action and setting and wardrobe. "Gone With the Wind" is like that. Wow. It's absolutely breathtaking, and a true classic. And some movies are smaller, just a more personal story, that doesn't need much more than the people involved to get the point across. "Rain Man" is that kind of a movie. In the film, Tom Cruise's character discovers that he has an autistic brother, played by Dustin Hoffman. The journey, how these two get to know each other, and get to understand themselves, and what is important in life, is just beautiful. It strikes a chord because we all have relationships in our lives from which we can learn about ourselves and our connection to the world. -*Lissa Coffey*

> "When you're making a movie, you can't think anybody
> will ever see it. You've just got to make a movie
> for the values it has. The greatest films were made
> because someone really wanted to make them. And,
> hopefully, the audience will show up, too."
> -Clint Eastwood

I am a huge movie fan! I go to see lots of different types of movies, not just the big blockbusters. It is really an incredible art form, to tell a story with words and pictures, to evoke emotion, to entertain. There is a movie that is now on DVD called "What the Bleep Do We Know?" This is definitely not your standard action-adventure flick, though it is filled with lots of action and adventure. It's about Life! It's about Consciousness. What got me is that so many of the concepts in the film are really big concepts, and somehow the filmmakers managed to present them in such a way that the audience is just riveted. It's part documentary, part story, part animation, and totally worthwhile. It's clear that the filmmakers felt that this was an important movie to make, and that's why they did it. Not to sell tickets, or get this huge box-office, but to express what they felt were important things for people to talk about. This is a great way to live our lives, to be in our "dharma" – do what you need to do, what you feel is important to do, not for the applause, or the critics, or the money, and see what happens. *-Lissa Coffey*

Flowers

> "Earth laughs in flowers."
> -Ralph Waldo Emerson (1803-1882)

Flowers are an expression of joy. It seems like a miracle that the earth can produce such a variety of species, so colorful, vibrant and full of life. Is it any wonder that we've made such a tradition of giving flowers in courtship? Sometimes flowers say what words cannot. *-Lissa Coffey*

> "Consider the lilies of the field, how they grow; they
> neither toil nor spin; yet I tell you, even Solomon in all
> his glory was not arrayed like one of these."
> -Jesus (A.D. 1st cent.) Matthew 6:28

Consider the effortlessness with which flowers grow and bloom and share their glory. We are like flowers, each individual, each unique - and yet, how often do we try to change our colors to fit in with a particular landscape? We can learn from the simplicity and beauty of nature. We can choose to bloom where we are planted. *-Lissa Coffey*

> "Beautiful, tender flowers grow upon the lava lips of
> Mono craters, pines ascend their ashy slopes, and it is
> just where the glaciers have crushed heaviest that the
> greatest quantity of beautiful life appears."
> -John Muir (1838-1914)

Life has a way of showing up. Grass makes its way through cracks in a sidewalk. Daffodils poke through previously frozen ground to find the sun. We might think of flowers as delicate and fragile, but they are strong, and full of life! -*Lissa Coffey*

"Where is the fountain that throws up these flowers in a ceaseless outbreak of ecstasy?"
-Rabindranath Tagore (1803-1882)

The source - the fountain - from which this vast array of beauty is born, is the same source that gives us life. And the spirit in which these amazing displays of ecstasy are created is the same spirit with which we were brought to this place and time. We are here to grow, to bloom, to share our gifts with the world. -*Lissa Coffey*

"Thou canst not stir a flower Without troubling a star."
-Francis Thompson (1859-1907)

There is a connection between the flowers, the stars, the rivers, between all of life. There is an exchange of energy that takes place that can help us to thrive. When we tend to a garden, we encourage growth. The flowers on our table make us smile. The fruits we eat nourish our bodies. It's all good. -*Lissa Coffey*

Food

"Food is an important part of a balanced diet."
-Fran Lebowitz

Fran Lebowitz is known for her funny outlook on life – but let's look at the truth in this statement. If we think of our "diet" as everything on our "plate" then that would include relationships, work, fun, and yes, food – among other things! It's a balance of things that keeps us healthy. There's an old saying that "man does not live by bread alone," meaning that the other gifts of life – love, friendship, music, etc., also give us sustenance. -*Lissa Coffey*

"Dinner, a time when one should eat wisely but not too well, and talk well but not too wisely."
-W. Somerset Maugham

One way we can honor ourselves and our food is by paying attention to what we eat. Start the meal with gratitude. Enjoy the company of people you love. Share with each other, both the food and the conversation. Pause after the meal to rest and digest before transitioning to another activity. -*Lissa Coffey*

"I feel a recipe is only a theme, which an intelligent cook can play each time with a variation."
-Madame Benoit

Cooking is a wonderful way in which we can express our creativity. We can improvise with herbs, experiment with color and presentation. My friend Cheryl Sindell has a wonderful book that shows us how cooking can be fun and playful – and also intuitive! It's called "Cooking Without Recipes." That's the way I like to cook, by what tastes good to me. I rarely stick to any recipe! *-Lissa Coffey*

"Food for all is a necessity. Food should not be a merchandise, to be bought and sold as jewels are bought and sold by those who have the money to buy. Food is a human necessity, like water and air, and it should be as available."
-Pearl S. Buck, 1967

Food is probably the most basic of human needs. It's one way that we take care of each other. I think of when I would go over to my grandmother's house. She loved to feed me! Somehow it made her feel good to see me eat. There is a website now that we can visit, and just by "clicking" food is provided to people who need it most. It doesn't cost us anything because it is advertiser sponsored. This is just one example of how people are coming together to help alleviate the hunger problem in the world. *-Lissa Coffey*

"Tell me what you eat, and I will tell you what you are."
-Anthelme Brillat-Savarin (1755-1826)

The more popular version of this saying is: "You are what you eat." That's easy to understand in terms of food. We know what's good for our bodies. But think of what we eat in terms of what we consume in the media, and the marketplace, too. Are we buying and using products that are good for ourselves and the environment? Are we reading, watching shows, and expressing ourselves in ways that are beneficial to humanity? Food for thought! *-Lissa Coffey*

Forgiveness

"The forgiving state of mind is a magnetic power for attracting good."
-Catherine Ponder

Forgiveness tends to be one of those things that is easy to say, but hard to do. We get caught up in the hurt and pain and for some reason we don't want to let that go. But forgiveness is freeing – it is healing, and it brings with it all kinds of life lessons and spiritual growth. And that is always good. *-Lissa Coffey*

"Forgive all who have offended you, not for them, but for yourself."
-Harriet Uts Nelson

When we hold on to our grudges, when we refuse to forgive, the only one we are really hurting is ourself. Why cause ourselves unnecessary pain? Where is the spiritual lesson in that? We can choose to release these grievances and choose to create a miracle. Forgiveness is a gift we give ourselves. *-Lissa Coffey*

**"To forgive is the highest, most beautiful form of love.
In return, you will receive untold peace and happiness."**
-Robert Muller

Think of this from a purely economical point of view. When you invest in blame, judgement, criticism and victimization, what do you receive in return? Does an attempt at making someone else feel bad bring any real benefit to you personally? Or could it actually cause you harm? Now, knowing that we are each responsible for our own choices and responses, think about this: When you invest in forgiveness, acceptance, understanding and harmony, what do you receive in return? Here there are many rewards! Among them: peace of mind, coherence, stability and love. *-Lissa Coffey*

**"Dream of your brother's kindnesses instead of
dwelling in your dreams on his mistakes. Select his
thoughtfulness to dream about instead of counting up
the hurts he gave."**
-A Course in Miracles

Whatever we turn our attention to increases. So focusing on the good increases the good. Our "reality" is just a perception of things as they are – so choose to look at what we want more of. There is always more than one way of seeing, or thinking about someone or someone's behavior. *-Lissa Coffey*

"To err is human; to forgive, divine."
-Alexander Pope

I've heard this quote dozens of times, but I never knew who said it! We are spiritual beings living in human form. We are capable of all things divine – and prone to all things human. We make mistakes. We mess up, we blow it – and sometimes stupidly, too. But the divine in us knows that this is all a part of the process, that we are growing and learning and finding our way every day. When we forgive ourselves, and others, we are tapping into that pure potential of divinity within each one of us. *-Lissa Coffey*

Fortune

**"The day of fortune is like a harvest day,
We must be busy when the corn is ripe."**
-Goethe (1749-1832)

There are times when everything just seems to come together. It seems easy, almost like magic! When that happens, we're going with the flow. We're in tune with nature.

There's a saying that luck is when preparation meets opportunity. When we've taken the steps, planted the seeds, and tended the garden, then we have to expect that at some point our efforts will make a difference. Are we ready when it's time to reap the rewards? *-Lissa Coffey*

"When fortune closes one door, it opens another."
-Sa'di (A.D. 1213? – 1292)

We've heard some version of this particular quote used for many different scenarios. Its purpose is to show us that there is always something more. There are no endings, only new beginnings. Is that lucky for us? It's nature's design! *-Lissa Coffey*

"Fortune can neither give to any man honesty, diligence, and other good qualities, nor can she take them away."
-Sallust (86? – 34? B.C.)

Whatever fortune we have, or don't have, does not affect who we are. Who we really are, our spirit, is unchangeable. Our behaviors may change, our roles may change, or environments may change – how we express ourselves is our choice. Fortune has no influence on our spirit one way or another. *-Lissa Coffey*

"The fortunate circumstances of our lives are generally found, at last, to be of our own producing."
-Oliver Goldsmith (1728-1774)

Fortune could be thought of in terms of money ("I made a fortune last year!" The Fortune 500, etc.) or in terms of luck (fortune cookies, "I had the good fortune to know him" etc). Either way, since we create our lives, we are ultimately creating the fortune in our lives – so we have to give ourselves credit where it is due! *-Lissa Coffey*

"To be thrown upon one's own resources, is to be cast into the very lap of fortune; for our faculties then undergo a development and display an energy of which they were previously unsusceptible."
-Benjamin Franklin (1706-1790)

Sometimes something we see as misfortune at the time can turn out to be one of the best things that has ever happened to us. Maybe it's a wake-up call – something that spurs us on to achieve. Whatever it is, we have to have faith that all of the resources we need we already have. We can do anything. *-Lissa Coffey*

Freedom

"Freedom is not won on the battlefields.
The chance for freedom is wonthere. The final battle
is won or lost in our hearts and minds."
-Helen Gahagan Douglas (1945)

It is essential for our souls to feel free. We need freedom of expression, freedom of choice, to learn and grow. And yet, so many of our brothers and sisters all over the world live without that freedom. We are all one, and we feel their pain. Amidst the politics and controversy, what can we do? We can hold them in our hearts and in our minds, lift them up and know the Highest Truth for all of us. We can express gratitude for the freedom that we experience every day. *-Lissa Coffey*

"That is the truly beautiful and encouraging aspect of
freedom; no one struggles for it just for himself."
-Fanny Lewald, in Hanna Ballin Lewis, "The Education of Fanny Lewald" (1871)

If there is a lesson in our struggle for freedom, (and there always is a lesson, in any struggle) then it is that there is no separation between us. We are all one. We are not truly free until each and every one of us is free. *-Lissa Coffey*

"I believe in freedom – social, economical, domestic,
political, mental and spiritual."
-Elbert Hubbard

Freedom is all-encompassing; you can't have one "kind" of freedom without all the others. I remember Deepak Chopra talking about the 25 qualities of the Unified Field. Scientists have studied this Field, which could also be called "all of nature," and identified 25 qualities that it has. Because we are one with this Field, these are qualities inherent in each of us, too. Number 24 on the list: Freedom. *-Lissa Coffey*

"To have freedom is only to have that which is
absolutely necessary to enable us to be what
we ought to be."
-Ibn Rahel (Medieval Christian chronicler, lived in Egypt)

One of my children's songs has a line in it that says: "You gotta be you and you gotta do what you love to do." That's freedom. Freedom lets us be ourselves. We often take freedom for granted – it feels so natural to us. But we need to recognize it every once in awhile, and celebrate it. *-Lissa Coffey*

"A man is either free or he is not. There cannot be any
apprenticeship for freedom."
-Imamu Amiri Baraka, in Kulchur

There is no middle ground with freedom. It's an all or nothing proposition. And it is a great responsibility. We can practice it, live it, respect it, and grow from the experience of freedom every single day of our lives. -*Lissa Coffey*

Friendship

**"Those friends thou hast, and their adoptions tried,
Grapple them to thy soul with hoops of steel."**
-Shakespeare

One of the greatest gifts we are given in this lifetime is the gift of friendship. Our friends are our treasures! We learn so much from each other. Think about the first friend you ever had. Remember the joy you felt just hanging out and playing together? Chances are that the friends we had in childhood are different than the friends we have today. People change and grow and move away and go on to lead separate lives. But we remember those friends, and they remember us! We learned from them then, and are where we are now in part because of those friendships. -*Lissa Coffey*

"The only way to have a friend is to be one."
-Ralph Waldo Emerson

Friendship is ours to give. It is a gift that multiplies when it comes back to us. Friends help us to be more of who we are, they help us to feel our connection to the world. With the support of friends we can achieve more, enjoy more, and appreciate more. And we can do the same for our friends! Friendship works both ways. -*Lissa Coffey*

**"Each friend represents a world in us, a world possibly
not born until they arrive, and it is only by this meeting
that a new world is born."**
-Anais Nin

Have you ever noticed that some new friends you don't just "meet," but you "recognize?" It's as if we can see ourselves in that person. Maybe it's chemistry, feeling that connection of oneness - or maybe it's memory of a past life together or something. Whatever the reason, the discovery of this new friendship often leads to great things. Find out just why you were brought together. There are no coincidences! -*Lissa Coffey*

**"However deep our devotion may be to parents, or to
children, it is our contemporaries alone with whom
understanding is instinctive and entire."**
-Vera Britain, Testament of Youth (1933)

Some people say that we can't choose our parents or our children, but we can choose our friends. I don't know if that is entirely true. I think there is some reason we have the family that we have, either by divine agreement or for learning purposes.

I also think that our friends are our friends for a reason, too. We're making choices all the time, and our friends are making choices, too. And somehow, those choices brought us together. And because we are brought together, we grow. We experience more of what life is about. Understanding is huge! To find a friend who truly understands is a magnificent gift. *-Lissa Coffey*

"Friendship's a noble name, 'tis love refined."
-Susannah Centlivre, The Stolen Heiress (1703)

It's interesting that one of the top-rated TV shows right now is called "Friends." I think it's because that's what we all want. We all want people in our lives whom we love and who love us back. People we can count on, people we can laugh with, people who appreciate us for who we are. The theme song for that show says: "I'll be there for you" and that says so much! We need to cherish our friends, both old and new, and pay attention to those relationships, and nurture them because they are important to us. *-Lissa Coffey*

Future

"The future... is something which everyone reaches at the rate of sixty minutes an hour, whatever he does, whoever he is."
-C.S. Lewis (1898-1963)

C.S. Lewis had a very practical way of looking at the future. In this description, the future could be seen as the great equalizer. The truth is that the future belongs to each of us, and it is up to us how we approach it. The possibilities are endless! *-Lissa Coffey*

"The future belongs to those who fuse intelligence with faith, and who with courage and determination grope their way forward from chance to choice, from blind adaptation to creative evolution."
-Charles E. Merriam (1876-1953)

Our present was at one time our future. We got here because of the choices we made. As we continue to learn and grow, we are better equipped to make the kinds of choices that bring us to the future we envision for ourselves. *-Lissa Coffey*

"The only certain thing about the future is that it will surprise even those who have seen furthest into it."
-E.J. Hobsbawm

Surprise! The future is that realm of uncertainty – beautiful, and a little scary, but would we have it any other way? Wouldn't life be totally boring if we knew all the time exactly what was going to happen? The future can change with a thought. *-Lissa Coffey*

"The future is made of the same stuff as the present."
-Simone Weil, 1968

It's so amazing how true this is... so many times I meet people and our experiences in life have been so similar – it's almost like we're all living the same life – maybe in different places, or different times, but the lessons we learn are universal. And the lessons don't change. We've heard them time and time again, it's just up to us to assimilate them into our lives until we "get it." *-Lissa Coffey*

"If we can recognize that change and uncertainty are basic principles, we can greet the future and the transform-ation we are undergoing with the understanding that we do not know enough to be pessimistic."
-Hazel Henderson (1981)

One of my favorite books of all time is Martin Seligman's "Learned Optimism." It is a classic, and it makes so much sense. The subtitle is "How to Change Your Mind and Your Life." It's just a matter of looking at things, including the future, differently. It can make a huge difference in how we experience things. *-Lissa Coffey*

Gardening

"My garden is an honest place. Every tree and every vine are incapable of concealment, and tell after two or three months exactly what sort of treatment they have had. The sower may mistake and sow his peas crookedly: the peas make no mistake but come and show his line."
-Ralph Waldo Emerson (1803-1882)

How does your garden grow? Remember that line from a nursery rhyme? Now we can see how it applies to the 'big picture.' What choices are we making? What colors are we choosing for our palette? Do we have some vegetables in the mix? Some fragrant flowers? Are we showing our garden enough tender-loving-care? We will harvest our rewards, and they can be as bountiful as we want them to be! *-Lissa Coffey*

"All gardeners live in beautiful places because they make them so."
-Joseph Joubert (1754-1824)

This I'm looking at "gardening" in the bigger sense of the word. There's a reason why we understand the philosophy: 'You reap what you sow' - in gardening nothing is more true! When we plant radishes, we can't expect gardenias to spring up. This life is our garden, and we can tend to it, and make it a beautiful place to be. *-Lissa Coffey*

"When I used to pick the berries for dinner on the East Quarter hills I did not eat one till I had done, for going a-berrying implies more than eating the berries. They at home got only the pudding: I got the forenoon out of doors and the appetite for the pudding."
-Henry David Thoreau (1817-1862)

Here's an example of how the journey can be more important than the destination! Thoreau is known as a naturalist. He had a great affinity for nature, and loved to write about it. Sure, the pudding must have been a nice treat, but I can see where Thoreau felt that the adventures that led up to the pudding made it all the more delicious! *-Lissa Coffey*

"Grandma spent much time 'working in the garden.' She called it that, but it wasn't like work. It was a kind of formative being present, intensely aware – that combination of willing and of gloating, simultaneously, that is creation."
-Bertha Damon, 1938

Both of my grandmothers had that "green thumb" that is so coveted by gardeners. And my mother and my sister have it, too. Gardening really is a kind of meditation. It is a beautiful way to be close to Spirit – to co-create, to nurture and to guide these little plants to full glory. I think of the joy that these women get from 'working in the garden' and I wonder what I'm doing inside on my computer! *-Lissa Coffey*

> "I wanted no one lifting a finger in that garden unless he loved doing it. What if Fred had hired a man to dig those trenches and it had turned out that he didn't love to dig? Who could eat that kind of asparagus?"
> -Ruth Stout, 1955

We are so intricately connected and with each other that we can feel a person's emotions. It's the same way with the earth – we are just as connected with this planet, so why wouldn't 'it' be able to feel our emotions as well? In the movie 'Like Water for Chocolate' there is a scene where a girl is broken-hearted. As she cooks, her tears fall into the stew, and when the family eats the stew, they start to cry. When we're sick with a cold, the famous remedy is chicken soup – but what is the 'magic' ingredient that makes the soup so healing? The love that the cook puts in there! These are illustrations of how our emotions, or how our intent, can affect our environment, and the people in our lives. In a way, we are gardening all the time. *-Lissa Coffey*

Genius

> "You may have heard people repeat what I have said, 'Genius is one percent inspiration, ninety-nine percent perspiration.' Yes, sir, it's mostly hard work."
> -Thomas Alva Edison (1847-1931)

Often we associate genius with intelligence. But according to Edison, it is much more than that. There are a lot of really smart people in this world – but how many of them really channel that intelligence into something bigger than themselves? How many can say that they have worked so hard that their efforts have created something that benefits all of mankind? These are the true geniuses. *-Lissa Coffey*

> "The sum total of excellence is good sense and method. When these have passed into the instinctive readiness of habit, when the wheel revolves so rapidly that we cannot see it revolve at all, then we call the combination genius."
> -Samuel Taylor Coleridge (1772-1834)

Given this explanation, we all have the potential for genius. I think a genius is someone who has worked so hard at something that they make it look easy, effortless. In Howard Gardner's book, "Frames of Mind: The Theory of Multiple Intelligences," he identifies seven kinds of intelligence, and he recently added an eighth. Genius can be found in any field, and it shines as a bright example for all of us. *-Lissa Coffey*

"When nature has work to be done, she creates a genius to do it."
-Ralph Waldo Emerson (1803-1882)

We are so intricately connected with nature. And nature has so much organizing power and so much intelligence that we can tap into! We can harness that energy, we can flow with it and create anything we can imagine. We can work together with nature, for the good of nature, and all of us. *-Lissa Coffey*

"Genius... means little more than the faculty of perceiving in an unhabitual way."
-William James (1842-1910)

Ah! How true! It's thinking "out of the box" or "breaking the mold!" It's breaking that karmic cycle of doing the same thing, the same way, over and over again. Genius is originality! *-Lissa Coffey*

"Does it not appear to you that versatility is the true and rare characteristic of that rare thing called genius – versatility and playfulness? In my mind they are both essential."
-Mary Russell Mitford, 1813

Versatility, flexibility, enthusiasm – these are all traits that I would associate with genius. You've got to be able to go with the flow, take what comes and adapt – and you've got to love what you're doing to be able to keep doing it until you reach the desired results. It's hard work, and it's also insight, seeing "inside" and having that vision that keeps you going. *-Lissa Coffey*

"It is characteristic of genius to be hopeful and aspiring. It is characteristic of genius to break up the artificial arrangements of conventionalism, and to view mankind in true perspective, in their gradations of inherent rather than of adventitious worth. Genius is therefore essentially democratic, and has always been so."
-Harriet Martineau, Society in America, 1837

This is so cool. There are geniuses at Ivy League schools, no surprise there – and there are geniuses who are in kindergarten. It doesn't matter about age, or gender, education or nationality – the potential for genius is everywhere equally. It's in all of us, right now! *-Lissa Coffey*

"The real wonder is not that one man should be a genius, but that every man should not be."
-Mary Austin, Everyman's Genius (1925)

The potential for genius is within all of us. Genius can be expressed in so many different ways. Howard Gardner has come up with the theory of Multiple Intelligences – and he has named 8 of the in his books. Genius can show up in athletics, in music, in mathematics, in a "green thumb" – in so many different ways! We can develop genius, we can pursue it. *-Lissa Coffey*

> **"Does it not appear to you that versatility is the true
> and rare characteristic of that rare thing called
> genius – versatility and playfulness? In my mind
> they are both essential."**
> -Mary Russell Mitford, 1813

Can you just imagine Benjamin Franklin putting the key on the kite – and flying it out in the storm – the guy had to have had a sense of playfulness! And think about modern day geniuses, like Bill Gates and Steve Jobs playing with their inventions in the garage, dreaming up programs to come up with home computers. There must have been set-backs all along the way, but the ability to be versatile, flexible, to go with the flow had to have kept them going when other would have given up. *-Lissa Coffey*

> **"Genius is the talent for seeing things straight – seeing
> them as they are, without any warping of vision.
> Flawless mental sight! That is genius!"**
> -Maude Adams, 1907

Genius is able to see things that are there, that others overlook. It's not "rose-colored glasses" or "x-ray vision" – it's more like heightened perception. Seeing the big picture, and the details at the same time. *-Lissa Coffey*

> **"True genius doesn't fulfill expectations, it shatters them."**
> -Arlene Croce, Afterimages, 1976

We hear a lot lately about "out of the box" thinking – that's what genius is. There are no boundaries, no limits – there is unlimited potential, including potential for greatness. I don't think genius is so rare as it is so rarely expressed. We have these expectations that we place on ourselves, or that are placed on us, and we tend to go just that far. But, oh, the possibilities that are out there for us! *-Lissa Coffey*

Gentleness

> **"There is nothing stronger in the world than gentleness."**
> -Han Suyin, 1952

Think of some of the people in this world who have been an example to us of gentleness: Jesus Christ, Mother Teresa, the Dalai Lama. These people also demonstrate great strength. Gentle does not mean weak. Gentleness is kind and loving. It is a quality which grows and expands in us as we recognize and live in love. *-Lissa Coffey*

> **"Remember
> the bread you meet each day
> is still rising
> Don't scare the dough."**
> -Macrina Wiederkehr, 1979

Our lives are a work in progress. We're all doing the best we can. It helps to be nurturing, and encouraging to one another. But if we can't do that, the least we can do is to be gentle. Allow for the process to happen. *-Lissa Coffey*

"Never take anything in life but flowers, and from flowers, only the perfume."
-Emilie Carles, 1977

We can be gentle with our place on the earth, with our role on the planet. Flowers give us their beauty, and their fragrance. They are happy to share – it is their dharma, their purpose! When we are in nature, we can give respect, and not interfere. *-Lissa Coffey*

"Tenderness is greater proof of love than the most passionate of vows."
-Marlene Dietrich, 1962

What we do carries more weight than what we say. If we mean what we say, how do we show it? When we're talking about love – it means being gentle, and tender, and loyal and available. Think of how we respond to a sleeping baby – we cuddle and whisper and walk softly. It's in our nature to show love by being gentle. *-Lissa Coffey*

"There never was any heart truly great and generous that was not also tender and compassionate."
-Robert South (1634-1716)

Each of our heroes, in life and in literature, throughout history – no matter how strong – has a gentleness to him or her, an openness, a sincerity that shows us that this person really cares. Spiderman is so popular right now because he's not just this "larger than life" character who has amazing powers – but because he's also basically a nice guy. He loves his family, and he struggles to do the right thing. He doesn't like to see people hurt. He's not all about the money or the recognition; he really wants to help. Who wouldn't love a gentle soul like that? *-Lissa Coffey*

Giving

"The greatest grace of a gift, perhaps, is that it anticipates and admits of no return."
-Henry Wadsworth Longfellow (1807-1882)

Give without hesitation. Give without expectation. Give freely of yourself, and watch. There are miracles just waiting to happen. *-Lissa Coffey*

A man there was, though some did count him mad, The more he cast away, the more he had."
-John Bunyan (1628-1688)

So many people have said the same thing: when you give, you receive. Whatever it is that you want in your life, give that. Somehow, it comes back to you, in a bigger and better way. Somehow, what you are looking for finds you. You have to put it out there; it has to circulate. Rather than hold on to something, set it free. Let it live, let it breathe, let it grow. Giving is good for everyone. -*Lissa Coffey*

> "The one desire which grows more and more is to give… Giving and receiving are at bottom one thing, dependent upon whether one lives open or closed. Living openly one becomes a medium, a transmitter; living thus, as a river, one experiences life to the full, flows along with the current of life, and dies in order to live again as an ocean."
> -Henry Miller (1891-1980)

Let's look at the process of giving, and how much the simple, and natural, act of giving contributes to our spiritual growth. Giving opens us up, it opens our hearts. The more we give, it seems, the more we want to give, because we experience that current in our lives and are energized by it. It just feels good! -*Lissa Coffey*

> "When I give I give myself."
> -Walt Whitman (1819-1892)

Most of us have too much "stuff." We could probably give half of it away and not even notice. It doesn't "mean" anything to us. Giving isn't necessarily just distributing stuff into another person's hands. The best gifts are thoughtful and heart-felt. The best gifts are personal, given with the receiver's needs and wants in mind. The best way to give is to give of ourselves. -*Lissa Coffey*

> "We are rich only through what we give, and poor only through what we refuse."
> -Anne-Sophie Swetchine (1869)

God's gifts to us are bountiful! Yet how many of them do we recognize, how many do we use? All the riches of the world are available to us right here and right now. We have only to graciously accept them into our lives. Is there any work of art more valuable than a sunset? It is ours to gaze upon every day! Giving makes us rich, by allowing us to experience the good we can do in the world. Receiving God's gifts makes us rich, because we understand that there is nothing that we lack. -*Lissa Coffey*

Goals

> "It is not enough to take steps which may some day lead to a goal; each step must be itself a goal and a step likewise."
> -Goethe (1749-1832)

We learn about the importance of setting goals, and we know how good it feels when we reach those goals. But at the same time, we need to remember that each step is an important part of our progress. We need to recognize this, and celebrate that we are moving forward. We are learning and growing every day.
-*Lissa Coffey*

"The going is the goal."
-Horace Kallen, 1952

This is another way of saying that the journey, not the destination, is our goal. We're hear to be in the game, so we might as well play. Sometimes we have a good run, sometimes we score, and sometimes we fall down. As long as our heart is in it, we're making progress. -*Lissa Coffey*

"The final goal of human effort is man's self-transformation."
-Lewis Mumford (1895-1990)

What I love about this quote is that it says "self-transformation," not just "transformation." Transformation is change, growth. We can't change anyone but ourselves. We can't grow for anyone but ourselves. When we realize, as a whole, how important it is for us to transform individually, and we each take responsibility for this, then great change will occur globally. -*Lissa Coffey*

"What we truly and earnestly aspire to be, that in some sense we are. The mere aspiration, by changing the frame of the mind, for the moment realizes itself."
-Anna Jameson, 1855

We wouldn't aspire to something if it wasn't within our capability to achieve it. We can see, both literally and figuratively, ahead as far as we want to go. Because we can perceive something means that it is already a part of us. Distance, whether in time or space, is all relative. -*Lissa Coffey*

"An ignorance of means may minister To greatness, but an ignorance of aims Makes it impossible to be great at all."
-Elizabeth Barrett Browning, 1851

A lot of times we hear stories about entrepreneurs who say they didn't know just how they were going to make their business work, they just knew they were going to do it. They had a goal, and worked toward that goal diligently. When we keep our "eye on the prize" it's easier to let obstacles fall by the wayside. We become creative in our quest.
-*Lissa Coffey*

God

For a While
We have all come to the right place.
We all sit in God's classroom.
Now,
The only thing left for us to do, my dear,
Is to stop
Throwing spitballs for a while.
-Hafiz

We're here to learn, and we're learning whether we realize it or not! All of our experiences, all of our adventures, disappointments, joys and grievances... they're all lessons. Sometimes they whisper in our ears, sometimes they shout in our faces - the message is there. Do you hear it? Are you listening? It's time to stop "throwing spitballs" and pay attention! God Is. -*Lissa Coffey*

"God is a circle whose center is everywhere, and its circumference nowhere."
-Empedocles

God is omnipresent, without borders, without limitations. Everywhere we go, God Is. Everything we see, God Is. Everything we touch, smell, hear, taste and sense... it's all God's creation. When we tap into the God energy that is with us here, now, and always - then we are without limitations as well. There is nowhere that God is not. God is all-encompassing, we can never be outside of God's circle. -*Lissa Coffey*

"Nature is too thin a screen; the glory of the omnipresent God bursts through everywhere."
-Emerson

"Glory" is a great word! Glory, glory, Halleluah! :-) It's a glorious day today and everyday that we see it as such. God doesn't hide, the glory of God is vibrant and wants to be experienced! Enjoy it! -*Lissa Coffey*

"We know God easily, if we do not constrain ourselves to define him."
-Joubert

We could wax on and on about all that God is... because God is All there is! But it seems that any definition, any kind of label we could attribute to God, is limited by its meaning. So we just need to know that God Is. That's it. God Is. -*Lissa Coffey*

"God's gifts put man's best dreams to shame."
-Elizabeth Barrett Browning

There is so much more to life and to living than we could ever comprehend. All we can do is to keep growing, keep learning, keep stretching our capacity for wisdom, and trust that all that we need to know is available to us when we need to know it. We can dream big dreams, and know that there is yet more beyond that, even if we can't see it right now. *-Lissa Coffey*

Good

"What good shall I do today?
What good have I done today?"
-Benjamin Franklin (1706-1790)

Benjamin Franklin used to start his day with the first question, and end his day with the second. He consciously set out to do good, every single day. And he checked back with himself to make sure that he followed through. It was important to him. Good here is a noun, used in the way that he wanted to make some contribution. We've seen the grand contributions that Franklin has made to the world, but I'm sure that given his philosophy, there was much more good that he did that we are not aware of: lives he touched, people he helped. What a wonderful example to us! *-Lissa Coffey*

"To do good without ulterior motive is a generous and
almost divine thing in itself."
-Francesco Guicciardini (1483-1540)

Ah! Too many times the "what's in it for me?" creeps up when we are in a position to do some good. We wonder if it is worth the effort, and the time it takes, to go out of our way. But when we really do good, without expectation of any reward or reciprocation, it feels good. And isn't that the best compensation anyway? *-Lissa Coffey*

"Waste no more time arguing what a good man
should be. Be one."
-Marcus Aurelius (A.D. 121-180)

There are so many debates about what "good" is, and man's nature, whether we are "wired" for good or selfish motives. But does it matter? We all have our own definitions of what good is. If we'd just live up to that, this world would be a better place. Do good, be good – whatever that means to you! *-Lissa Coffey*

"By doing good we become good."
-Rousseau (1712-1778)

Our actions help to create our reality. Do we think good thoughts? Do we do good things? Do we help out? By doing good, we see ourselves as good, and then that is our reality. When we can see it in ourselves, we can see it in the world. *-Lissa Coffey*

"To be good is to be in harmony with oneself."
-Oscar Wilde (1854-1900)

The words that follow "I am..." help us to define ourselves. We strive for harmony, and balance, within our own physiology and within our world. Good is positive, and healthy – healthy for our minds and bodies and emotions and self-esteem. -*Lissa Coffey*

Grace

"It is the grace of God that helps those who do everything that lies within their power to achieve that which is beyond their power."
-Abraham Joshua Heschel (1907-1972)

The grace of God: is there anything more powerful than that? And it is available to us all the time. God's grace is here to help us, and when we help others, when we're doing the best we can, we can see that grace kick in and allow us to accomplish amazing things. -*Lissa Coffey*

"The breeze of God's grace is blowing continually. You have to set your sail to catch that breeze."
-Swami Prabhavananda (1893-1976)

I have a beautiful little niece named Grace. When I read this quote, it was easy for me to think, "The breeze of God's Grace is blowing continually," because, like most children, Grace has a lot of energy. She's always dancing around, full of joy and light, and it's so contagious. You can't help to catch that breeze and sail along with her. Children are wonderful reminders to us of the beauty and fun that are a part of our world every day. -*Lissa Coffey*

"The state of love is the state of grace."
-N. Sri Ram (1899-?)

This is the simplest definition of "grace" that I found. Webster's defines grace as: "an attractive or pleasing quality; good will." And yet there are so many meanings attached to such a little word. There is the "grace" period, which means a temporary extension of a deadline. There is the "grace" that we say at the dinner table before we eat. There is the "grace" of a dancer's movements, or a swan's gentle glide across a pond. All of these are wonderful things. Look and see where you can find grace in your life today. -*Lissa Coffey*

"All is waiting and all is work; all is change and all is permanence. All is grace."
-Barbara Grizzuti Harrison (1984)

All is grace – yes, that's it! Everything, the all – it's a blessing, it's a virtue. I wrote a book called "Getting There With Grace" and my editor titled the book after it was already written. I thought it was really interesting that she chose that particular word, "grace." And when I thought about it, it made perfect sense. Grace to me conveys a sort of ease, an effortlessness. And that's the way it is when we understand that we're not in it alone. We're never alone. All of creation, ALL of nature, is here to support us in our dreams and desires. *-Lissa Coffey*

"Grace comes into the soul, as the morning sun into the world; first a dawning; then a light; and at last the sun in his full and excellent brightness."
-Thomas Adams (1640)

First we glimpse it, then we recognize it, then we know it as ours. Then we embrace it, and bask in its beautiful glow. And then it starts to radiate from us, and we see it as a part of who we are. This is the process of our spiritual growth. With grace comes love and patience and acceptance and reverence. It's awesome! *-Lissa Coffey*

Gratitude

"A grateful thought toward heaven is of itself a prayer."
-Lessing

What other topic could be better for Thanksgiving week than Gratitude? This is a reminder for us all to count our blessings. Thanksgiving is a traditional American holiday, which used to be all about giving thanks for the bounty we receive. Lately it's been referred to more often as "Turkey Day" and the main activity is the football game on TV! Let's turn our thoughts, and our hearts, toward heaven, and express gratitude. *-Lissa Coffey*

"It is another's fault if he be ungrateful, but it is mine if I do not give. To find one thankful man, I will oblige a great many that are not so."
-Seneca

The only way to truly give is to give without expectation. And that includes any expectation of gratitude! We may not see, or hear, the immediate results of our giving, but the universe does. Whatever we give is ultimately a gift to ourselves. We can be grateful for the opportunity to give, to better ourselves and our environment without expectations. *-Lissa Coffey*

"When thankfulness o'erflows the swelling heart, and breathes in free and uncorrupted praise for benefits received, propitious Heaven takes such acknowledgement as fragrant incense, and doubles all its blessings."
-Lillo

We give without expectation, and we give thanks without expectation... and then watch in amazement and wonder at all the gifts we receive from the universe. It is a beautiful thing.

Tonight I am attending a special Interfaith service of light. Many different faiths and religious holidays will be represented, and the common theme among them all is gratitude on this Thanksgiving eve. I am grateful for this spiritual community, and the opportunity for all of us to come together and give thanks. -*Lissa Coffey*

"O Lord, who lends me life, lend me a heart replete with thankfulness."
-Shakespeare

I read a comic strip this morning and had to laugh - a grown son was disappointed that his parents were taking a vacation over the Thanksgiving weekend. His wife said that she was glad that the parents would be enjoying themselves. The son said: "Thanksgiving is not about enjoying yourself, it's about family!"

No matter where we are in life, either physically or spiritually, today is a day for some recognition of our blessings. And our families, whether they are our genetic family, our church family, our neighbors or friends, help us to grow. Some families create conflict, but conflict often leads to growth, understanding and acceptance. Other families provide unconditional love and support when we need it the most. We have the relationships we have for a reason. And if we're truly honest with ourselves, we know that we're given exactly what we need, when we need it... even if we don't think so at the time! -*Lissa Coffey*

"It was easier to do a friendly thing than it was to stay and be thanked for it."
-Louisa May Alcott, Little Women

For many of us, giving comes easy - we are natural "givers." But for some reason it is not as easy for us to be on the receiving end. We feel awkward, uncomfortable. Why is that? Do we feel that we are undeserving? Look at it this way: by receiving a gift, or accepting someone's gratitude graciously, we are actually giving one of the most valuable gifts of all! We are GIVING that person the opportunity to GIVE! Allow them that. Without receiving, there is no giving - the two go hand in hand. So accept the "thank yous" that come your way with a loving heart - and enjoy how good it feels to be appreciated. And you'll also see how good it feels for that other person to express gratitude. -*Lissa Coffey*

Greatness

"All rising to great place is by a winding stair."
-Francis Bacon (1561-1626)

Ever noticed how it is harder to climb up than it is to climb down? It's a tough go, each step is a challenge, and the higher you go, the harder it gets because you get tired and sore from working so hard. But the air gets more clear, and the view gets better – there are many advantages to "rising above." Sometimes we can take those stairs two at a time – but most often it's just a matter of putting one foot in front of the other to make continual progress. -*Lissa Coffey*

"Great men are they who see that spiritual is stronger than any material force, that thoughts rule the world."
-Ralph Waldo Emerson (1803-1882)

Could this be how we can distinguish between the great and the average? This is an important component of greatness – the ability to know that strength within, and the intelligence to use that strength rather than to rely on outside adornments (a title, a paycheck, a uniform or a vehicle) to get things done. *-Lissa Coffey*

"Self-confidence is the first requisite to great undertakings."
-Samuel Johnson (1709-1784)

It all starts with us – right where we are. We have the capacity for greatness, we have the ability to achieve and accomplish whatever it is that we set out to do. But do we know this? Do we believe it? Do we act as if this is true? Or do we hesitate, procrastinate, or hedge our bets? We must be confident and forge ahead if we are going to get anywhere. And how far we go is simply a matter of how fast we move and how long we keep going! *-Lissa Coffey*

"Keep away from people who try to belittle your ambitions. Small people always do that, but the really great make you feel that you, too, can become great."
-Mark Twain (1835-1910)

People who are "great" feel no jealousy or competition with others. They understand that there are no limits, that there is no lack. A little encouragement and support go a long way toward helping someone pursue, and eventually achieve, his ambitions. It feels good to hear someone say: "if I can do it, you can do it! *-Lissa Coffey*

"There is no greatness where simplicity, goodness and truth are absent."
-Leo Tolstoy (1828-1910)

Is goodness a prerequisite for greatness? I think so. Greatness is different from power, from fame. It's something that is not completely defined, but is instantly recognized. It cuts across lines of age, race and gender. We all have the potential for greatness. *-Lissa Coffey*

Happiness

"If you observe a really happy man, you will find him
building a boat, writing a symphony, educating his
son, growing double dahlias or looking for dinosaur
eggs in the Gobi Desert. He will not be searching for
happiness as if it were a collar button that had rolled
under the radiator, striving for it as a goal in itself. He
will have become aware that he is happy in the course
of living life twenty-four crowded hours of each day."
-W. Beran Wolfe

Of course, happiness is something that we all want for ourselves and those we love.
But happiness is not something that we can pursue. Happiness is something that
finds us! When we are expressing ourselves, living a life filled with love, we can't help
but feel the happiness that is always around us. *-Lissa Coffey*

"If my heart can become pure and simple like that of a
child, I think there can be no happiness greater than this."
-Kitaro Nishida

If we want to be reminded about what happiness looks like, all we have to do is go to
the park and watch a child at play. Here is a great example of being "in the moment!"
Innocent, loving, sweet - that's how happiness feels. It is a wonderful thing to be
child-like... Children know that there is a lot to be happy about without even thinking
about it. *-Lissa Coffey*

"If you are unhappy, you are too high up in your mind."
-Carl Jung

Happiness is a choice. We can CHOOSE to be happy! If we are not choosing happiness,
what are we choosing? Happiness is one of those things that many of us tend to shy
away from. Maybe because we are afraid that happiness doesn't last - that if there is
"happy" there is bound to be "unhappy" at some point. But it only works that way if
our happiness is attached to someTHING or someONE. When we understand that our
happiness is inside ourselves, and we can tap into it independently of any situation
or scenario, then we can allow ourselves to choose happiness anytime! *-Lissa Coffey*

"Happiness is a present attitude - not a future condition."
-Hugh Prather

How many times have we heard: "I'll be happy WHEN... I get that new job, new relationship, new car, computer, etc." WHY??? Why are we postponing our happiness? When we live for the future, happiness never comes... because happiness can only be experienced in the present moment. Choose to be happy NOW, because now is the only time there is. *-Lissa Coffey*

"Many persons have a wrong idea of what constitutes true happiness. It is not attained through self-gratification but through fidelity to a worthy purpose."
-Helen Keller

It is true that no one can make you happy except yourself. So, how do we do this? First, we make a choice to be happy. Then, we express ourselves in a way that helps others. When we see the difference that we can make in the world, when we see that there is something that we can do to make this world a better place, we feel worthwhile - and we can't help but feel happy about our contribution. *-Lissa Coffey*

Heart

"Do not worry about what others are doing! Each of us should turn the searchlight inward and purify his or her own heart as much as possible."
-Mohandas K. Gandhi (1869-1948)

We talk about how the heart thinks, and how the heart is intuitive - and we also understand that the heart has a conscience. We ask what is in someone's heart, meaning that we want to know their intentions. But we can't do anything about anyone else's heart. We can only work on ourselves, and learn to tune in to our own heart's wisdom and desires. *-Lissa Coffey*

"The tiny flame that lights up the human heart is like a blazing torch that comes down from heaven to light up the paths of mankind. For in one soul are contained the hopes and feelings of all Mankind."
-Kahlil Gibran (1883-1931)

Love is strong, love is powerful - love makes all things possible. This same strength is within each one of us. Physically, our heart is the "engine" that drives our whole body. Emotionally, love is what keeps us going. Love lights the way for us. *-Lissa Coffey*

"We distrust our heart too much, and our head not enough."
-Joseph Roux (1834-1886)

We say: Listen to your heart. Follow your heart. But do we take our own advice, or do we overthink and rationalize? Where does intuition come from? We feel it in our gut or know it in our hearts. Too often we ignore it, thinking that we know better, that logic says something different. Our heads can argue, we can debate an issue with ourselves and end up more confused than ever. But our heart doesn't waver. It offers a clear direction. When we take the time to tune in, its message is simple. *-Lissa Coffey*

"Nobody has ever measured, even the poets, how much a heart can hold."
-Zelda Fitzgerald, 1945

The heart is associated with love. How much love can we hold in our hearts? What is our capacity for love? It is immeasurable! There's not a limit on how many people we can love, or how much we can love, or how deeply we can love. Love can't be quantified. *-Lissa Coffey*

"The heart outstrips the clumsy senses, and sees - perhaps for an instant, perhaps for long periods of bliss -- an undistorted and more veritable world."
-Evelyn Underhill, 1955

The heart has its own intelligence. Paul Pearsall wrote an amazing book called "The Heart's Code" where he talks about all the research he has done that proves that the heart actually "thinks." This is not just an organ in our body that serves a function for us to live. The heart is a sophisticated tool that can help us to live better, more beautifully. *-Lissa Coffey*

Heaven

"We must... make the kingdom of God a reality in this world by works of love."
-Albert Schweitzer (1875-1965)

Heaven. Each of us has our own idea of just what that is. But whatever we think Heaven is, it is an ideal. We can't point to it on a map, but we can conjure it up in our minds. And we can create a kind of heaven on earth through works of love. Love makes all things possible. We know what love is, and we know how heavenly this world can be when love prevails. *-Lissa Coffey*

"The world to come is not only a hereafter but also a herenow."
-Abraham Joshua Heschel (1907-1972)

Heaven is not just "out there" but it is "in here." Heaven is not just "someday" but it is "now." We can "get there" but we can also "be here!" Be present in the moment and recognize Heaven all around. Everything we see, touch, experience... it is all such a blessing, it is all such a gift. *-Lissa Coffey*

> **"Heaven is always pictured as a community – never as made up of individuals who live in boxes, which they call homes, where they lock themselves in by locking others out."**
> -Elbert Hubbard (1856-1915)

We hear this all the time. We're all in this together. Heaven is not a lonely place; ideally, it's a place where everyone lives in harmony. We can create heaven on earth by reaching out to each other, helping one another, supporting, accepting, and loving one another. We can open our doors, and open our hearts, to a new vision of community. *-Lissa Coffey*

> **"The kingdom of God is within you."**
> -Jesus (A.D. 1st cent.) Luke 17:21

Where is Heaven? Within you. Within me. Within each one of us, right here and right now. We don't have to look anywhere outside of us to find God's love. All of God's possibilities and blessings are at hand – we have but to recognize this divine Truth to make use of it. *-Lissa Coffey*

> **"Heaven is neither a place nor a time."**
> -Florence Nightingale (1913)

So, what is Heaven? It's something different to each of us. Maybe it's the joy that comes from watching your team win the World Series. Maybe it's the passion you feel when you look into your spouse's eyes. Maybe it's the laughter on a family outing, or the sweetness of hot fudge over an ice cream sundae. There is no set definition of Heaven – it's whatever we feel it is at the moment. And it is always available to us. *-Lissa Coffey*

Helping

> **"What do we live for if not to make life less difficult for each other?"**
> -George Eliot

When we look for our dharma, our purpose in life, we recognize it when we can affirmatively answer the following questions: Is this something I love to do? Is this something that helps others? Of course there is a huge range of things that qualify as helpful, and we can't all be Mother Teresa. But we can each contribute to making the world a better place, and spreading some light, love and laughter in our own unique way. *-Lissa Coffey*

> **"The service we render others is the rent we pay for our room on earth."**
> -Wilfred Grenfell

Helping other is not just an obligation; it's a responsibility. Are we making a difference in the world, or are we just taking up space? There are opportunities for service presented to us every day, and these are also opportunities for our own learning and growth. It can be something simple, or something grand, and when we rise to the occasion we know we've done something good, because we feel good. *-Lissa Coffey*

"We cannot live only for ourselves. A thousand fibers connect us with our fellow men."
-Herman Melville

When we help one person, we're helping all people – and we're helping ourselves. Because of our intricate connection with each other – we feel it on some deep primordial level. And it works the other way, too. When one of us is hurt, all of us are hurt. Because of technology and advances in communications, we can understand better how something like a war, way on the other side of the world affects each one of us. We see the war; we feel the emotions. People we love are far away from us, and our hearts are with them, and their families. We can help them with our thoughts and prayers. *-Lissa Coffey*

"We cannot hold a torch to light another's path without brightening our own."
-Ben Sweetland

We're all connected. By helping another, we're helping ourselves! And for that reason, we need to be able to ask for help when we need it, too. By allowing someone to help us, we are actually giving that person the opportunity to learn and grow! It's good to help out, and it's good to seek help when we need it, too. We're all in this together! *-Lissa Coffey*

"Believe, when you are most unhappy, that there is something for you to do in the world. So long as you can sweeten another's pain, life is not in vain."
-Helen Keller

A basic human need is to feel needed. When we are feeling unhappy, we can step outside of ourselves and do something to help someone else. Once we see the effect that our actions have in the world, how our helping does some good, we are reminded how much we truly are needed. We are here for a reason. There are so many things we can do to help, we just have to get out there and do them! *-Lissa Coffey*

Home

"The ornament of a house is the friends who frequent
it. There is no event greater in life than the appearance
of new persons about our hearth, except it be the
progress of the character which draws them."
-Ralph Waldo Emerson (1803-1882)

People come and go from our lives. And as we change and grow spiritually, we begin to notice that we draw people to us for special reasons. Maybe we have something to offer a friend that no one else can. Maybe a friend has a gift, or a lesson, for us that we wouldn't have found on our own. There are no coincidences. It's all part of our journey to experience these people and events at just the time when we are supposed to. Welcome them! -*Lissa Coffey*

"Home, home on the range,
Where the deer and the antelope play;
Where seldom is heard a discouraging word,
And the skies are not cloudy all day."
-Brewster Higley (19th cent, 1873?)

This is where we live; this is our home. Wherever we are, wherever we go, this planet is ours to enjoy and take care of. All of nature calls for us to notice. Whether we sleep under a roof or under a canopy of stars, we live here together – with the animals and trees and all of creation. -*Lissa Coffey*

"A home is not a mere transient shelter: its essence
lies in its permanence, in its capacity for accretion and
solidification, in its quality of representing, in all its
details, the personalities of the people who live in it."
-H.L. Mencken (1880-1956)

"Home" itself is a very spiritual word – as it contains the primordial sound "om." And the words associated with home: like "mom" and "father" have the "ah" sound. These words because mantra-like to us in that they represent a kind of security, a peace, a presence. Our homes are a reflection of how we express ourselves, and how we feel about ourselves. Look around and see what your home says about you – and what your home says to you! -*Lissa Coffey*

"A house is no home unless it contain food and fire for
the mind as well as for the body."
-Margaret Fuller (1845)

A home is more than a place of shelter. It is a place of comfort, a place of peace. This is where we can take refuge from the world, where we can relax, and where we can grow. A home can be a "safe environment" where we can learn without fear of criticism, and where we can explore and express our feelings. The person, or people, inside that space is what makes a house a home. -*Lissa Coffey*

"Mid pleasures and palaces though we may roam,
Be it ever so humble, there's no place like home."
-John Howard Payne (1791-1852)

Even after the most marvelous vacation – we usually return and say "it's so good to be home!" There's something about the comfort and familiarity about our own personal space that keeps us coming back. Remember Dorothy clicking her heels together in The Wizard of Oz? It doesn't have to be anything grand or spectacular. Just having our own little defined area makes us feel a part of something bigger. I love what Jimmy and Rosalind Carter have started with Habitat for Humanity. By helping to build homes for families that need them, they're giving so much more than financial assistance. They're giving a sense of pride and permanence that is invaluable.
-Lissa Coffey

Honesty

"Honesty is better than any policy."
-Immanuel Kant (1724-1804)

Policy is open to interpretation. Honesty is clear, and simple. When we live honestly we are governed by our own conscience, we answer to ourselves. Relationships based on honesty have clear channels of communication, which generate openness and trust.
-Lissa Coffey

"Make yourself an honest man, and then you may be
sure there is one rascal less in the world."
-Thomas Carlyle (1795-1881)

There are so many things in this world that we would like to change, if only we could. Yet so much is out of our personal control. What we can work on, at any given moment in time, is changing our own behavior. It starts with a decision. *-Lissa Coffey*

"The shortest and surest way to live with honor in the
world, is to be in reality what we would appear to be;
and if we observe, we shall find, that all human virtues
increase and strengthen themselves by the practice
and experience of them."
-Socrates (469-399 B.C.)

The most important aspect of being honest is being honest with ourselves. This involves self-trust, and self-knowledge. It is important to learn who we are, and to express who we are freely. No masks, no illusions. *-Lissa Coffey*

"Men are disposed to live honestly, if the means of
doing so are open to them."
-Thomas Jefferson (1743-1826)

It is our nature to be honest. Look at how everything else in the world expresses itself. We don't expect antelope behavior from a lion, that would be silly. And yet many times we go around being untrue to ourselves. We are strong, beautiful, creative – so let's not be afraid to show it! *-Lissa Coffey*

"No legacy is so rich as honesty."
- William Shakespeare (1564-1616)

Being called honest is a compliment. And it feels good to hear that someone appreciates that about us. It's because we value honesty, it's important to us. We like to be dealt with fairly and honestly. Honesty engenders trust, which builds strong relationships. *-Lissa Coffey*

Humor

"Mirth is like a flash of lightning, that breaks through a gloom of clouds, and glitters for a moment; cheerfulness keeps up a kind of daylight in the mind, and fills it with a steady and perpetual serenity."
-Joseph Addison (1672-1719) British Essayist

Truly spiritual people are light-hearted and filled with joy! They love a good laugh and are the first to share a smile. These are the kinds of people who brighten our day just by showing up. How much we can learn from this! We're all connected, so it makes sense that if one person is "up" it helps all of us to rise up. Let's be the person who shines through the clouds today. *-Lissa Coffey*

"Humor is emotional chaos remembered in tranquility."
-James Thurber (1894-1961) US humorist, illustrator

Do you remember the TV show "My World and Welcome to It?" It starred William Windom as James Thurber. This was many years ago, so it may be that he played a James Thurber "type," (I was very young and can't remember the details. ;-) I loved that show! And I loved how the lesson was that there was always something to laugh at, some funny way of looking at something that we might not have thought of. Sometimes when we're going through something really awful or embarrassing, we'll look at one another and say: "Someday we'll look back on this and laugh." And doesn't that happen! Some of our funniest moments come out of our most human foibles. We are funny people, and we can enjoy ourselves. *-Lissa Coffey*

"I think laughter may be a form of courage... As humans we sometimes stand tall and look into the sun and laugh, and I think we are never more brave than when we do that."
-Linda Ellerbee

We can rise above all of our problems. We are bigger than any of them anyway! When things get rough, we have a choice – we can be devastated and beat down, or we can face it head-on and say: "Okay, here we go again. I can take it. I can learn from this. I am growing and I can handle this!" Having a good sense of humor gets us through a lot. It's just a different way of looking at things, one that recognizes the power that we have over our problems, not the other way around! *-Lissa Coffey*

> **"Sexiness wears thin after a while and beauty fades,**
> **but to be married to a man who makes you laugh every**
> **day, ah, now that's a real treat!"**
> -Joanne Woodward

Sure, Joanne Woodward can talk – she's married to Paul Newman! But look what she really values in her husband: his sense of humor. Our sense of humor will take us far in this life. Laughter is like medicine – it keeps us healthy and feeling good. It's a way of experiencing joy, and a joyful life is a spiritual life, recognizing and appreciating our connection with the Divine. *-Lissa Coffey*

> **"When humor goes, there goes civilization."**
> -Erma Bombeck

We need humor to balance out all the other "stuff" that is going on in the world every day. Where would we be without our ability to laugh at ourselves. Situation comedies have always been popular on TV because they depict "situations" that we've all been in and can relate to – but they do it in such a way that we can see how funny the whole thing is! Today look at the world this way: "My Life is a SitCom!" Of course, you are the star of the show! And all your friends are relatives are supporting players. I'll bet you'll find lots of punch lines in the script! *-Lissa Coffey*

Ideas

"Every new idea has something of the pain and peril of childbirth about it."
-Samuel Butler (1835-1902)

It seems like ideas are a dime a dozen, there are so many of them out there. But the real value comes from the execution of those ideas! Ah! How many times have we seen some invention or some new contraption and said: "I thought of that!" Yes, and someone else did, too- and the difference is that someone took that idea and ran with it, and made it a reality. It's easy and fun to sit around and brainstorm. The "pain and peril" comes from the work that is involved in developing the idea into something that is viable, something that is tangible. *-Lissa Coffey*

"Ideas come from God."
-Albert Einstein (1879-1955)

Ideas are so ethereal- we wonder where they come from, how we "get" them. There is one school of thought that says that there are no new ideas- that every idea ever conceived is floating around in the universe and it is up to us to tap into that intelligence, and kind of "download" it into our consciousness. It makes sense that ideas come from God. But then we have to wonder if God "gives" us these ideas, or if we go out there and "find" them from our own creative pursuits. *-Lissa Coffey*

"You talk of our having an idea; we do not have an idea. The idea has us, and martyrs us, and scourges us, and drives us into the arena to fight and die for it, whether we want to or not."
-Heinrich Heine (1797-1856)

When we get a really good idea, we can tell that it is a really good idea because it won't let go of us. We think about it, dream about it, and pursue it until we can make it a reality. It's like the Universe is tapping on our shoulders, saying: "This is it, come on, let's go!" How could we resist? *-Lissa Coffey*

"The man with a new idea is a Crank until the idea succeeds."
-Mark Twain (1835-1910)

Imagine the ridicule that the Wright Brothers must have had to put up with. But did that deter them? Obviously not! Anything new and innovative might be regarded with fear or suspicion because it is untried, unproven. I guess it's just a part of our human nature to be skeptical. Thank goodness there are those among us who follow their dreams regardless of their critics! From just one idea, when it blooms, many seeds spring forth, and a whole garden of ideas can then grow and flourish! That's progress. And we can do the same thing spiritually, too. -*Lissa Coffey*

"Now some people when they sit down to write and nothing special comes, no good ideas, are so frightened that they drink a lot of strong coffee to hurry them up, or smoke packages of cigarettes, or take drugs or get drunk. They do not know that ideas come slowly, and that the more clear, tranquil and unstimulated you are, the slower the ideas come, but the better they are."
-Brenda Ueland, If You Want to Write, 1938

The quality of the thoughts we have, and the ideas we get, is reflected in our lifestyle. Whether it's writing, or selling, or manufacturing, or any kind of business that we're in, we're dependent upon fresh ideas to keep us moving forward. When we're aware of that, and make time and space in our lives to nurture ideas through silence and meditation, our lives become that much more peaceful and efficient. -*Lissa Coffey*

Illusion

"Belief in the absence of illusions is itself an illusion."
-Barbara Grizzuti Harrison, 1992

What is real? What is illusion? These are two of the biggest questions we're faced with in this lifetime. Especially today, when we have TV and "reality TV" – who is real and who is putting on a show? But one thing we know is that there are indeed illusions, and it's just a matter of each one of us figuring out for ourselves what is real, what is important, what is ever-lasting. -*Lissa Coffey*

"If you ever do a survey, you'll find that people prefer illusion to reality, ten to one. Twenty, even."
-Judith Guest, 1976

There seems to be a lot of escapism in our society. We like to go to movies and get lost in a story. We like to visit places like Disneyland, called "the happiest place on earth." As much as we can enjoy these excursions, we can't live in Fantasyland. But what we must understand is that reality can be just as blissful. We can create our lives so that we experience joy, love, peace, anytime we want to. -*Lissa Coffey*

"Our greatest illusion is to believe that we are what we think ourselves to be."
-Henry Amiel (1821-1881)

Who do we think we are? We go around acting like human do-ings, with families, jobs, cars, mortgages. But is this our reality, or is it an illusion, a play? There's an ancient Indian saying that explains that we are actually spiritual beings having a human experience. Let's think of ourselves from that perspective, and see how things change for us. *-Lissa Coffey*

> "And so we plow along, as the fly said to the ox."
> -Henry Wadsworth Longfellow (1807-1882)

This quote makes me smile. It's a funny illustration of illusion. It's good to keep a sense of humor about ourselves. Life can be hard, but we can still laugh. Sometimes we think we're going through something really painful, awkward, or difficult – and we look at each other and say "some day we'll look back on this and laugh" – and that immediately lightens the situation because we know it's true! Life is full of experiences. Sometimes we're the ox and sometimes we're the fly. *-Lissa Coffey*

> "We, the undisciplined in discernment of the inward, knowing nothing of it, run after the outer, never understanding that it is the inner which stirs us; we are like one who sees his own reflection but not realizing whence it comes goes in pursuit of it."
> -Plotinus (A.D. 205-270)

The outer: the job, the money, the big screen TV – but what makes us go in pursuit of that? Who makes us go in pursuit of that? Eventually the same thing that drives us to go after "the outer" finds that it is not satisfied. With maturity and experience we learn that the inner world holds treasures for us far more valuable than we ever could have imagined. The veil of illusion is lifted when we tap into the power of love. *-Lissa Coffey*

Immortality

> "The voice of Nature loudly cries,
> And many a message from the skies,
> That something in us never dies."
> -Robert Burns (1759-1796)

Nature illustrates its message to us in so many beautiful ways. The cycles of the seasons – the sun rising every day – the rainbow after the storm. Life is beautiful and bold, precious and strong – and such a ride! Nature mirrors our Spirit. Nature nurtures our Soul. *-Lissa Coffey*

> "Be the first to say something obvious and achieve immortality."
> -Marie von Ebner-Eschenbach (1830-1916)

I had to smile when I read this quote! It's so funny because it rings true! There are universal truths in life – certain things that are said over and over again – and maybe the first person who makes the statement gets the credit for it, and the others are left to quote this person. But knowledge and wisdom is available to all of us – whether we read it in a book, or obtain it through meditation. Probably everything that needs to have been said, has been said already – but by saying it again, in a different way, time, or place, someone hears it for the first time. Truth resonates. Truth is immortal no matter who says it. *-Lissa Coffey*

"Life is real! Life is earnest!
And the grave is not its goal;
Dust thou art, to dust returnest,
Was not spoken of the soul."
-Henry Wadsworth Longfellow (1807-1882)

This is from one of my favorite poems "A Psalm of Life" – it's the one that also expresses:

"Lives of great men all remind us
We can make our lives sublime
And departing, leave behind us
Footprints in the sands of time.
Let us then be up and doing,
With a heart for any fate,
Still achieving, still pursuing,
Learn to labor and to wait."

Longfellow said it so well – and his words live on, appropriate for anytime or place, because they echo the truth so beautifully. *-Lissa Coffey*

"This World is not Conclusion.
A Sequel stands beyond –
Invisible, as Music –
But positive, as Sound."
-Emily Dickinson (1862)

I just love this! We close our eyes and it is there, beautiful music – undeniable. It's that faith that even though we can't see something, it exists. It is within it, it is all around us. *-Lissa Coffey*

"We feel and know that we are eternal."
-Benedict De Spinoza

Immortality is a big word that is open to so much interpretation. What does it mean to you? This is a good one for the discussion boards! Instinctually, we know that there is some degree of immortality to life. Whether it's in memories, or history, we each make kind of some impression on this world just with our presence. And when we add to it the work that we do, and the love we share, there's a part of ourselves that lives on far beyond our time here on earth. *-Lissa Coffey*

Independence

"I've lived a life that's full
I've traveled each and ev'ry highway,
And more, much more than this,
I did it my way."
-Paul Anka "My Way" (song, 1969)

When Frank Sinatra sang this song, didn't you believe him? He sang it like he meant it, and I think he really did! It's important for us to be able to look back on our lives and reflect on our independence. Every decision we've made, right or wrong, has been ours alone, and we need to take responsibility for that. I, for one, am doing it "my way!"
-Lissa Coffey

"The first of earthly blessings, independence."
-Edward Gibbon (1737-1794)

Independence is a big word, and one that held a lot of meaning for our forefathers who wrote the Declaration of Independence 227 years ago. It seems like a long time ago, but then it's so relatively recent compared with some of these quotes we read here, some dating back thousands of years. I remember when our country celebrated it's bicentennial in 1976. In my hometown, Palo Alto, California, all the fire hydrants were painted red, white and blue to celebrate! I was just a little kid then, so I don't think I really understood the significance of that day. But I do now. Independence is indeed a blessing. *-Lissa Coffey*

"The greatest thing in the world is to know how to belong to oneself."
-Montaigne (1533-1592)

Independence could also be called self-reliance, or self-sufficiency. We must know that we are each whole and complete. We can count on ourselves, we belong to ourselves.
-Lissa Coffey

"What is independence? Freedom from all laws or bonds except those of one's own being, control'd by the universal ones."
-Walt Whitman (1819-1892)

It shows great spiritual maturity to be independent, to know that universal laws prevail. There's a self-referral that goes on with true independence. We answer to ourselves. We don't need the written out, voted and agreed on laws to guide our behavior- we know the right thing to do, and we do it. It doesn't need to be written in a book, it's written in our hearts. *-Lissa Coffey*

> "No bird soars too high, if he soars with
> his own wings."
> -William Blake

I guess this is another way of saying "Go for it!" This makes me think of my favorite book, Jonathan Livingston Seagull by Richard Bach. Jonathan was certainly independent. He lived by his own rules, he learned and grew beyond the expectations of society, because he felt compelled to do so. He followed his heart, and he later became a teacher, passing his wisdom on to younger generations seeking inspiration. Why be content to walk, or even run, when it is in us to soar? We get to make the choice because we are independent thinkers. -*Lissa Coffey*

Individuality

> "A child develops individuality long before
> he develops taste."
> -Erma Bombeck, 1971

Life is funny – and people are funny – isn't great that we can laugh at ourselves? We all go through ages and stages – and somehow we make it through. Our individuality shines through the more we learn and grow. -*Lissa Coffey*

> "Individuality... lies at the root of all progress."
> -Mohandas K. Gandhi (1869-1948)

We often ask ourselves in our spiritual practice the "who am I?" question. Three little words, and such a big question! We learn more about this every day as we learn more about the world we live in. It becomes "who am I and what can I do to help?" "What makes me different?" "What are my unique qualities which I can use to make a contribution to the world?" And as we learn and grow we progress, and the world progresses right along with us. -*Lissa Coffey*

> "Though all men be made of one metal, yet they be not
> cast all in one mold."
> -John Lyly (1554?-1606)

I've always heard this "broke the mold" quote and now I know where it came from! Yes, we're all made up of the same "stuff": bones, water, muscle tissue, etc. But each one of us is completely and totally unique and individual. Our looks contribute to our individuality, but mostly it's our character, our values, our interests, our ideas, and our opinions – the "intangible stuff" that "defines" who we are. We are creating our lives, and our individuality, every day. -*Lissa Coffey*

> "Always remember that you are absolutely unique.
> Just like everyone else."
> -Margaret Mead (1910-1978)

We are all One, and we are all individuals – we are each an individual expression of the Spirit that animates us. It is because of our differences, and our uniqueness, that we can help each other and learn from each other. We each have something to contribute – because we are each a part of the Whole. And yet, we are whole and complete within ourselves, and we have that in common with everyone else! *-Lissa Coffey*

"In proportion to the development of his individuality, each person becomes more valuable to himself, and is, therefore, capable of being more valuable to others."
-John Stuart Mill (1806-1873)

I think we've all heard the advice: "Just be yourself." To do that we have to know whom that "self" is! It is in the process of our growth that we develop our individuality, and that we understand and accept who we are - and at the same time, create for ourselves the life we want to live. As we learn more about ourselves, we can appreciate our worth, and see all that we have to share with the world. *-Lissa Coffey*

Industry

"If you have great talents, industry will improve them: if you have but moderate abilities, industry will supply their deficiency. Nothing is denied to well-directed labor: nothing is to be obtained without it."
-Sir Joshua Reynolds (1723-1792)

Whether you call it industry, or action, there's no substitute for good, old-fashioned effort. There is definitely a place for thinking positively. And that must be followed up with planning and organizing. Then steps must be taken to implement the plan. All this is industry, and we can use it to create, to make things happen! *-Lissa Coffey*

"Far and away the best prize that life offers is the chance to work hard at work worth doing."
-Theodore Roosevelt (1858-1919)

Work worth doing hardly seems like work at all – it's a pleasure! Doing good work makes us feel alive. It's wonderful to be able to contribute, to be able to make an impact, make a difference. Any work you love doing, any work that helps people, or makes the world a better place in any way – that is work worth doing. *-Lissa Coffey*

"The hope, and not the face, of advancement is the spur to industry."
-Henry Taylor (1800-1886)

Advancement is moving forward, improvement, growth. We are driven to industry, attracted to it, because we know how much further we have to go, and how much further it can take us. *-Lissa Coffey*

**"It is not enough to be industrious, so are the ants.
What are you industrious about?"**
-Henry David Thoreau (1817-1862)

What is your passion? Where do you put your energy? There are choices we have to make everyday about how we spend our time. Think about it, and choose wisely. There is so much we can do, but we can't do it all at once! *-Lissa Coffey*

"There is no substitute for hard work."
-Thomas Alva Edison (1847-1931)

Good advice from someone who knows! We can take Edison's word for it because we know he worked hard. And we know the work he did produced some amazing results! But, Edison didn't just work hard; he worked smart. He was organized, and had a plan, and he didn't give up. *-Lissa Coffey*

Insight

"I was always looking outside myself for strength and confidence, but it comes from within. It is there all the time."
-Anna Freud

The word insight itself, "in-sight," explains its meaning. It is looking within, and seeing what is there. Our strength, confidence, wisdom, creativity, beauty, power – all of it – comes from within. We carry it with us. When we are aware of its presence we can more easily bring it forward. *-Lissa Coffey*

"You need to claim the events in your life to make yourself yours. When you truly possess all you have been and done, which may take some time, you are fierce with reality."
-Florida Scott-Maxwell

All of the experiences we've gone through in life have brought us to where we are right now. When we look at the lessons learned, we understand that it's all part of the process. We can't change the past, and we can't control the future, but we can live in this moment, aware and grateful for the person we are today. *-Lissa Coffey*

"I've learned from experience that the greater part of our happiness or misery depends on our dispositions and not on our circumstances."
-Martha Washington

I think it was Abraham Lincoln who later said: "We're about as happy as we make up our minds to be." Events and circumstances change all around us, all the time. And yet our spirit remains present throughout. In difficulties, it doesn't retreat to wait on more ideal times. We can choose our attitude. So why not choose to garner insight and make the most of any condition? *-Lissa Coffey*

> "Have regular hours for work and play; make each day
> both useful and pleasant, and prove that you understand
> the worth of time by employing it well. Then youth
> will be delightful, old age will bring few regrets, and
> life will become a beautiful success."
> -Louisa May Alcott

As we go through life, learning and growing, we gain insight. And often what we see is that the formula for success, and happiness, is really very simple. *-Lissa Coffey*

> "You can change your beliefs so they empower your
> dreams and desires. Create a strong belief in yourself
> and what you want."
> -Marcia Wieder

Believe in yourself. Be yourself. Wise words, but do we take them to heart? Do we even understand the deep meaning of these words? First we need to know who we are. When we recognize and acknowledge the wisdom, strength and beauty that is within us, we understand that we can't be anything less. Our dreams and desires are empowered by our faith and conviction. *-Lissa Coffey*

Inspiration

> "Stung by the splendour of a sudden thought."
> -Robert Browning (1812-1889)

Robert Browning describes inspiration so poetically. And isn't that exactly what it feels like? Inspiration seems to come out of nowhere – but we really know exactly where it comes from – Spirit. In fact, the word itself means "in spirit." So when we are tuned in with that divine energy, we are open to receiving that "splendour" at any time. And it is beautiful. *-Lissa Coffey*

> "The most beautiful thing in the world is, precisely,
> the conjunction of learning and inspiration."
> -Wanda Landowska, in Denise Restout, ed., Landowska on Music (1964)

This is what spiritual growth is all about. When we are inspired to learn we grow so much. Our inspiration is our calling to grow, to bloom. It is a gift; it is a blessing. *-Lissa Coffey*

> "I am one who, when Love inspires, attend, and
> according as he speaks within me, so I express myself."
> -Dante (1265-1321)

Writers and artists often speak lovingly of their "muse." Love is a muse that all of us share. What could be more inspiring? When we are "in love" we are "in spirit," we feel our connection with God. Yet that connection is omnipresent. So when we feel that connection, we can have that same feeling of being "in love" and use it to inspire our selves! *-Lissa Coffey*

"Don't loaf and invite inspiration.
Light out after it with a club."
-Jack London (1876-1916)

Inspiration can come to us... but more often it is something we go out and find. And we can find it just about anywhere! Spirit is everywhere, in everything. We may have to change our scenery once in awhile to wake us up to that fact. But look around – we are living amongst the richest treasures of spirit all the time – choose to be inspired. *-Lissa Coffey*

"My affirmations or utterances come to me ready-made
– not forethought – so that I occasionally awake in the
night simply to let fall ripe a statement which I had
never consciously considered before, and as surprising
and novel and agreeable to me as anything can be. As
if we only thought by sympathy with the universal mind,
which thought while we were asleep. There is such a
necessity [to] make a definite statement that our minds
at length do it without our consciousness."
-Henry David Thoreau (1817-1862)

We are in spirit, and therefore inspired, all the time, even in our sleep. All we need to do is recognize this, and use what is available to us. *-Lissa Coffey*

Instincts

"It is our business to go as we are impelled."
-D.H. Lawrence

We are attracted to what we are attracted to for a reason. We want what we want for a reason. We are drawn in a certain direction for a reason. These are all clues as to our purpose in life. Our instincts work to bring us to our desires. They don't come to us so much as we go to them through our actions and efforts. *-Lissa Coffey*

"Common sense is instinct. Enough of it is genius."
-George Bernard Shaw

We know what is good for us. That's common sense. We don't even have to think about it. When we apply that same common sense, that same instinct, to the big things in our lives then they can come just as easily, just as effortlessly for us. The universe is made up of infinite intelligence, and we can tap into it if we would just get out of our own way. *-Lissa Coffey*

"A goose flies by a chart which the Royal Geographical Society could not improve."
-Holmes

There are so many examples in nature of animals that follow their instinct. It is really our nature to do so. So why do we fight it? We think we know better? We are equipped with this instinct for a reason. It's our radar, and it's build into our system. We just have to use it. *-Lissa Coffey*

"The truth of a thing is the feel of it, not the think of it."
-Stanley Kubrick

We know when something feels right. Our body sends us that signal of comfort when we are making a good decision. And when we have that feeling of discomfort, then something is wrong. It's a signal for us to choose again. The "feel" of it leads us to the truth. If we had to make a decision solely based on thinking, we may come to an entirely different conclusion. There are too many other factors to consider, and our mind weighs the alternatives. Easier, and quicker, to "go with the gut" in many cases, and basically follow our instinct. *-Lissa Coffey*

"Instinct is intelligence incapable of self-consciousness."
-John Sterling

I like John Sterling's definition of instinct. It sounds like thinking with our heart, rather than our head. Sometimes in our head we over-think, and maybe that's where the self-consciousness comes in. Our ego second guesses us. But the way our hearts think it's pure; it's instinctual. Paul Pearsall wrote a book called "The Heart's Code" that explains a lot of this. It's a remarkable concept. *-Lissa Coffey*

Integrity

"Society has no bribe for me, neither in politics, nor church, nor college, nor city."
-Ralph Waldo Emerson (1803-1882)

Society challenges us all the time. We're here in this human existence to learn and to grow, and facing these challenges is one way for us to do that. What wins out, temptation or conviction? Integrity has a lot to do with it. Like Jiminy Cricket sings: "always let your conscience be your guide." *-Lissa Coffey*

"I wanted to try to live in accord with the promptings which came from my true self. Why is that so difficult?"
-Hermann Hesse (1877-1962)

Promptings come from the true self all the time. But are we listening? Are we responding? There is so much clutter and confusion in the world that too often we aren't tuning in to that still small voice inside. And yet that's where all the wisdom is, with the true self. First we need to listen, and then we can live in accord with those promptings. *-Lissa Coffey*

"Integrity without knowledge is weak and useless, and knowledge without integrity is dangerous and dreadful."
-Samuel Johnson (1709-1784)

So of course it follows that integrity with knowledge is strong and powerful. We're here to learn and to grow. When we educate ourselves we become better decision makers. And when we back up our wisdom with integrity we can change the world. *-Lissa Coffey*

"Integrity and firmness are all I can promise. These, be the voyage long or short, shall never forsake me, although I may be deserted by all men; for of the consolations, which are to be derived from these, under any circumstances, the world cannot deprive me."
-George Washington (1732-1799)

There must have been many reasons why our founding fathers chose George Washington to be the first president of the United States. And it is likely that one of those reasons was that he was a man of integrity. When we have integrity, we earn respect and trust. These are important qualities in a leader. *-Lissa Coffey*

Polonius: This above all: to thine own self be true, And it must follow, as the night the day, Thou canst not then be false to any man."
-Shakespeare (1564-1616), Hamlet

Integrity is meaning what you say, it's doing what you say you will do. It's being honest, but more than that, it is staying true to what you believe to be right, just, and fair. When we know who we are, integrity comes easily. We expect nothing less of ourselves. *-Lissa Coffey*

Intelligence

"Intelligence is not something possessed once for all. It is in constant process of forming, and its retention requires constant alertness in observing consequences, an open-minded will to learn and courage in re-adjustment."
-John Dewey (1895-1952)

IQ tests are one measurement of intelligence. It is interesting to note that one person's score on a test can change, indicating that the person's intelligence can change. We can actually teach ourselves to think smarter. One way to do this is through meditation, tapping into the wisdom of the universe. *-Lissa Coffey*

"The mind can store an estimated 100 trillion bits of information – compared with which a computer's mere billions are virtually amnesiac."
-Sharon Begley et al (in Newsweek, 1986)

Technology may attempt to keep pace with the mind, but no computer will ever be as intelligent as a human being. A computer represents just one kind of intelligence, while we wonderful creatures also exhibit emotional intelligence, spiritual intelligence, physical intelligence, and so much more that's just not programmable into a mere machine. *-Lissa Coffey*

"I not only use all the brains I have, but all I can borrow."
-Woodrow Wilson

We don't need to know everything. Isn't that great? What a burden it would be to carry around all that information constantly. And yet everything we could ever need, or want, to know is available to us at any time. All we have to do is ask! We are here to help each other, we are our own greatest resource. *-Lissa Coffey*

"Intuition becomes increasingly valuable in the new information society precisely because there is so much data."
-John Naisbitt

Data and information are computed in the mind. When intuition comes into play then we are thinking with our heart. Using our mind and our heart together we tend to make much more intelligent decisions. *-Lissa Coffey*

"Intelligence alone, without wisdom and empathy for suffering, is hollow."
-John G. Stoessinger

Intelligence is a wonderful trait, it serves us well in so many ways. And yet, wisdom, which is knowledge seasoned with experience, and compassion, which is heartfelt empathy, makes us all the more intelligent. *-Lissa Coffey*

Interdependence

"One life stamps and influences another, which in turn stamps and influences another, on and on, until the soul of human experience breathes on in generations we'll never even meet."
-Mary Kay Blakely, 1989

Yes, we are independent, as people and as a nation, and at the same time we are interdependent. We rely on each other. We support and sustain one another. Each person, independently, makes contributions that have far-reaching effects. It's the pebble in the pond example, where the ripples are felt for a long time after the stone has landed. -*Lissa Coffey*

"Whatever we do to any other thing in the great web of life, we do to ourselves, for we are one."
-Brooke Medicine Eagle, 1991

The great web of life – this amazing connection that binds us together. These days when we hear "web" we think of the worldwide web. And this is a great analogy for how we can really move beyond space and time to experience our connection with one another. I had a service question for aol recently, and ended up speaking with a technician in India! We had a great conversation. He solved my problem and I showed him my whatsyourdosha.com website. Although Ayurveda is somewhat new to us here in the west, it's a part of everyday life in India, and he was pleased that we are finally "getting" it! -*Lissa Coffey*

"There's a thread that binds all of us together, pull on one end of the thread, the strain is felt all down the line."
-Rosamond Marshall, 1943

We have an inherent obligation to help out. When someone is in pain, that hurt affects more than just that one person. By reaching out, by showing compassion, by doing whatever we can to ease the burden, we make it better for all of us. Love lifts, love heals, love lightens. Whether it's right here at home, or across the world, there are so many opportunities to make a difference. -*Lissa Coffey*

"All that is due to us will be paid, although not perhaps by those to whom we have lent."
-Marie von Ebner-Eschenbach, 1893

I guess you could say that what comes around, goes around, and why not in a good way? Think of it as some kind of karmic bank account that keeps track of our good deeds. We don't have to keep score, the universe takes note! So we don't have to think about it, we just have to take action, help out, do our best to make the world a better place for all of us. It all works out. -*Lissa Coffey*

"We all act as hinges – fortuitous links between other people."
-Penelope Lively, 1987

Hinges open doors! Isn't this great? We have the power, and the privilege, to open doors for people, to create opportunities, to make life better! And when we work together, doors come flying open, one right after the next. It can be easy if we are "open" to helping each other. -*Lissa Coffey*

Intuition

"You must train your intuition - you must trust the
small voice inside you which tells you exactly what to
say, what to decide."
-Ingrid Bergman

Jewel sings a song called "Intuition." It's gotten me thinking about intuition, instinct, hunches… it's all the same thing. The lyrics in the song say: "Follow your heart, your intuition, it will lead you in the right direction." Great advice- but like much great advice, do we always take it? I think we try to second guess ourselves too much. When Ingrid Bergman says we must train our intuition, I think she really means that we must train ourselves to listen to that voice, and hear what it has to say. *-Lissa Coffey*

"Trust your hunches… Hunches are usually based on
facts filed away just below the conscious level.
Warning! Do not confuse your hunches with wishful
thinking. This is the road to disaster."
-Dr. Joyce Brothers

We can look at intuition either scientifically or spiritually, but it is there, and significantly so, nonetheless. When we get our minds involved, analyzing our hunches, that's where we get ourselves into trouble. We think too much, when sometimes we need to just "feel." *-Lissa Coffey*

"By learning to contact, listen to, and act on our intuition,
we can directly connect to the higher power of the
universe and allow it to become our guiding force."
-Shakti Gawain

Where is this intuition coming from? Whether it's from the deep recesses of our memory or from the intelligence of the universe, it is worth listening to. Maybe we can't explain intuition, but we can see the benefits of it at work in our lives. *-Lissa Coffey*

"Instinct is the nose of the mind."
-Madame De Girardin

I love this! The nose doesn't "think" - it just senses- our brain then translates what scent is coming through. Our instinct is the same way- sometimes we don't know why we know something, but we just do. So rather than try to translate or decipher this information in the brain, it might do us well to just go with it every once in awhile, and find out just where our intuition leads us. *-Lissa Coffey*

"I go by instinct… I don't worry about experience."
-Barbra Streisand

This is such a powerful concept. Look at how this relates to the work community. One resume may be loaded with experience, while another has just the bare bones. Is that more important than the impression the job candidate makes in the interview? When we meet someone face to face we get a "feel" for how we can relate to that person, how we would like to be around that person every day in the work environment. These are the kinds of things that can't be put down on paper, we have to use our instincts.
-*Lissa Coffey*

Joy

"Joy is not in things; it is in us."
-Richard Wagner

"Real joy comes not from ease or riches or from the praise of men, but from doing something worthwhile."
-Sir Wilfred Grenfell

It is with true joy that we release this inaugural newsletter into the universe!
-Lissa Coffey

"Winning is important to me, but what brings me real joy is the experience of being fully engaged in whatever I'm doing."
-Phil Jackson

Phil Jackson is the coach for the NBA Champion Lakers, and he obviously has a winning attitude. When you watch him on the court, you can see that he is fully engaged in coaching his team. He is focused, involved and very "in the moment." Joy has a way of inherently bringing success with it! Where do you find your joy? Go there! Immerse yourself and reap the rewards. *-Lissa Coffey*

"Joy is not in things; it is in us."
- Richard Wagner

Joy is always present, but do we choose to see it, feel it, experience it? Make that choice today... choose to let joy bubble up and express through you! How many times have we heard "have a good day!" and thought nothing of it? We can have a good day every day, it's simply a matter of making that conscious decision. By recognizing love, peace, and joy, just by bringing it into our awareness, we lift the energy around us and make the world a better place. *-Lissa Coffey*

"O world, I cannot hold thee close enough!"
-Edna St. Vincent Millay, 1917

That kind of joy, that kind of love for the world, is contagious. One person, whose love radiates outward, can elevate the feelings all around. Have you ever seen someone whose smile can light up a room? It's like that. The world responds to the way we respond to it. Be joyful! *-Lissa Coffey*

> ### "Joy is the holy fire that keeps our purpose warm and our intelligence aglow."
> -Helen Keller, 1905

We can find joy in anything we do. Joy is something that comes from within our selves, not from any other source. It fuels us, feeds us, nourishes us. *-Lissa Coffey*

> ### "Joy is a net of love by which you can catch souls."
> -Mother Teresa, 1975

Joy is attractive. When we "give" joy, what we are actually doing is helping someone to experience the joy that is already there. Joy is internal. We may see something beautiful, or fun, or silly, and that may trigger us to feel joy. But the joy is not in the thing; it is in us. *-Lissa Coffey*

> ### "You have to sniff out joy, keep your nose to the joy-trail."
> -Buffy Sainte-Marie, 1975

What makes you feel happy? What brings you joy? Do you get enough of that? Keep your nose to the joy-trail. Whatever helps joy to fill you up, to make you feel that you're in exactly the right place, exactly where you are supposed to be in this place and time, that is something you want to revisit often. *-Lissa Coffey*

> ### "People need joy quite as much as clothing. Some of them need it far more."
> -Margaret Collier Graham, 1906

Joy is a tonic; it is like a vitamin. It keeps us strong and moving forward. It helps us keep things in perspective. Because we know joy, we know that whatever bad times we go through are only temporary. There is balance. *-Lissa Coffey*

Kindness

"Only kindness matters. We are God's hands."
-Jewel

Ask anyone what they value most in a person, what they remember most about a person, and chances are that they will say 'kindness.' Kindness always makes such a positive and lasting impression! Why is that? Is it because we encounter it all too rarely these days? Being kind is such a simple gesture, yet it is one that is often disregarded. Let's make an effort today to recognize kindness in others, and to express kindness ourselves. *-Lissa Coffey*

"Kindness is wisdom; there is none in life but needs it, and may learn."
-Bailey

It is truly amazing that as we learn and grow and attain more wisdom, that we understand more and more the real value of the most simple things in life. Kindness is precious. It is healing and life-affirming and contagious! And kindness is readily available at all times. If there were a prescription for happiness, kindness would be one of the ingredients. It all starts here - show kindness and see what happens!
-Lissa Coffey

"Ask thyself, daily, to how many ill-minded persons thou hast shown a kind disposition."
-Marcus Antonius

Therein lies the challenge! Sure, we can be kind to children and animals. We can be kind when someone is kind to us. But to maintain our centeredness and be kind in spite of conflict, animosity, anger - ah, there's our real opportunity for spiritual growth! *-Lissa Coffey*

"Deeds of kindness are equal in weight to all the commandments."
-Talmud

A kind word, a smile, a friendly gesture - sometimes that's all it takes to totally turn someone's day around. If we can turn a day around so easily, couldn't we turn a life around? We can certainly turn our own lives around. It's these little things that add up in big ways and make the big differences in the world. *-Lissa Coffey*

"Heaven in sunshine will requite the kind."
-Byron

It is our nature to be kind. And most of the time, kindness comes easily to us, especially when we're on the path and everything is going our way. The difficulty comes when we encounter an obstacle - maybe a large, rude, imposing obstacle! Those are the times we need to remind ourselves to be kind. Those are the times that some may say we are "tested." How kind are we really? How patient? How loving? How understanding? Because we are human, there may be times when we need to make a greater effort to express kindness. But the more often we do so, and see the far-reaching effects that kindness has, the easier it gets. *-Lissa Coffey*

Language

"How did language develop? In much the same way as an economic order develops through the market - out of the voluntary interaction of individuals, in this case seeking to trade ideas or information or gossip rather than goods and services with one another."
-Milton Friedman and Rose Friedman, 1979

Whatever language we speak, it's our way of communicating with one another. Language is a means of translating our feelings and emotions into words so that we can be understood. When we can master a language, then we can be more clearly understood, and we can more clearly understand, too. There's always more to learn, about words, and about each other. *-Lissa Coffey*

"There have been periods in the history of the various cultures, when the language of spirituality was clear, accurate and exhaustive. At the present time it is muddled, inadequate to the fact and dangerously equivocal. Lacking a proper vocabulary, people find it hard, not only to think about the most important issues of life, but even to realize that these issues exist."
-Aldous Huxley (1894-1963)

This is really interesting to think about. Is our language of spirituality clear, accurate and exhaustive? So many times, when asked about our beliefs, it seems it's hard to put into words. It's difficult to define any big concept like that because the meanings of words can vary based upon the experience of each person. But we have to start somewhere. It might be a good exercise to write up some of our own definitions just to see what kind of language we come up with to express ourselves. We might just discover something about ourselves long the way, too. Start with these: love, joy, peace, faith. *-Lissa Coffey*

"Language is power... Language can be used as a means of changing reality."
-Adrienne Rich

The words we say carry weight, carry meaning. And it's not only which words we say but the way that we say them, too. Look at the "spin" that can be put on things in advertisements and in political speeches. There are ways that we can make this concept work for us in our spiritual growth. Affirmations, for example. We use words and language to change our thinking, and we can change our lives. We create our own reality. *-Lissa Coffey*

> **"England and America are two countries separated by
> the same language."**
> -George Bernard Shaw (1856-1932)

This is so funny, and so true! I had this experience when visiting Australia. I felt a little bit like Alice in Wonderland! I could understand every word that people spoke, and yet many times I had no idea what they were talking about! The Australians still use the more traditional English terms, and somehow in America we've found another way. Is it a boot or a trunk? A bonnet or a hood? A footpath or a sidewalk? A trolley or a cart? A serviette or a napkin? And there is the same kind of communication "gap" between American adults and teenagers a lot of times... Is it good, bad or sweet? Hot, hip or cool? I could go on and on, but as they say, "a rose by any other name would smell just as sweet." What matters is that we talk with each other, the rest is "details!"
-Lissa Coffey

> **"I never taught language for the purpose of teaching
> it; but invariably used language as a medium for the
> communication of thought; thus learning of language
> was coincident with the acquisition of knowledge."**
> -Anne Sullivan (1866-1936)

My older son is going into his junior year in high school, so he's starting to study for the SAT tests and doing all the preparation that he has to do to get ready because those scores are so important when it comes to applying to colleges. When I spoke with a tutor about it, he said that students who are well-read typically do better on the test. That is because they develop a larger vocabulary, and a broader base of general knowledge. That makes sense to me. When we read we learn, and when we learn we expand our use of language. *-Lissa Coffey*

Laughter

> **"Laughter is the lightning rod of play,
> the eroticism of conversation."**
> -Eva Hoffman

Look in any women's magazine and you'll find some sort of survey that ranks "sense of humor" as one of the most attractive qualities in a person. We love to laugh, and we love people who can make us laugh! Laughter builds wonderful connections between us. We let down our guard and allow ourselves to just enjoy the moment. *-Lissa Coffey*

> **"Man is the only creature endowed with the power of
> laughter; is he not also the only one that deserves to
> be laughed at?"**
> -Lord Greville

And why does man deserve to be laughed at? Because we take ourselves entirely too seriously! Think about it – we're running around with our ear glued to a cell phone, dashing through parking lots, stressing about deadlines. All the while missing what's really important in and all around us. And we do this daily. We can't help it, we're creatures of habit! Well, it's time to get into some new habits, and we can start by realizing just how silly we really are! *-Lissa Coffey*

> **"Life can be wildly tragic at times, and I've had my share. But whatever happens to you, you have to keep a slightly comic attitude. In the final analysis, you have got not to forget to laugh."**
> -Katharine Hepburn

Most of comedy is built on tragedy – the slip on the banana peel, the pie in the face, the big misunderstanding. And we laugh because we can relate – we've been there. In movies there can only be so much drama before we're offered up some "comic relief." Writers know that audiences need a break in their emotions or they just go numb. Yes, life is tragic, and life can also be hysterically funny. Have you ever had one of those things happen where you say: "We're going to look back on this and laugh one day?" We all have. And you know what? That day does come when we laugh – and it feels good. *-Lissa Coffey*

> **"A good laugh is as good as a prayer sometimes."**
> -L.M. Montgomery

Laughter heightens our senses so that we feel joy. And when we feel joy, we feel our connection with God. Having that feeling of oneness is like a prayer, it's comforting, it's cleansing. Laugh, and share the joy. *-Lissa Coffey*

> **"A good laugh is sunshine in a house."**
> -William Makepeace Thackeray

Norman Cousins discovered personally, and wrote eloquently, about the healing power of laughter. Laughter is good medicine. When we laugh, we can't help but feel good. We feel good around people who laugh, people who enjoy life and can express themselves so freely. Here's a little story I heard that might get you giggling: A wealthy man dies and goes to Heaven. He brings with him all of his earthly belongings when he meets St. Peter at the gate. St. Peter says: "Oh, my... you know, you can't bring any of that in here." The man pleads his case, he worked so hard for everything and can't bear to leave it all behind. Finally St. Peter agrees to discuss the situation with his boss, who says, "Fine, let him bring in just one suitcase." The man is overjoyed! He goes through everything and loads up one of his largest bags and presents it to St. Peter for inspection. It is filled to the brim with solid gold bars. St. Peter looks at his quizzically and says: "You brought pavement?" *-Lissa Coffey*

Leadership

**"What you cannot enforce,
Do not command!"**
-Sophocles (496? – 406 B.C.)

The laws of nature are always at play. There are some things that we just can't control, nor would we want to! When we're in the flow, we realize that right action takes place, in its own way and in its own time. Let God lead, and we'll end up exactly where we want to be! -*Lissa Coffey*

**"The task of leadership is not to put greatness into humanity,
but to elicit it, for the greatness is already there."**
-John Buchan (1875-1940)

Great leaders see the greatness in the community. They understand what the community has to offer and they seek ways to express that. We can each be a leader, right where we are, just by noticing all the good around us, and bringing it to the attention of others. -*Lissa Coffey*

"Great leadership arises out of great conflict."
-James MacGregor Burns

In turbulent times, we often find that the best is brought out in us. When there is a need, we rise to the occasion. All of our natural instincts kick in and we help, and serve, and show compassion and empathy. It happens time and time again. But we don't need to wait for a crisis to help each other. There are opportunities for us to do so every day. -*Lissa Coffey*

**"Divide and rule, the politician cries;
Unite and lead, is watchword of the wise."**
-Goethe (1749-1832)

It has been said a million different ways, a million different times: we're all in this together. Great leaders understand this and show us just how much we have in common. Together, with all of our talents and intelligence working as one, we can accomplish so much, more so than we ever could alone. -*Lissa Coffey*

"Do not wait for leaders; do it alone, person to person."
-Mother Teresa

Now is the time for us to take initiative. We could wait forever for someone to tell us what to do – or we could just go out and do what we know needs to be done! We are each the leaders of our own lives. We decide. We choose. -*Lissa Coffey*

Learning

"What we learn to do, we learn by doing."
-Aristotle (384-322 B.C.)

There's a difference between theory and practice. We may know how to meditate – all the technical points and benefits of meditation that we hear so much about. But until we actually meditate ourselves, we haven't really learned anything about it! On a recent episode of the TV comedy "Frasier," Frasier and his brother were trying to learn how to ride a bike by reading a book. Now we know how silly that is! And yet, that's the same kind of thing we often do in our spiritual practices. We read about prayer, and chanting, and mantras – but to really "get it" we've got to do it! -*Lissa Coffey*

"A primary method of learning is to go from the familiar to the unfamiliar."
-Glenn Doman, How to Teach Your Baby to Read, 1964

Simple steps. And yet the unfamiliar often scares us, so that first step is the most difficult! Why not just step into the unknown? If we really want to grow, we've got to learn, and that means that we might have to start doing things differently to make space for that in our lives. No risk, no reward. -*Lissa Coffey*

"It is impossible for a man to begin to learn what he thinks he knows."
-Epictetus (A.D. 55? – 135?)

The most important ingredient in learning is an open mind. We need to approach each experience willing to take in the lesson and see the growth in ourselves. We can begin anytime, we can begin right now! -*Lissa Coffey*

"You learn more from getting your butt kicked than from getting it kissed."
-Tom Hanks

We often call life experiences the "school of hard knocks" because we learn from going through those rough times. And we end up being better people because of it! As hard as it may be at the time, we can be grateful for the tough times, because they give us the opportunity to learn and grow. -*Lissa Coffey*

"I am still learning."
-Michelangelo (1475-1564)

Michelangelo was a master – no one would dispute that. And yet, he knew there was always room for growth. I think we go around a little too confident in our own skills, and then we get reminded that we still have much to learn. We drive around everywhere, especially here in Southern California, almost on auto-pilot, not really aware of what we're doing... until one day we get a ticket, and our attention turns to the laws of the road while we're sitting in traffic school. There are spiritual laws that we know about, too, but are we paying attention to those? We can always learn more. *-Lissa Coffey*

Leisure

"Nothing excellent can be done without leisure."
-Andre Gide (1869-1951)

One of my favorite quotes is from Emerson who said: "Nothing great was ever achieved without enthusiasm." There seems to be a magic formula for success and excellence. We need down-time and a good attitude! This leisure time lets us clear our minds and think more efficiently. It helps us keep things in perspective. Haven't we all had the experience where we're working so hard, struggling to solve a problem and the answer is just not coming to us? And then, we take some time off and do something else and the answer just pops into our head! There is a purpose to this, and it is divine! *-Lissa Coffey*

"Leisure is the mother of Philosophy."
-Thomas Hobbes (1588-1679)

Remember the "Leisure Suits" that were so popular in the 70's? As if we needed the appropriate attire to lounge around in... It seems funny now, but it was so stylin' then! But maybe the real point was that we didn't necessarily need the suits, but we did, and do, need the leisure. In some strange way, that was brought to our attention. It might benefit us psychologically to "suit up" – whether it's in our yoga pants or in our pajamas, to spend some time down time, some time to clear our minds so that we can open our minds to deep thought. *-Lissa Coffey*

"He enjoys true leisure who has time
to improve his soul's estate."
-Henry David Thoreau (1817-1862)

Spiritually, we know that there is no such thing as time. And yet, here we are, living this existence, and we have these constraints to deal with. There is only so much time, so many hours in a day, so many vacation days in a year. So, how do we spend out time? And more importantly, how do we spend our precious leisure time? If we take Thoreau's advice, we spend that time in spiritual pursuits, and then we understand how wonderful leisure can really be. *-Lissa Coffey*

"Leisure requires the evidence of our own feelings,
because it is not so much a quality of time as a peculiar
state of mind... What being at leisure means is more
easily felt than defined."
-Vernon Lee, "About Leisure," Limbo, 1908

By this definition it sounds like leisure is the opposite of stress. Ah! So, maybe there is an antidote after all! Perhaps we can choose to work leisurely and enjoy the time we spend getting things done - rather than work under stress, wishing we were doing something, anything ELSE! Perhaps it is a state of mind, one that we can tap into for our own benefit. -*Lissa Coffey*

"Leisure, some degree of it, is necessary to the health
of every man's spirit."
-Harriet Martineau, Society in America (1837)

A woman said this, so we can assume that she naturally meant every man and woman's spirit! And this is so true. We care for the health of our body by eating right and exercising. We care for our mental health by learning new things and solving problems. The best way to care for the health of our spirit is to enjoy some time at leisure, doing what we love to do. It's refreshing and invigorating! -*Lissa Coffey*

Letters

"Our correspondences have wings – paper birds that fly
from my house to yours – flocks of ideas crisscrossing
the country."
-Terry Tempest Williams, 1991

In the broader sense, correspondence could be all forms of written communication, including e-mails! With the internet, it's not exactly paper birds, but electronic ones, making their way into computers all over the world. Because of technology, the world has been made smaller, closer. We have the opportunity to meet people we never might have met before, and to learn things and share experiences in ways that were not available to us in the past. -*Lissa Coffey*

"Why is it that you can sometimes feel the reality of
people more keenly through a letter than face to face?"
-Anne Morrow Lindbergh, 1971

Sometimes we allow ourselves to open up more when we write out our feelings. We have time to think more, to choose our words carefully, to really express what it is we want to say. And when we read someone's letter, we have the time to absorb the words, to give it thought and consideration. -*Lissa Coffey*

"There's no finer caress than a love letter, because it
makes the world very small, and the writer and reader,
the only rulers."
-Cecelia Capuzzi, 1987

A love letter is the ultimate in romance. It's something to be cherished, and read over and over again. When we really make the effort to put into words how we feel about someone, that brings us clarity, and it brings meaning to the relationship. Letters of love can be written to our children, or our parents, or to anyone we love and appreciate. *-Lissa Coffey*

"Letter-writing on the part of a busy man or woman is the quintessence of generosity."
-Agnes Repplier, 1926

Old-fashioned letter writing is almost a lost art. But think of the beauty of actually putting pen to paper and composing thoughts! How personal, how rare. This is entirely different that jotting off a quick e-mail, and cc'ing everyone on your list. This is different from buying a card printed with "Hallmark" sentiments. We're all busy, but when we take the time to write a letter, it is a wonderful gift that we are giving. *-Lissa Coffey*

"I am much fonder of receiving letters, than writing them: but I believe this is no very uncommon case."
-Mary Lamb, 1802

Remember when we were little, and the whole experience of going out to the mailbox was magical? And those days when we received mail of our very own were so special, like a surprise! Receiving letters is still special, and it's good to remind ourselves of that. We can actually make someone's day by writing them a letter. Just that small act of kindness, of attention, can bring a smile that lights up the world. *-Lissa Coffey*

Life

"Trust life, and it will teach you, in joy and sorrow, all you need to know."
-James Baldwin (1924-1987)

You know the punch line when someone asks: "Got any questions?" and someone answers back, "Yeah, what's the meaning of life?" We laugh because we know that's not exactly what the first guy was expecting to hear... and also because we know that it is the BIG question we've all come here to find out... and because we know that there are no easy answers! It's the same for all of us. But at some point we figure out that we don't NEED to know everything. We understand that we can trust the process enough to know that life is here for us and that we will learn all we really need to know along the way. *-Lissa Coffey*

"Life is like playing a violin solo in public and learning the instrument as one goes on."
-Samuel Butler (1835-1902)

Can't you just picture that? It's so true! Here we are, living our lives, not really knowing what we're doing until actually doing it. We're finding our way, step by step, day by day. We will stumble, hit some sour notes, learn a few lessons, and write our own songs. An audience may reject our music, or embrace it, but we keep on playing because the instrument is there for us. And someday, with enough practice, we will be a master life-liver, a virtuoso! *-Lissa Coffey*

> ## "Life is what happens to you
> ## While you're busy
> ## Making other plans."
> -John Lennon (1940-1980)

We go about our lives trying really hard to keep everything in order, all the plates spinning: jobs, family, friends, community responsibilities, etc. But every once in awhile something happens that is beyond our reach, out of our control. Maybe someone we love gets sick, or we have a bad financial setback. Now our attention is elsewhere, and it seems that everything else gets out of balance, too. The truth is that we can't control everything, and that we probably wouldn't be any good at it if we could! But we can control our responses to these unexpected situations. We can use our problems as opportunities to learn and to grow. These are the times when we find that reserve of strength that was there all along. We discover more of who we really are, and what we're really capable of. *-Lissa Coffey*

> ## "I slept and dreamt that life was joy.
> ## I awoke and saw that life was duty.
> ## I acted and behold, duty was joy."
> -Rabindranath Tagore (1861-1941)

There's no doubt that life can be hard. And yet life is poetic. What we learn in our time here is beautiful. All that we really take with us is the wisdom we garner. Life is full of joy. We were blessed, against all odds, to be here, in this time and place, in this particular circumstance. It is our duty to live this life and to get all that we can from the experience. *-Lissa Coffey*

> ## "To live is the rarest thing in the world. Most people
> ## exist, that is all."
> -Oscar Wilde (1854-1900)

We need to ask ourselves: Are we living the life that we want to live? If not, then make some changes! Life is too short, life is too precious, to miss out on. Every moment is holy. It is there for us to embrace. How many moments go by without notice? Are we spending our time analyzing the past, which is done and gone – or planning for the future, which is changing every instant? Or are we living, truly LIVING in this moment, NOW, where our life is taking place? It is not enough to exist, choose to live! *-Lissa Coffey*

Light

> "Even if our efforts of attention seem for years to be producing no result, one day a light that is in exact proportion to them will flood the room."
> -Simone Weil

Sometimes our spiritual progress is like a dimmer and brighter control – one of those knobs where we can make the light gradually grow brighter. And sometimes it seems like we're putting in all of this work and nothing is happening. It can be a little frustrating. But something is happening, we just can't see it yet. It's like something going on behind-the-scenes, and when the light finally hits us, it's so bright we have to wear shades! -*Lissa Coffey*

> "Science and art may invent splendid modes of illuminating the apartments of the opulent; but these are all poor and worthless compared with the light which the sun pours freely, impartially, over hill and valley, which kindles daily the eastern and western sky; and so the common lights of reason and conscience and love are of more worth and dignity than the rare endowments which give celebrity to a few."
> -William Ellery Channing (1780-1842)

The light of day, the morning sun steaming through our window gives us a sense of newness, and optimism. We share the sun, it warms each of us without playing favorites. Songs are written about the sun, and the happiness it brings. -*Lissa Coffey*

> "Light is the symbol of truth."
> -James Russell Lowell (1819-1891)

There are two kinds of "light" in the English language. One is the visual, the light we get from the sun or a lamp, that lets us see. This kind of light is indeed a symbol of truth, because the truth lets us see, nothing is hidden. The other kind of "light" is a measurement of weight, the opposite of "heavy." This, too, could be called a symbol of truth. The truth makes us free, and we feel light because we don't have to carry the heavy burden of hiding a secret. -*Lissa Coffey*

> "The eye's light is a noble gift of heaven! All beings live from light; each fair created thing, the very plants, turn with a joyful transport to the light."
> -Johann Christoph Friedrich von Schiller (1759-1805)

Light is life, and it is life-giving. Light is eternal, and ever present. Darkness is merely the absence of light. We reach for the light. It represents goodness, and power. In cartoons when someone has an idea we see a lightbulb over their head – the light has gone on! When someone is smart we say they are "brilliant." -*Lissa Coffey*

"Light! Nature's resplendent robe; without whose
vesting beauty all were wrapt in gloom."
-James Thomson (1700-1748)

The whole world is made up of opposites. Dark and light are just one pair. And we really can't have one without the other. When light hits the earth it creates shadows. Day turns to night, and the light comes again in the morning. Even in the darkness of night the stars shine their light. We wouldn't be able to see the stars without the darkness. Even though there are opposites, it's all good. It's all a gift. *-Lissa Coffey*

Living

"The flower is the poetry of reproduction. It is the
example of the eternal seductiveness of life."
-Jean Giraudoux

The flower: so simple, elegant, and sweet. It is a symbol of beauty, and a representation of life expressing itself. We are drawn to them. It's no wonder that we love to give and receive flowers. *-Lissa Coffey*

"This is the true joy in life, the being used for a
purpose recognized by yourself as a mighty one;
the being thoroughly worn out before you are
thrown on the scrap heap."
-George Bernard Shaw

There's a lot of living to do in this life! It's one thing to go out and have adventures and experience all the fun there is to be had. But at a certain point in time we discover our purpose, the certain something that we feel compelled to do that gives our life meaning. And when we're totally involved in our purpose and giving of ourselves, there's no better feeling. *-Lissa Coffey*

"Life is not having been told that the man has just
waxed the floor."
-Ogden Nash

Whoops! It's those surprises that make life interesting. We never know what is just around the corner for us. And isn't that wonderful? We live with uncertainty, so good things can happen at any time. *-Lissa Coffey*

"Is not this the true romantic feeling – not to desire to
escape life, but to prevent life from escaping you."
-Thomas Wolfem

We can live life "in love" all the time. When we love our life, and ourselves, we are filled to the brim with joy and peace. We overflow with wonder that spills out to the world and makes it a better place to be. *-Lissa Coffey*

> **"The vanity of human life is like a river, constantly**
> **passing away, and yet constantly coming on."**
> -Alexander Pope

It's interesting to look at little children and think: "I was once that age!" We all start out as babies, fresh and new to the world. And now here we are as adults, shaping the world, making decisions that affect the future, a future which will one day be the present to these babies who will one day be adults. And life goes on. We're connected now and always. *-Lissa Coffey*

Longevity

> **"'Tis very certain the desire for life**
> **Prolongs it."**
> -Lord Byron (1788-1824)

Life is good. Love it! Eat it up – devour it like a sweet peach and let the juice dribble down your chin. We have so many beautiful sights to see, sounds to hear, wisdom to learn, and it's all right in front of us – and it's all within us at the same time. *-Lissa Coffey*

> **"If there is one single secret to long life,**
> **that secret is moderation."**
> -George Gallup (1901-1984)

It's amazing how far good common sense gets us. Moderation is that middle path. It's balance. We have a lot to balance in this life - our diets, our relationships, our workload, our checkbooks. When things are in balance then we are less stressed, we're better able to cope with the little stuff that comes up. Moderation may take some maintenance, but maintenance is a lot easier to handle than repair. *-Lissa Coffey*

> **"Katharine: A light heart lives long."**
> -William Shakespeare (1564-1616) Love's Labour's Lost, 1594

It's no secret that stress takes its toll on us mentally, physically and emotionally. When we learn to handle stress more effectively, to lighten our load, or "lighten up," then we feel better. Studies have shown that a good attitude goes a long way in increasing our longevity. *-Lissa Coffey*

> **"What counts is not the years in your life**
> **but the life in your years."**
> -Adlai E. Stevenson (1900-1965)

We often hear "You're as young as you feel" or "You're as young as you think you are!" Think about it. How important is our chronological age anyway? It's just a marker of time. Of course we need to take care of ourselves, and we also need to go out there and experience life, to challenge ourselves, to live Life with a capital "L!" *-Lissa Coffey*

"The brain is the organ of longevity."
-George Alban Sacher (1917- 1981)

Longevity here means not only length of life, but vitality, too, both health and happiness-wise. Why is longevity important? Because the more time we have here on earth, the more opportunity we have to learn and to grow. That's what we're here for. That's what it's all about. So we might as well make the most of the years that we have, get it all in! -*Lissa Coffey*

Love

"Love is the central flame of the universe, nay, the very fire itself."
-Ernest Holmes

Of course, during this Valentine's week, our focus is on "love." What else is there, really? A Course in Miracles says that there are only two things in this life - love and fear... and when it all comes down to it, there is really just love. For just a little word, LOVE is a huge concept. Love is our greatest motivator, our deepest inspiration. No wonder love is so often associated with fire, and desire, and burning passion. It warms us, heals us, frees us. -*Lissa Coffey*

"We may think of the Divine as a fire whose outgoing warmth pervades the Universe."
-Plotinus

Many people say God IS love. And love certainly pervades the Universe. Love is something we all understand, something we can all relate to. Every mother knows what it means to love a child. Every person is capable of giving and receiving love. In A Course in Miracles, fear is defined as the absence of love. Much like darkness is the absence of light. Let's light that fire, and light up the world with our outpouring of love! -*Lissa Coffey*

"Love is a fire and I am wood."
-Rumi

Love has been the subject for poets throughout the ages. In contemporary times, think of how many songs we hear that are all about love! According to the lyrics, "Love is all there is," and "Love can move mountains." Love brings us to the movies, where we can see love acted out larger than life and feel our emotions stir. We are drawn to love because that is what we all crave more of. And we crave love because that is what we are made of! Love brings us to our true nature. We are consumed by it because we want to know who we really are, and love allows us to experience that. -*Lissa Coffey*

"All's love, yet all's law."
-Robert Browning

Love and Law are two sides of the same coin. Everything is love, and at the same time, everything has that organizing power that we can totally count on. There is a reason why we love someone or something. There is a creative purpose to our love. We are not under some spell like the characters in "A Midsummer Night's Dream." We love who we love because God, the Universe, brought us together to learn and grow and experience more of our Selves. Love is divine, and yet love is totally practical.
-Lissa Coffey

> "Some day, after we have mastered the winds,
> the waves, the tides and gravity, we shall
> harness... the energies of love. Then, for the
> second time in the history of the world, we
> will have discovered fire."
> -Pierre Tielhard de Chardin

Is there anything more powerful than love? Love is creative; with love we can accomplish anything. With love we have accomplished everything! Love is the great up-lifter, the strongest force there is. Love heals. Love grows. Love is the basis for life itself. Love is invisible, and yet ever-present. Love is the most valuable gift we will ever give or receive, and yet love is perfectly free. *-Lissa Coffey*

Luck

> "Luck to me means hard work - and realizing what is
> opportunity and what isn't."
> -Lucille Ball (1911-1989)

So, it's not just hard work, it's also being smart about it- discriminating between which chances we take, and which we don't. It's knowing what it takes to be ready for an opportunity and doing the necessary preparation for it. *-Lissa Coffey*

> "Luck is not chance-
> It's Toil-
> Fortune's expensive smile
> Is earned - "
> -Emily Dickinson (1830-1886)

We hear time and time again that good luck is all about hard work. But isn't life like that, too? We get out of it what we put into it. *-Lissa Coffey*

> "Good luck is another name for tenacity of purpose."
> -Ralph Waldo Emerson (1803-1882)

Is there such a thing as luck? It's hard to argue against it. So much of what we go through can be explained away by luck, either good or bad. One famous saying is that luck is when preparation meets opportunity. I think most of the time we find,

or even create, our own luck, just by being ready for it. What if you knew that today was your lucky day? Where would you go, or what would you do, to find your luck?
-Lissa Coffey

"It is a great piece of skill to know how to guide your luck even while waiting for it."
-Baltasar Gracian (1601-1658)

Go ahead and carry that four-leaf clover, or pick up that lucky penny- it couldn't hurt! But meanwhile, we need to take the necessary steps to create our own opportunities. By being opening to what presents itself, we become lucky - we recognize when the universe is working to help us realize our goals, and we go along with that plan.
-Lissa Coffey

"How can you say luck and chance are the same thing? Chance is the first step you take, luck is what comes afterwards."
-Amy Tan, The Kitchen God's Wife, 1991

We need to be ready and willing to take that chance when it comes along - seize the day - take hold of the opportunity! And then, see what happens! Whether or not it turns out the way we had hoped, maybe that has something to do with luck. But we'll never know unless we try. And we'll learn and grow and stretch ourselves by taking those chances - and isn't that lucky anyway? *-Lissa Coffey*

Meaning

**"The world is not divine sport; it is divine destiny.
There is divine meaning in the life of the world; of
man, of human persons, of you and of me."**
-Martin Buber (1878-1965)

Sometimes we just have to pause and ask "why?" Think about it. There are no accidents, there is meaning everywhere. There is this organizing power at work in the world. We have our place in the world, and our tasks to complete. The people we meet, the people we love, are all a part of our lives for a reason. We can learn from all of our experiences, and become better people from living life consciously and meaningfully. *-Lissa Coffey*

**"There is no meaning in life except the meaning man
gives his life by the unfolding of his powers,
by living productively..."**
-Erich Fromm (1900-1980)

Each day we learn and grow, we are unfolding our powers! Doesn't that sound great? We're getting better and stronger and more powerful the more that we discover about ourselves. By living productively, by using our time on this planet well, we find meaning in our lives. We are not meant to be a mere observer – we are meant to participate. We are given powers to use, not to let stagnate. *-Lissa Coffey*

**"Life is not meaningful... unless it is serving an end be-
yond itself; unless if is of value to someone else."**
-Abraham Joshua Heschel (1907-1972)

How many times have we heard the phrase: "There's more to life than..."? We KNOW there is more to life, more than pettiness, or selfishness, or indulgence, or whatever! We find value in life when we reach out and go beyond our comfort zone – when we help others, when we see how our work resonates out into the world. Life is full of opportunities for us to find meaning, and to create meaning. *-Lissa Coffey*

**"The need to find meaning in the universe is as real as
the need for trust and for love, for relations with other
human beings."**
-Margaret Mead (1972)

It's the age-old question: What is the meaning of life? Living this quest is as natural as breathing. It's how we learn and grow, all a part of the process of life. We reach out to each other, for comfort, for love, for definition. And many times it is in our relationships that we find the meaning that we seek. *-Lissa Coffey*

"One needs something to believe in, something which one can have whole-hearted enthusiasm. One needs to feel that one's life has meaning, that one is needed in this world."
-Hannah Senesh (1938)

It's that passion, that purpose, that spurs us forward in life. We know that there is more to life than just paying the bills and hanging out. But that "more" is different for each one of us. Understanding that Life has meaning is one thing, but we must also understand that our own lives have meaning. We're here for a reason. And it's up to each one of us to discover just what that reason is and to embrace it whole-heartedly! *-Lissa Coffey*

Meditation

"When one devotes oneself to meditation, mental burdens, unnecessary worries, and wandering thoughts drop off one by one; life seems to run smoothly and pleasantly."
-Nyogen Senzaki

Through the process of meditation, of going into the silence, to that "higher place"- we get a different perspective of the world. We see the "big picture" and our place in it. We understand our connection to God, and to each other. Life runs more smoothly because we allow it to, that's the way it is meant to be! *-Lissa Coffey*

"You are used to listening to the buzz of the world, but now is the time to develop the inner ear that listens to the inner world. It is time to have a foot in each world, and it can be done."
-Saint Bartholomew

It's all about balance. Rather than getting inundated by the buzz of the world, we can tune in to the silence, turn on that higher frequency and experience what really matters. And then the beauty of meditation is that we bring that experience of stillness back into our activity, and find that life is just so much easier and more fulfilling. We are better able to feel the joy that is always there. *-Lissa Coffey*

"The very best and utmost attainment in this life is to remain still and let God act and speak in thee."
-Meister Eckhart

All the wisdom of the universe can be found in silence, can be experienced through meditation. When we are quiet, we allow spirit in, we are in-spired! This is how we get the answers we seek, this is how God communicates with us. -*Lissa Coffey*

"Meditation is the action of silence."
-Krishnamurti (1895-1986)

Meditation is, quite simply, one of the best things we can do for ourselves and our spiritual growth. Our souls need silence the way our bodies need the air we breathe. Because we are so bombarded with activity and "noise" in our busy lives, we much actively pursue this silence. We must seek it out, and take it in, and then we will understand the good that is does for us. -*Lissa Coffey*

"The gift of learning to meditate is the greatest gift you can give yourself in this life. For it is only through meditation that you can undertake the journey to discover your true nature, and so find the stability and confidence you will need to live, and die, well. Meditation is the road to enlightenment."
-Sogyal Rinpoche, The Tibetan Book of Living and Dying, 1992

There are so many different ways of meditating. The key is to find one that works for you and then practice it regularly. It is through the regular practice of meditation that we experience its benefits. We learn more about ourselves, and our world, and can see things so much more clearly and calmly. -*Lissa Coffey*

Memories

"The past with its pleasures, its rewards, its foolishness, its punishments, is there for each of us forever, and it should be."
-Lillian Hellman

During the holiday season it's easy to wax nostalgic. We tend to remember holidays because we take photos and keep them in albums. We get together with friends and family and create memories. We remember because during that time we are in the moment, and enjoying ourselves, so the feelings remain long after the time is past. -*Lissa Coffey*

"Fortunate are the people whose roots are deep."
-Agnes Meyer

When trees have deep roots they don't fall over as easily. It works the same with people. Our roots help to support us, and to keep us strong when the wind blows hard. Our roots can nourish us. It's up to us to grow these roots for ourselves – with our friends, our family, our community and our memories. -*Lissa Coffey*

"As the dew to the blossom, the bud to the bee,
As the scent to the rose, are those memories to me."
-Amelia C. Welby

Granted, not all memories are pleasant. But those that are sweet, are cherished. We keep those memories close to us, and they bring us comfort and joy. I think about when my kids were little and I smile. *-Lissa Coffey*

"How we remember, what we remember, and why we re-member form the most personal map of our individuality."
-Christina Baldwin, 1977

Memory is selective. Whether it's conscious or unconscious, there are things that just stick in our minds and then they pop up at various times, called upon or not. We carry memories around with us all the time, they are a part of our history, a part of us. *-Lissa Coffey*

"It is memory that provides the heart with impetus,
fuels the brain, and propels the corn plant from
seed to fruit."
-Joy Harjo, 1991

Memory is part of the karmic cycle. Memory creates a desire, which then causes us to take action. That action then creates another memory, and we go around again. In the movie "March of the Penguins" we could see how the penguins had some kind of genetic memory that took them on the same journey year after year. It's memory that makes birds fly south for the winter. In this way our memory can help us learn and grow. *-Lissa Coffey*

Moderation

"Moderation multiplies pleasures."
-Democritus (460-370 B.C.)

When we don't have to worry about the extremes, we can enjoy the ride so much more. We can have a clear view from both sides, we can breathe freely, we can coast every once in awhile on the smooth surface. We appreciate all the little things along the way that make the journey so pleasurable. *-Lissa Coffey*

"Enough is as good as a feast."
-John Heywood (1497-1580)

This is as true of food as it is of anything in our lives! It is important to learn how to simplify. How many pairs of shoes does one closet need, really? There is a difference between collecting and hoarding. There is freedom in learning to let go. Get rid of some shoes and gain space! Gain organization! Gain good karma by donating to charity. Learn to say "when" because enough is really enough. *-Lissa Coffey*

**"Moderation is the silken string running through the
pearl-chain of all virtues."**
-Joseph Hall (1574-1656)

Does moderation sound boring? Often we go for the extremes – the ultimate high, the melodrama, whatever is exciting and gets our juices pumping. But those extremes come with life anyway, we don't need to go looking for them. Moderation is looking for that balance, that middle-road that keeps us a little more sane, a little more grounded. *-Lissa Coffey*

**"The pursuit, even of the best things,
ought to be calm and tranquil."**
-Marcus Tullius Cicero (106-43 B.C.)

Moderation in our temperament is essential to our health and well-being. It is exhausting going from euphoria when something goes right to depression when something goes wrong. Our middle ground here comes from knowing that external forces do not influence our emotions. We decide how to react, we can choose to accept that we really are okay no matter how things go. *-Lissa Coffey*

"To climb steep hills requires a slow pace at first."
-William Shakespeare (1564-1616)

We all have goals in mind, something that we are working towards. Life is more a marathon than a sprint. We have to pace ourselves, and make sure we don't get worn out. Sure, we give it our all, but there are times when we put on the steam and other times when we ease off to organize. With this kind of moderation, we can make it as far as we want to go. *-Lissa Coffey*

Moments

**"Each moment we live is a new and unique moment
of the universe, a moment that never was before and
never will be again."**
-Pablo Casals

I was given this quote when I was sixteen, and I have it displayed in my office today. Being "in the moment" is one of those things that is so easy to say, yet sometimes so hard to do. The moments seem to pass by us so quickly. We find ourselves saying: "Where did the time go?" So it's important to stay present, and to recognize the value of those moments. In spirit, there is no time or place... but we're here, in this physical body, on this earth, for a reason. Here there is time, here there are moments – moments we can hold and treasure, moments where we can learn and grow. *-Lissa Coffey*

**"Let me tell thee, time is a very precious gift of God, so
precious that it's only given to us moment by moment."**
-Amelia Barr

Have you ever watched a television game show? In most of the games, there is an element of time involved. You're up against the clock. You have 2 minutes to race through a grocery story, or 30 seconds to come up with the right answer. If you happen to be the person playing that game, you realize just how precious each one of those moments are! You focus your attention, and use the time wisely to win the game. Well, we're lucky that life is not a game show! We have all the time we need to learn and grow and accomplish what we need to in this life. And we can start anytime, so why not start now? The prizes are all around us, just waiting to be won.
-Lissa Coffey

"I always say to myself, what is the most important thing we can think about at this extraordinary moment."
-Francois de La Rochefoucauld

There are no ordinary moments – each moment is new and unique, so each moment is extraordinary. We can fill that moment with extraordinary thoughts, extraordinary deeds, extraordinary attention. We can choose to think of peace, to recognize beauty, to experience joy. This moment is ours, and we can choose what to do with it.
-Lissa Coffey

"A player's effectiveness is directly related to his ability to be right there, doing that thing, in the moment... He can't be worrying about the past or the future or the crowd or some other extraneous event. He must be able to respond in the here and now."
-John Brodie

John Brodie is the famous former quarterback for the San Francisco 49ers. How do I know this? My brother and my father were BIG fans when we were living in the Bay Area. Athletes know how important it is to be fully present in the moment when competing. There are too many factors that have to fall into place to succeed – and the only way to get them to do that is to be there: mentally, physically and spiritually.
-Lissa Coffey

"Love the moment and the energy of the moment will spread beyond all boundaries."
-Corita Kent

Love the moment. Isn't that great? As you're reading this, take one moment right now and love it, just simply love it. That energy is just extending beyond your circle of influence out into the world – whether you realize it or not! 'Spontaneous moment-loving': now there's a concept! Imagine how the energy of the whole planet would shift if we all did that at the same time... *-Lissa Coffey*

Morning

"How beautiful, how buoyant, and glad is morning!"
-L.E. Landon, 1933

Good morning! Reading positive messages is a great way to start the day, getting centered, remembering what is important. The break of day represents a kind of optimism. There is a newness, a freshness, as if time starts all over again. No matter what has happened the day before, we know the sun will come up and shine its light on us today. *-Lissa Coffey*

"The moment when first you wake up in the morning is the most wonderful of the twenty-four hours. No matter how weary or dreary you may feel, you possess the certainty that absolutely anything may happen. And the fact that it practically always doesn't, matters not one jot. The possibility is always there."
-Monica Baldwin, 1950

There is always some uncertainty to the day. Will it rain? Will it be sunny? And we don't know what surprises may come our way, big or small! But how fun to be able to participate in the process, to watch things as they unfold and to make choices and contribute. *-Lissa Coffey*

"I like breakfast-time better than any other moment in the day. No dust has settled on one's mind then, and it presents a clear mirror to the rays of things."
-George Eliot, 1859

Somehow we see things differently in the light of a new day. When we have a big decision to make, we often say "let me sleep on it," knowing that after a rest we'll have a fresh perspective and be able to think more clearly. *-Lissa Coffey*

"Morning prospective: imagination. Evening retrospective: memory."
-Ralph Waldo Emerson (1803-1882)

This is an entry that Emerson put in his journal one day. I love the way that Emerson expressed himself – so simply, and so beautifully. I can see him in the morning looking ahead, planning, creating, and writing. And in the evening, looking back at what was accomplished, remembering the good things in his life, expressing gratitude. *-Lissa Coffey*

"It's completely usual for me to get up in the morning, take a look around, and laugh out loud."
-Barbara Kingsolver

Our attitude has everything to do with how the day goes for us. When we approach our activities with a sense of fun and light-heartedness, it affects our environment, and the people around us. Time passes by more quickly, and we enjoy ourselves so much more. *-Lissa Coffey*

Motherhood

"You might not have thought it possible to give birth to others before one has given birth to oneself, but I assure you it is quite possible, it has been done; I offer myself in evidence as Exhibit A."
-Shiela Ballantyne, Norma Jean the Termite Queen (1975)

Since this is Mother's Day week, I thought we'd look at motherhood, and quotes from women about the subject. The whole concept of "giving birth" is fascinating. And I'm not talking about the biology of it, but rather the process of renewal. We can give birth to an idea. And when raising children we are helping them to give birth to themselves. As mothers, we help these young people to discover who they are. And if they could only see themselves through our eyes, they'd know. If we could see ourselves through our mother's eyes, we'd know. *-Lissa Coffey*

"The most important thing she's learned over the years was that there was no way to be a perfect mother and a million ways to be a good one."
-Jill Churchill, Grime and Punishment (1989)

There's always been this sort of pressure on mothers, from society and from ourselves. No matter what we do, how "good" we are, it never seems to measure up to how good we think we "should" be. Mothers take the heat, and are the subject of many sessions at the therapist's office! But we've got to remember that we're all just doing the best that we can. We are each on our own path, mother, son, daughter – and where our lives come together we live and grow and help each other the best that we can. *-Lissa Coffey*

"Nothing else ever will make you as happy or as sad, as proud or as tired, for nothing is quite as hard as helping a person develop his own individuality – especially while you struggle to keep your own."
-Marguerite Kelly and Elia Parsons, The Mother's Almanac (1975)

I can honestly say that I have learned more from the experience of parenthood than I have from any other experience in my life. There is nothing as challenging, or as rewarding, as raising a child – living with this growing and expanding young soul as it finds its place and recognizes its divinity. All of the trials and episodes and celebrations that we have been through have strengthened my spirit and given me daily evidence of God's presence. *-Lissa Coffey*

"Most of all the other beautiful things in life come by twos and threes, by dozens and hundreds. Plenty of roses, stars, sunsets, rainbows, brothers and sisters, aunts and cousins, comrades and friends – but only one mother in the whole world."

-Kate Douglas Wiggen, in Charles L. Wallis, ed., The Treasure Chest (1965)

We have the mother that we have for a reason. We have the children that we have for a reason. There are no accidents and no coincidences. Cherish your mother. Cherish her presence in your life for reasons known and unknown and beyond understanding. *-Lissa Coffey*

"No matter how old a mother is she watches her middle-aged children for signs of improvement."

-Florida Scott-Maxwell, The Measure of My Days (1968)

Does a mother ever stop being a mother? No. It's as simple as that. There is always a connection between us, there is always a feeling of "unfinished business" because a mother considers her child a "work in progress!" And with the most loving intention, she wants what is best for us. To all moms out there: "Mom, I have what is best for me, I have you for a mother. You taught me to make good decisions, and I want you to know that you can trust me to make the best decisions for myself. I love you. Happy Mother's Day! And yes, I will clean my room!" *-Lissa Coffey*

Motivation

"Where the willingness is great, the difficulties cannot be great."

-Niccolo Machiavelli

What compels us to do something? When our motivation comes from external factors, it can wax and wane depending upon the influence of those factors. But when our motivation is intrinsic, when it comes from within ourselves, it is strong, and we can use it to accomplish anything, to overcome any difficulties. *-Lissa Coffey*

"It seems to me we can never give up longing and wishing while we are alive. There are certain things we feel to be beautiful and good, and we must hunger for them."

-George Eliot

A longing and wishing keeps us motivated to move forward. We can use this motivation to achieve great things, whether they are personal or global goals. We can use this motivation to learn and to grow and to become a more peaceful planet. *-Lissa Coffey*

> **"We must each find our separate meaning in the
> persuasion of our days until we meet in the
> meaning of the world."**
> -Christopher Fry

On the surface, it looks like we are so very different. Men and women, different ages, races, cultures, backgrounds. Yet inside, we are so very much the same. We all search for meaning, we all long for peace, we all seek happiness. Our motivations are very similar. *-Lissa Coffey*

> **"I want to do it because I want to do it."**
> -Amelia Earhart

Sometimes motivation cannot be explained. It simply is. Maybe it's how we are guided in our spiritual growth. We each have our own road to travel, and we're making decisions which way to turn all the time. We're motivated to keep going, to see what is around that next corner. *-Lissa Coffey*

> **"There are only two stimulants to one's best efforts:
> the fear of punishment, and the hope of reward."**
> -John M. Wilson

Which is the greater motivator? Fear can't be all bad, everything has some purpose. Sometimes it can spur us into action. We can be motivated to overcome fear. And that, in itself, is a reward. A Course in Miracles says that fear is simply a lack of love. It is a void that can be filled. *-Lissa Coffey*

Music

> **"Music has charms to soothe a savage breast,
> To soften rocks, or bend a knotted oak."**
> -William Congreve (1670-1729)

No, that's not a typo. We've all heard it as "savage beast" but it really was said "savage breast." And I think it is more effective that way. A savage breast says to me, "an angry heart," and I can see that as being hard and cold. There is a lot of power there, but Congreve uses the word "charms" instead. Interesting... the power of music comes not from sheer strength but from its charms, from its subtle, gentle effect on our soul." *-Lissa Coffey*

> **"Heard melodies are sweet, but those unheard
> Are sweeter."**
> -John Keats (1795-1821)

When we listen very carefully to the silence we can hear the songs of the universe. These songs are playing all the time, yet we are unaware of them because so many other things are going on at the same time. When we take the time to slow down, and "tune in" to these beautiful sounds, we are enraptured. God is a musician." *-Lissa Coffey*

"Music is your own experience, your own thoughts, your wisdom. If you don't live it, it won't come out of your horn. They teach you there's a boundary line to music. But, man, there's no boundary line to art."
-Charlie Parker (1920-1955)

Whatever we create comes through us. It is our own expression of music, or any kind of art, that makes it unique and original. Music is a part of the universe, and when we take the time to listen, we can channel it through to our everyday lives. There are infinite possibilities before us, and music is one way that we can experience that. *-Lissa Coffey*

"Nothing recalls the past like music."
-Madame de Stael, Corinne (1807)

We've all had that experience of driving around in the car, flipping around the radio stations, when a certain song comes on that takes us back to our junior year in high school, the dance, the gym, our "crush" at the time. Music has a way of doing that. It creeps into our memory and imprints itself onto our psyche. When we hear a familiar song again, we can repeat the lyrics, even if has been years since we last heard it play. That's one reason why couples have "their song" – to remember the romance and take themselves back to the time when they were falling in love. *-Lissa Coffey*

"Music comes first from my heart, and then goes upstairs to my head where I check it out."
-Roberta Flack (1993)

Writing music is a spiritual experience. It comes from within and bubbles forth. I know people who are musical geniuses, expressing music is their dharma. It's an amazing experience when you're in your dharma, and doing what you're really supposed to be doing. It comes easily, effortlessly, with timeless awareness. And when you're done you look at what you've produced with amazement, like someone else must have done it. Where did this come from? The same place everything else comes from – God. *-Lissa Coffey*

Mystery

"If death is one mystery, life is another, greater one... We can only feel awe before a mystery that both is what we are and surpasses our understanding."
-Jonathan Schell

We're living this mystery every day! It can be fun, and exciting. Some of the best-selling books of all time are mysteries. We just love to figure things out, to use our minds, to put the pieces together so that they make sense. We're wired this way. So if we approach our lives with the same zest and fortitude, imagine the fun we could have! *-Lissa Coffey*

"The more unintelligent a man is, the less mysterious existence seems to him."
-Arthur Schopenhauer (1788-1860)

For concrete evidence of mystery, we could go to a library and count up how many topics we know nothing about. Even the most scholarly people, experts in their fields, understand that there is more for them to learn. The world just operates that way. It is changing and growing and evolving just as we are – so there will always be some mystery for us to happen upon. Existence is big, and it is ours to discover. *-Lissa Coffey*

"Mystery is not the denial of reason but its honest confirmation: reason, indeed, leads inevitably to mystery…: mystery and reality are the two halves of the same sphere."
-Walt Whitman (1819-1892)

It seems like we don't even know what we don't know! There is just so much to learn, so much to comprehend – so much that we don't understand. And when we find a new topic of study, we learn a little bit and it opens up a whole bunch of questions! In that way mystery is beautiful. It lets us know that there is always more to be revealed. *-Lissa Coffey*

"The true mystery of the world is the visible, not the invisible."
-Oscar Wilde (1854-1900)

This is a big concept. The invisible could be love, for example. Is that so mysterious? Love just "is." We know it, we feel it, we treasure it. We can count on it; it doesn't go away. But the visible, that can be transitory. We can ask, what is its purpose? What is our relationship to it? If we can accept the invisible as reality, we can look at the visible in another light. So, what is real? That is the mystery! *-Lissa Coffey*

"No object is mysterious. The mystery is your eye."
-Elizabeth Bowen, 1936

Like beauty is in the eye of the beholder, so is mystery. The questions we ask when we observe something are all our own. What is going on in our mind's eye? What definition are we giving to an object? What emotion are we attaching to it? And the miracle is that we can see and perceive an object! It's this whole process that is mysterious, and beautiful. *-Lissa Coffey*

Myth

"Mythology is much better stuff than history. It has form; logic; a message."
-Penelope Lively, 1987

I think there is some kind of an innate fascination with myth, and that's why it has been so prevalent throughout time. The best myths are well-crafted stores that we can relate to, and learn from. We remember these stories, repeat them, and pass them down through the generations. They have become an important part of our spiritual education. *-Lissa Coffey*

"The patterns and logic of fairy tale and myth correspond to those of dream."
-Joseph Campbell (1904-1987)

We couldn't have a week on myth without a quote from Joseph Campbell, a man who has studied and written about myth probably more than anyone else. We can see ourselves reflected in the myths that we create. And we create our lives following the recurring themes found in myth. It's art imitating life imitating art. The same stories are played out over and over again, whether it's Aesop, or Shakespeare, or Mark Twain or each of us individually doing the "writing." *-Lissa Coffey*

"I can find my biography in ever fable that I read."
-Ralph Waldo Emerson (1803-1882)

Some myths may be larger than life, but at their core they illustrate basic human needs and ambitions. We can see ourselves in the characters, and try out our options as they do. The archetypes of myth are our examples, our heroes, our role models, our teachers. We learn from their triumphs and tragedies, from their wisdom and from their mistakes. *-Lissa Coffey*

"I find nothing in fables more astonishing than my experience in every hour. One moment of a man's life is a fact so stupendous as to take the luster out of all fiction."
-Ralph Waldo Emerson (1803-1882)

I don't know who said "truth is stranger than fiction" but I have seen so many examples of things that have happened where I just shake my head and say: "You couldn't make this stuff up!" I have always been attracted to biographies and true stories for that very reason. Here we are, actually living some of the great myths of our time! Our history books are filled with them. Sometimes the lines are blurred, and we can't remember what is real and what is not. We take liberty with history to have it "make sense" to us. Can we believe what is reported to us in the news? Or is it just another story? It's up to each one of us to be informed, and make good decisions. *-Lissa Coffey*

"Myths have their magic power because they cast on
the screen of our imaginations the figures of the
heavenly constellations, immense projections of
our hope and capabilities."
-Robert Heilbroner

Myths make us question: "What are the possibilities?" Instead of thinking of the practical and mundane, they open up to us areas of grandeur and limitlessness! Our imaginations are there to help us create, and we are capable of creating our own reality. So, why not dream big? *-Lissa Coffey*

Names

Juliet: "What's in a name? That which we call a rose
By any other name would smell as sweet."
-Shakespeare (1564-1616)

Shakespeare has a point here in that a name is a label, and in many cases, merely an identifier. But at the same time, those letters, and syllables, come to signify something to us that is meaningful. The word alone conveys the meaning that we have attached to it. *-Lissa Coffey*

"Let us make distinctions,
call things by the right names."
-Henry David Thoreau (1817-1862)

Language is an art and a science. We have so many words for things, each of which distinguishes itself in some particular way. As we learn and grow, we become more discerning. We understand the differences between the details, and why they are valuable. *-Lissa Coffey*

"We do what we must,
and call it by the best names we can."
-Ralph Waldo Emerson (1803-1882)

Do you ever find yourself at a loss for words? Sometimes things can be beyond description. We can feel them, but it is difficult to express the significance or the impact they have on us. Sometimes we can communicate best in the silence, without letting words get in the way. *-Lissa Coffey*

"What signifies knowing the Names,
if you know not the Natures of things."
-Benjamin Franklin (1706-1790)

It's fascinating when we look at the etymology behind words. So many words really match the object they represent. When we look at the botanical names of plants, we find that the Latin root refers to the nature of the particular flower. I love reading baby name books because they lend insight into the origin of a person's name. As we grow, our name changes and evolves with us. We may have a nick-name when we're little, and choose something more formal when we get older. We may pick up names given to us by our friends and loved-ones. Many of us change our names when we marry. And when we have children, we take on the name "Mom" or "Dad." I know several people who have chosen a new name for themselves to reflect who they are today. It's our prerogative, since we know ourselves best. *-Lissa Coffey*

"The boy who, when asked how many legs his calf would have if he called its tail a leg, replied, "Five," to which the prompt response was made that calling the tail a leg would not make it one."
-Abraham Lincoln (1809-1865)

Slapping a label on something does not change its nature. Just because someone is called a fool does not make him one. Neither does calling someone a genius give him a high IQ. Although we may have many different labels hoisted upon us at different times in our lives, we are not limited by any one of them. It's our choice how we want to identify ourselves. *-Lissa Coffey*

Nature

"Nature is an endless combination and repetition of a very few laws. She hums the old well-known air through innumerable variations."
-Ralph Waldo Emerson (1803-1882)

Interesting that Emerson calls Nature "she." Maybe because we think of Mother Nature. The idea, though, is that nature is something we can count on. As unpredictable as nature can be, we do know that the sun will rise, the seasons will change, that rivers will flow to the sea. There are these laws in effect that go beyond our powers of human manipulation. Nature is much bigger than we are, and yet, at the same time, it is an essential part of who we are. The same laws that govern nature affect us as well. *-Lissa Coffey*

"Nature is ever at work building and pulling down, creating and destroying, keeping everything whirling and flowing, allowing no rest but in rhythmical motion, chasing everything in endless song out of one beautiful form into another."
-John Muir (1838-1914)

Who taught the grass to grow, or the bird to sing? Who makes the wind blow, or told the lion roar? It is nature. It is nature being true to Itself. Does the bird aspire to roar? Or the lion "really want to direct?" We can learn from nature, to be true to ourselves, to let our natural talents and instincts shine in endless song. And then, to grow and change and go with the flow, knowing that all of our roles in this life eventually turn from one beautiful form into another. *-Lissa Coffey*

> **"Nothing in nature is isolated. Nothing is without
> reference to something else. Nothing achieves meaning
> apart from that which neighbors it."**
> -Goethe (1749-1832)

Everything we have, everything we see, everything we are, has its roots in nature. We are all made up of the same basic materials! Look at your desk, the paper, wood and wicker that come from the trees, which grow from the earth. We feel disassociated from nature when we work in an office, and yet we can never get away from it. The water that runs through the rivers, and through our taps, and through our bodies, is all a part of nature. We are connected to the planet, and to each other, in ways seen and unseen. *-Lissa Coffey*

> **"Ah, dear nature, the mere remembrance, after a short
> forgetfulness, of the pine woods! I come to it as a
> hungry man to a crust of bread."**
> -Henry David Thoreau (1817-1862)

Nature can nourish us, refresh us, and replenish us. Time spent with nature helps to still the mind, to quiet the activity of our thoughts. Nature provides us with everything we need for our bodies with its bounty of fruits, grains and vegetables. Yet nature's "food for thought" – its pure silence, is just as necessary for our health, mentally, physically and spiritually. *-Lissa Coffey*

> **"The natural world is dynamic. From the expanding
> universe to the hair on a baby's head, nothing is the
> same from now to the next moment."**
> -Helen Hoover, The Waiting Hills, 1963

It is true that we are constantly changing. We understand and even welcome change when it comes to nature. We look forward to the warmth of Summer after a rainy spring. We do not mourn when Autumn turns to Winter – because we realize that it is time moving forward, that it is all a part of the cycle necessary for growth and evolution. And still, as humans, we tend to resist change, to deny it, or fight it. But Nature and its laws understand that we all fit into the big picture, and so we are along for the ride, like it or not! We might as well enjoy it, appreciate it, and learn and grow from the experience. *-Lissa Coffey*

Openness

"Happiness is something that comes into our lives through doors we don't even remember leaving open."
-Rose Wilder Lane

Open doors let in light, and fresh air, and opportunity. An open mind allows in new ideas and fresh outlooks. And an open heart invites friendship and acceptance and love. *-Lissa Coffey*

"Change is the watchword of progression. When we rite of well-worn ways, we seek for new. This restless craving in the souls of men spurs them to climb, and to seek the mountain view."
-Ella Wheeler Wilcox

Being open means being open to change. Change shakes up the old and moves life forward. Change helps to broaden our horizons and gives us a chance to experience new things. *-Lissa Coffey*

"When we are listened to, it creates us, makes us unfold and expand. Ideas actually begin to grow within us and come to life."
-Brenda Ueland

When we feel really listened to, we're more likely to open up and be honest with another person. And when we listen, people are more likely to open up to us, too. Communication is active, and reciprocal. *-Lissa Coffey*

"I always keep myself in a position of being a student."
-Jackie Joyner-Kersee

There is always more to learn, and if we're open to learning we'll find we learn something every day. We're all students of life, and this earth is one big open class-room. There's no monitor to take role, but we do learn more when we show up fully. *-Lissa Coffey*

"Giving opens the way for receiving."
-Florence Scovel Shinn

We open up space in our lives when we give. And that space is filled with exactly what we need at the time. Giving without expectation creates a positive energy, it opens up a flow that allows us to accept what comes to us. *-Lissa Coffey*

Opportunity

"A wise man will make more opportunities than he finds."
-Francis Bacon (1561-1626)

Opportunity. We often hear the phrase "opportunity knocks." How convenient it would be if that were the way it happened all the time! More often than not, our opportunities have been cultivated. We seek them out, rather than waiting for them to come calling on us. We prepare ourselves so that we can both create, and recognize, opportunities. *-Lissa Coffey*

"While we stop to think, we often miss our opportunity."
-Publius Syrus (85-43 B.C.)

Is this impulsive? Maybe. But it is also intuitive. Life tends to move really quickly - so when we recognize an opportunity that we've been waiting for, why overthink it? At a certain point, we've just got to say "I'm ready" and go for it! *-Lissa Coffey*

"You got to get it while you can."
-Janis Joplin (1943-1970)

Go for it. Just do it. May hay while the sun shines. Never put off until tomorrow what you can do today. Carpe Diem. Our opportunities are out there and the universe is urging us to scoop them up enthusiastically - we hear it time and time again!
-Lissa Coffey

"If you have many Irons in the Fire, some will burn."
-Thomas Fuller (1654-1734)

"Many Irons in the Fire, some must cool."
-James Kelly (18th cent.)

While we're out there creating opportunities for ourselves, we may find that we're juggling multiple projects, hoping that some will catch on and make it big. Take a look at the two quotes above - all these Irons in the Fire - some will burn, and yet some must cool. Why? Because we can't possibly pay attention to all of them. More "Irons" does not necessarily give us a better chance of success. We have a limited quantity of time - so when we have to spread it among several Irons, then the quality of time is reduced. It only makes sense that the Irons that are given both quantity and quality of Fire will burn the brightest. *-Lissa Coffey*

"The doors of Opportunity are marked 'Push' and 'Pull'."
-Ethel Watts Mumford, 1902

It is interesting that opportunity is often associated with a door - but a closed door doesn't get us anywhere. It is through an open door that we must walk to get somewhere. What is on the other side of the door? Unlimited possibilities! But we'll never know what they are until we get up and open that door to see for ourselves! -*Lissa Coffey*

Optimism

"Thou hast seen nothing yet."
-Cervantes (1547-1616) Don Quixote

"You ain't seen nothin' yet."
-Jimmy Durante (1893-1980) Entertainer. His signature line.

"You ain't heard nothin' yet."
-Al Jolson (1886-1950) His signature line.

What is ahead for us? We don't know for sure, but we do know there is still a lot to be experienced. We can look forward with optimism. Studies have shown that optimists live longer, healthier, happier lives. We can choose to see the glass as half-full, and as wholly satisfying. Think today's going to be a good day? You ain't seen nothin' yet! -*Lissa Coffey*

"I've got to admit it's getting better It's a little better all the time."
-John Lennon (1940-1980) and Paul McCartney (1942-) "Getting Better" 1967

When we learn to look at the world optimistically, we see that there is some evolution going on, some growth spiritually that just naturally takes place. We might lose sight of it at times, but because we are growing spiritually, things ARE getting better! And they're getting better all the time. -*Lissa Coffey*

"From every scrap you make a blanket."
-Rose Chernin, in Kim Chernin, "In My Mother's House" (1983)

When life gives you lemons... you know the rest. The sweet lemonade quenches our thirst. We can turn around a situation to benefit us. When life gives us scraps, we can make a blanket! That is so beautiful... a blanket represents warmth, security, comfort. We can literally make something real, something substantial and useful from what might be perceived as "nothing." Look around, what scraps can we turn into blankets today? -*Lissa Coffey*

"An optimist is the human personification of spring."
-Susan J. Bissonette, in Reader's Digest (1979)

A person with a good attitude is the kind of person we all want to be around. He or she knows how to bring warmth and light to any situation. We can be that kind of a person, too. It's just a matter of looking at things positively, of finding the good that others might not see. Good is always there, and it grows when we put our attention on it. *-Lissa Coffey*

"I don't believe in pessimism. If something doesn't come up the way you want, forge ahead. If you think it's going to rain, it will."
-Clint Eastwood

Our thoughts have so much power - we can color our day, and our world, with the thoughts that we think. So why not think optimistically? Why not think only of the best, the brightest, the most beautiful outcome in any given situation? We can make it happen. Anything is possible, ANYTHING... so let's not defeat ourselves before we've even started by thinking negatively. Be an optimist, and let those optimistic vibes out into the world today! *-Lissa Coffey*

Originality

"The will to originality is not the will to be peculiar and unlike anybody else; it means the desire to derive one's consciousness from its primary source."
-Nicolas Berdyaev (1874-1948)

Originality is not being unlike anything or anyone else, it is being totally true to who we are. And who we are is a unique, original, expression of God. We've got this whole "one-of-a-kind" thing going on without even trying! All we have to do is to be ourselves. *-Lissa Coffey*

"People are always talking about originality; but what do they mean? As soon as we are born, the world begins to work upon us, and this goes on to the end. What can we call our own except energy, strength, and will? If I could give an account of all that I owe to great predecessors and contemporaries, there would be but a small balance in my favor."
-Goethe (1749-1832)

Some people say that there is nothing original anymore, that it's all "been done." But how can that be? There are infinite possibilities out there, even the "same thing" can be done in infinitely different ways. The originality comes from ourselves, and what we bring to the task at hand. We can be inspired from those whose work has come before, but we can never re-create it in exactly the same way. *-Lissa Coffey*

**"Originality consists not only in doing things differently,
but also in 'doing things better.'"**
-Edward C. Stedman (1833-1908)

I think that this is what inventors have in mind when they come up with all these original concepts. It's all about progress, growth, building on what has been done before and expanding on what we have learned. And isn't life like that, too? With human relationships, and our own spiritual growth, we want to "do things better" and improve ourselves and our circumstances. We read books, and take advice, but how we apply it is individual and original to ourselves. *-Lissa Coffey*

**"True originality consists not in a new manner
but in a new vision."**
-Edith Wharton, The Writing of Fiction, 1925

Each of us has eyes through which we see the world, and no two visions are exactly alike. But because we are conditioned to go along with the crowd, our vision gets blurred, and starts to look like everyone else's. When we close our eyes, tap into our Source, and let Nature's creativity and intelligence flow through us, we can restore our vision and our originality. We allow our inner artist to shine through! *-Lissa Coffey*

"Originality is... a by-product of sincerity."
-Marianne Moore, in Vogue, 1963

Sincerity is honesty, truth, meaningfulness. And when we share who we really are, we are absolutely original and true to ourselves. What a wonderful thing it is to be an original! *-Lissa Coffey*

Paradoxes

**"Heaven and earth do nothing
Yet there is nothing they do not do."**
-Chuang-Tzu (369-286 B.C.)

There is a spiritual principle that opposites are found together - and this can be so profound! These paradoxes make us take pause, and think. Isn't life interesting?
-Lissa Coffey

"All cases are unique, and very similar to others."
-T.S. Eliot (1888-1965)

I find this to be true every day of my life. We're each living our individual lives, going about our business, and our families- and when we take time to connect with each other, we find out that so often we're going through the same things! We can relate to each other, because in a way we're living out the same scenarios. It helps to share our experiences, rather than to feel that we're in it alone. *-Lissa Coffey*

"God hides things by putting them near us."
-Ralph Waldo Emerson (1803-1882)

Isn't this so true? It's one of those "forest for the trees" examples. There is joy and love and beauty all around us, and right inside of us... and yet where do we look? Many of the great spiritual teachers answer every question they are asked with the same statement: "Look within." They might say it in hundreds of different ways, but the meaning is the same. It's so simple, and yet so complex- what a paradox! *-Lissa Coffey*

**"Almost anything you do will be insignificant, but it is
very important that you do it."**
-Mohandas K. Gandhi (1869-1948)

If you look at the universe from the beginning of time - (and yet was there a beginning?) until as far as we can imagine into the future - each little action we take may be considered insignificant. And yet, it's not. Every action we take has some impact on our spiritual growth. It might seem like little tiny baby steps when we're wanting to take great leaps and bounds- but each step, large or small, is significant nonetheless. We've got to keep going. *-Lissa Coffey*

> "There is a Law of Reversed Effort. The harder we try
> with the conscious will to do something, the less we
> shall succeed. Proficiency and the results of proficiency
> come only to those who have learned the paradoxical
> art of doing and not doing, or combining relaxation
> with activity, of letting go as a person in order that
> the immanent and transcendent Unknown Quantity
> may take hold. We cannot make ourselves understand;
> the most we can do is to foster a state of mind, in
> which understanding may come to us."
> -Aldous Huxley (1894-1963)

In "The Seven Spiritual Laws of Success" Deepak Chopra writes about "The Law of Least Effort" and tells us that we can actually do less, and accomplish more. He talks about working with the natural intelligence of nature, going with the flow. If you haven't read the book before, I recommend it- it's one of those books you can read over and over again and get something different out of it each time. Nature is a great example for us - it doesn't struggle, it just is. Eagles don't wish to be tigers, tigers don't try to fly. *-Lissa Coffey*

Parents

> "How true Daddy's words were when he said: 'All children
> must look after their own upbringing.' Parents can
> only give good advice or put them on the right paths,
> but the final forming of a person's character lies in
> their own hands."
> -Anne Frank (1929-1945)

We could place blame, point fingers, wallow in pain from all the things that "should" have been "if only" blah blah blah... But there comes a time when we must stand on our own two feet and recognize that we create our own future. We create our own present. We have choices to make every day. Look within. Find that strength and move on. *-Lissa Coffey*

> "If there is something that we wish to change in our chil-
> dren, we should first examine it and see whether it is not
> something that could better be changed in ourselves."
> -Carl Jung (1875-1961)

All relationships are a mirror for us. Is there something we want to change about our parents? Our friends? Our spouses, or ex-spouses? Maybe we need to see if that is something we can change in ourselves. We have the relationships that we have so that we can learn more about ourselves. We don't always want to admit it, but we learn something even from the people who we see as a negative influence in our lives. And when we learn the lesson that negative turns into a big positive! *-Lissa Coffey*

> "Trust yourself. You know more than you think you do."
> -Benjamin Spock (1903-1998)

Dr. Spock was speaking here about parenting – but doesn't this apply to just about anything in life? We know stuff! Instinctually, intuitively, and intellectually – we have the tools to figure it out if it's not immediately obvious to us. *-Lissa Coffey*

> **"My parents were both, in their way, very loving and indulgent. Just the fact that I had the presumption to become an artist is rather ridiculous, isn't it, with no qualifications except that I felt treasured as a child."**
> -John Updike

The power and influence that adults can have on children is simply amazing. We can look back on our lives and see which adults have helped us, through their love and support and encouragement, to grow in our chosen careers. And it's not so much the career that is supported and encouraged, but the person. It's the Wholeness – seeing and knowing that this person is treasured for who they are, without imposing any qualifications on what this person wants to do. *-Lissa Coffey*

> **"Children begin by loving their parents; as they grow older they judge them; sometimes they forgive them."**
> -Oscar Wilde (1854-1900)

Whether or not we have children ourselves, we have parents. And, like it or not, our parents have had a huge influence in how we define ourselves. The relationship is a complex one, but it is essential to our growth. It is a part of God's design. We have the parents we have for a reason. As we learn and grow we view these people in our lives, and our relationship with them, in different, more expanded, ways. *-Lissa Coffey*

> **"Are anybody's parents typical?"**
> Madeleine L'Engle, 1988

I think a lot of us have this "idea" of parents in our heads – what parents "should" be. Maybe we got it from watching television sitcoms, or from seeing our friends' idealized families. But as adults we know that reality is all perception. What is "typical" after all? And is that what would propel us to learn and grow optimally? It's time to throw out the "should"s in our lives and start and accepting what is – "warts and all" as the saying goes! *-Lissa Coffey*

Passion

> **"Without passion man is a mere latent force and possibility, like the flint which awaits the shock of the iron before it can give forth its spark."**
> -Henri Amiel (1821-1881)

Passion is such a primal human trait. We all know what it is, what it feels like. Whether it is passion for a person, place, or activity, passion is what carries us forward to new and greater heights of life experiences. And it is through these experiences that we learn more about ourselves, and are able to express ourselves. Our passions show us who we are, and what we can do. -*Lissa Coffey*

"It is the soul's duty to be loyal to its own desires.
It must abandon itself to its master passion."
-Rebecca West (1985)

Something within us helps us to find our passions. It's not like a conscious choice, like looking through a catalog and picking a hobby or something. We are drawn to things that we feel passionate about. We can't help but move towards things that give us that drive, that energy, that life force that is so all-encompassing. We have the desires, and the passions that we have for a reason. And pursuing our passions is one of the most important things we can do while we're living our lives. -*Lissa Coffey*

"The fiery moments of passionate experience are the
moments of wholeness and totality of the personality."
-Anais Nin (1968)

Passion is often associated with fire. It feels "hot." It feels like it could consume us. We need to pay attention to the things that we feel passionate about. Our passions are tools which help us to learn and grow. When we are pursuing our passions we feel alive, we are living in the moment, taking it all in and savoring each experience. The are the times when we are more of who we really are, and we know it. -*Lissa Coffey*

"How little do they know human nature, who think they
can say to passion, so far shalt thou go, and no farther!"
-Sarah Scott (1750)

It's probably a very good thing that we can't stop our true passions! Passion is exactly what drove Einstein, Madame Curie, Mother Teresa, and many more people who have had a positive impact on our world! Passion helps us to progress; it keeps us going despite the invariable obstacles. Every great achievement began with someone's passion, and was carried forward by that momentum. -*Lissa Coffey*

"Passion is what the sun feels for the earth
When harvests ripen into golden birth."
-Ella Wheeler Wilcox (1888)

This is so beautifully said. That's one of the things that makes poetry so amazing – that with just a few words you can get an image, or a feeling across. We can imagine the sun's feelings, and recognize them as our own. This passion is fiery like the sun, but also strong and proud and everlasting. -*Lissa Coffey*

Past

"Let the past as nothing be."
-Abraham Lincoln (1809 - 1865)

There is a wonderful saying that "The past is history, the future is a mystery, but this moment is a gift, and that is why it is called the present." I don't know who said that, but I smile every time I hear it. We can't change the past - it's water under the bridge, water over the dam, and whatever other old saying you want to apply to it! It doesn't do us any good to dwell on our past misfortunes or mistakes, or beat ourselves up for our shortcomings. And it doesn't serve us to live in an idyllic past, wishing for days gone by. We can't go back. But we can go forward. We can learn from the past and make better choices for ourselves in the present, which will create a more promising future. *-Lissa Coffey*

"Your whole past was but a birth and a becoming."
-Antoine de Saint-Exupery (1900-1944)

We know that the nature of life is to grow. And so here we are. And we couldn't have gotten here without everything that has happened in the past. It is the same way for society as it is for individuals. Whatever has happened throughout history has had an impact on how we have grown and changed as a nation, and as a planet. We're all connected. And the more that we grow as individuals, the greater the impact will be on our communities and our countries. *-Lissa Coffey*

"What's past is prologue."
-Shakespeare (1574 - 1616) Antonio in The Tempest

I always love to find quotes by Shakespeare, because he says things so poetically. Here are four simple words, which strung together say so much! Prologue is background, it's the leading-up to what is happening NOW. While it is important to have that background, we need to understand that each act, each new scene of our lives, begins in this moment. The show goes on! *-Lissa Coffey*

"It is not that I belong to the past, but that the past belongs to me."
-Mary Antin, 1912

This is such a beautiful way to put it. We don't want to live in the past, but we are aware that the past has helped to create the life that we live today. I think most people, given the opportunity, would not change their pasts, even if it was a horrible time to live through. Because people who have had such experiences understand that their strength and resolve, and maybe even their optimism and appreciation of life, came from getting through those challenges. Everything that we have done, all the life that we have lived up to this point, has made us the people that we are today. *-Lissa Coffey*

"Each had his past shut in him like the leaves of a book known to him by heart; and his friends could only read the title."
-Virginia Woolf, 1922

It is interesting to think that we each have a past that we carry with us. No one else can see it, but it has shaped who we are. What the past has taught us shapes our character and influences our behavior, and in that way lends itself to the "title" of the book that people see when they look at us. And yet we know that "you can't judge a book by its cover." And more importantly, we know that each of us is still busy writing our books every day, adding pages every moment! -*Lissa Coffey*

Patience

"Patience is necessary, and one cannot reap immediately where one has sown."
-Soren Kierkegaard (1813-1855)

It is easy to understand that patience is important, and even necessary – but why is being patient such a hard thing to do?! It seems so contradictory to what we have learned about taking action... and yet, it is equally as essential. There is a time when we must sit back and do nothing, when we must allow nature to take its course and not impose our human conditions and expectations upon it. Being patient involves having faith, that inner knowingness that all is as it is because it is. -*Lissa Coffey*

"What is your need to eat the seed, When growth might be so sweet?"
-Ann Wickham, 1915

Ah, this sounds almost like an offer, doesn't it? Maybe we have a choice – instant, yet temporary satisfaction now – or a more long-lasting and genuine appreciation if we but wait a little bit. Patience brings its own rewards. When we are children, we want everything NOW! It is difficult for us to sit still and wait for anything. But as the years go by, we understand that some things are worth the wait. We begin to put great value on patience. -*Lissa Coffey*

"How poor are they that have not patience! What wound did ever heal but by degrees?"
-Shakespeare, Othello

Sometimes we need to just get out of our own way and let nature do its thing. The seasons know how to change. It does no good to try to "hurry things up" so we can fit in one more vacation or whatever! So many things in this world just take care of themselves. There is an organizing power to the universe. Shouldn't we allow this power to work for us? All we have to do is be patient. Everything will work out the way that it is supposed to. -*Lissa Coffey*

**"Patience is not passive: on the contrary it is active;
it is concentrated strength."**
-Edward George Bulwer-Lytton (1803-1873) English novelist

Look at people who are patient. Along with patience comes a kind of calm, a deep faith, a beautiful presence. Compared with people who are impatient – who seem stressed out, angry, and hurried. Who has more strength? The patient person can do anything because that person recognizes his or her connection with the Universe. Patience can move mountains! -*Lissa Coffey*

**"Steady, patient, persevering thinking, will generally
surmount every obstacle in the search after truth."**
-Nathaniel Emmons (1745-1840)

Aren't we all together in this search for Truth? Our quest for spiritual growth is impressive! And that's what will get us there – the way that we surmount those obstacles and continue on. We know that we must be patient with our journey, and patient with ourselves. We know that there is no "instant" answer, but that answers unfold before us with wisdom and grace. We know that our patience is rewarded continually as we grow and experience more of who we really are. -*Lissa Coffey*

Peace

**"Love is not a doctrine. Peace is not an international
agreement. Love and Peace are beings who live as
possibilities in us."**
-Mary Caroline Richards, (Centering, 1964)

This time of year, and particularly this year, I find myself thinking more about peace, and about peace on earth. If we are correct, and it all begins with each of us, then it is more important than ever to find peace within ourselves. We all know how to find that peace through our spiritual practices. So, practice, practice, practice! And then bring that beautiful peace out into the world where it is so needed. -*Lissa Coffey*

**"Our goal must be not peace in our time
but peace for all time."**
-Harry S. Truman (1884-1972) Informal remarks, Galesburg, Illinois, 1950

In turbulent times, where is our attention? On the problem? Or on the desired outcome? What can we do to help the world situation, while we are here comfortable in our homes and we know that others are suffering? We can't all go out and battle, nor would that help even if we could. We must think peace. We must bring our attention to peace. We must create a unified consciousness of PEACE ON EARTH, GOODWILL TO ALL. We must build a class consciousness of love and caring. Starting right here and right now, with each one of us. -*Lissa Coffey*

> "Speak, move, act in peace, as if you were in prayer.
> In truth, this is prayer."
> -Francis de S. Fenelon (1651-1715), Fr. archbishop

It is wonderful to think of peace as a prayer. Peace is one of those amazing things that grows when it is out in the light. Share peace, distribute it freely, be generous with your portions and there will be lots more to go around! *-Lissa Coffey*

> "I have found that life persists in the midst of
> destruction and therefore must be a higher law
> than that of destruction. Only under that law
> would a well-ordered society be intelligible
> and life worth living."
> -Mahatma Gandhi

With everything we've been through these past few months, these words ring true, loud and clear. Peace is a process, an ongoing movement that doesn't stand still. We are all a part of this process, and our contributions to a peaceful society make a difference. *-Lissa Coffey*

> "Peace is a daily, a weekly, a monthly process, grad-
> ually changing opinions, slowly eroding old barriers,
> quietly building new structures."
> -John F. Kennedy (1917-1963) United Nations address, Sept 1961

What I like about this quote is that while President Kennedy was obviously talking about the world situation, about establishing world peace, it also works really well if you apply the worlds toward INNER peace. Isn't this the process that we all go through to attain higher states of consciousness and become at peace with ourselves? We change our minds, and our thoughts, to reflect what we learn and experience. We gently and quietly build new patterns and practices that help to bring peace to both our inner and outer worlds. *-Lissa Coffey*

> "Sublime is the moment
> When the world is at peace
> And the limitless deep
> Lies bathed in the morning sun."
> -Hirohito (1901-1989) Untitled poem.

This is something we can all visualize. We've all had glimpses of what peace feels like. Imagine if everyone in the whole world could have that feeling all at the same time. Possible? As an optimist, I have to say yes. Peace is real, it is inherent in each one of us. And there are an infinite number of possibilities that could lead to world peace. One by one we are creating a world where peace comes naturally, and stays. *-Lissa Coffey*

Perception

> "Life does not consist mainly, or even largely, of facts
> and happenings. It consists mainly of the storm of
> thoughts that are forever blowing through one's mind."
> -Mark Twain

Isn't it amazing how we can each see the same thing in an entirely different way? It's because of our perceptions. Our past experiences help us to formulate some kind of definition to our current experiences. Yet we can change the way we look at things. We can choose a different perspective, see things from someone else's point of view, or from a higher vantage point. And when we broaden our scope and look at the "big picture" then we can see more clearly what is real. *-Lissa Coffey*

> "We do not see things as they are.
> We see them as we are."
> -The Talmud

We're each looking through different eyes, bringing our own experiences and emotions to whatever it is we're looking at. This is perception. Perception can change. The TRUTH remains the same... but do we see it? Do we see spirit in everything and everyone? We must recognize the spirit within ourselves and then we will see it reflected back at us everywhere we go! *-Lissa Coffey*

> "To a large degree "reality" is whatever the people
> who are around at the time agree to."
> -Milton H. Miller

Basically, the consensus of social perception is what shapes our "reality." What we see in the media is a reflection of what the general population has "agreed" is "the way things are." But... things are changing! There is a subtle shift towards a more spiritual life. Sociologists have recognized a growing number of people as "Cultural Creatives" who are leaders in developing all kinds of trends. All of us out there reading spiritual books, doing yoga, serving the community, showing kindness and pursuing our own spiritual growth - we are the cultural creatives! By sharing ourselves and our experiences, we are making a difference in the world... and the difference is good! *-Lissa Coffey*

> "Change your thoughts, and in the twinkling of an eye,
> all your conditions change. Your world is a world of
> crystallized ideas, crystallized words. Sooner or later,
> you reap the fruits of your words and thoughts."
> -Florence Scovel Shinn

Our perceptions are all in our mind. So it makes sense that if we change our mind, we change our perceptions. And when we change our perceptions, we change our reality! We can experience more of the Truth of this wonderful world, the beauty, the peace, the prosperity, the abundance, the clarity. Choose to see it. Choose to live it! *-Lissa Coffey*

**"If we could see the miracle of a single flower clearly,
our whole life would change."**
-Buddha

Our perception tends to be that growth is hard, that it is a struggle, that it is work. But the truth is that we are only making it hard on ourselves. We cling to the past, try to control our futures. Are we willing to get out of our own way and just let it be? It could be so simple! Look at the flower. Learn from the flower. We can bloom just as easily. *-Lissa Coffey*

Perfection

**"Perhaps the crescent moon smiles in doubt
at being told that it is a fragment
awaiting perfection."**
-Rabindranath Tagore (1861-1941)

I love this! Tagore has such a way with words. Imagine that moon, shining so brightly and proudly – knowing that it is what it is and that it is absolutely perfect just the way it is. Is there anything missing? Not a chance! Can we see our lives in the same light? They are perfect just the way they are right here and right now. *-Lissa Coffey*

**"Ring the bells that still can ring,
forget your perfect offering.
There's a hole in everything,
That's how the light comes thru."**
-Leonard Cohen

A big trend in decorating right now is making things looked aged, worn, or imperfect. This adds a sense of history and comfort to a room. The theory is that when everything is new and perfect, it isn't as relaxing to be in that space. Here we are, living in the space of our imperfect human form – let us see the beauty in our imperfections, that is where our souls shine through! *-Lissa Coffey*

**"Everything, by an impulse of its own nature, tends
towards its perfection."**
-Dante (A.D. 1265-1321)

Is it our nature to seek perfection? Or can we understand that it is our imperfections that make us perfect! We are here on this earth to learn and grow and experience. If we were already "perfect" what would be the point? If we were already perfect wouldn't we be bored? We can always strive towards being the best that we can possibly be as human beings – knowing that a perfect human being must by design be imperfect in some beautiful way. *-Lissa Coffey*

**"The true perfection of man lies,
not in what man has, but in what man is."**
-Oscar Wilde (1854-1900)

What man is. Not what man does, says, earns, drives, etc! Each of us, each man, woman and child, IS perfect, simply because we are. How cool is that? When we know the truth, and live it, then we know how cool it is, and how cool we are! *-Lissa Coffey*

> **"Perfection consists not in doing extraordinary things, but in doing ordinary things extraordinarily well. Neglect nothing; the most trivial action may be performed to God."**
> -Angelique Arnauld

Perfection is sometimes given a ranking – like a perfect "10" in gymnastics, or a 6.0 in a figure skating competition. But think about it. A lot of people can do a cartwheel, a lot of people can ice skate. These are not extraordinary things. But the way that they are executed in these world championships are! That's how we can have something to aspire to. Those athletes are the role models for "perfection" in that sport. And yet, those athletes always see room for improvement in some way or another. So, in life, as we aspire to perfection in our spiritual world – we have role models, too. We'd probably give Gandhi or Mother Teresa a "10" – but, they would be the first to say that they were not perfect! Part of our spiritual growth is recognizing that there's always more to learn. *-Lissa Coffey*

Perseverance

> **"Perseverance is failing nineteen times and succeeding the twentieth."**
> -Julie Andrews

We learn perseverance from an early age. When we first start to walk, we need to make several attempts before we finally get up on our feet and go somewhere. We're met with the encouragement and support of our loved ones, but the real reward is in the freedom of being mobile. When we persevere, and reach our goal, we see that the effort we put in was worth it. *-Lissa Coffey*

> **"Entrepreneurs average 3.8 failures before final success. What sets the successful ones apart is their amazing persistence. There are a lot of people out there with good and marketable ideas, but pure entrepreneurial types almost never accept defeat."**
> -Lisa M. Amos

Perseverance is stick-to-it-iveness! It's having that vision that success is not only possible, it is inevitable. It's having the fortitude to navigate the bumps in the road, and not let those bumps become road blocks. *-Lissa Coffey*

> "When life knocks you to your knees, and it will, why,
> get up! If it knocks you to your knees again, as it will,
> well, isn't that the best position from which to pray?"
> -Ethel Barrymore

Many times we may feel like we're in this all alone, that it's us against the world. But the truth is that the universe supports us in our endeavors. When we allow this power to lift us up, our burdens become lighter. We can tap into the wisdom, and the strength of the universe whenever we call upon it. *-Lissa Coffey*

> "When you get into a tight place and everything goes
> against you, til it seems as though you could not hang
> on a minute longer, never give up then, for that is just
> the place and time that the tide will turn."
> -Harriet Beecher Stowe

We have more strength, and more ability to persevere, than we give ourselves credit for. We are creative, and can come up with solutions. It takes courage to hang on. It takes faith to stick with it. But that is what we're made of. That is who we are. *-Lissa Coffey*

> "Learn to self-conquest, persevere thus for a time, and
> you will perceive very clearly the advantage which you
> gain from it."
> -Teresa of Avila

Self-control, self-determination, self-esteem. When it all boils down to it, our motivation to persevere must be intrinsic. It can't come from anything outside of us, it must come from within. When this happens we recognize our strengths, we recognize our potential. *-Lissa Coffey*

Persistence

> "Rome was not built in a day."
> -John Clarke (1596-1658)

I've always heard this quote, and never knew who said it, so I was happy to come across it this time around. How appropriate! In this fast-paced society we tend to expect instant gratification. How often do you hear people complain about how slow their computers are, or their dial-up, or the pizza guy? And all that spills over into our expectations for ourselves. We want that great job NOW, that dream relationship NOW, enlightenment NOW! But we have to remember that there is always divine timing involved. The seed needs time to sprout, the sprout needs time to grow. We are like that sprout that needs to keep pushing up the dirt, keep reaching toward the sun. We're growing every day. *-Lissa Coffey*

**"Diamonds are only chunks of coal,
That stuck to their jobs, you see."**
-Minnie Richard Smith, 1947

I love this because it applies in so many ways. Writers go about submitting their work and it gets rejected so many times, that they end up feeling like a chunk of coal! Or that their work, which they poured so much of their heart into, is just a chunk of coal. But, ah, when they stick to the job, keep writing, keep submitting - someone recognizes the beauty. The diamond comes shining through! We just can't give up, no matter what business we're in, or what we are going for. Our persistence pays off. *-Lissa Coffey*

"Dripping water hollows a stone."
-Lucretius (99-55 B.C.)

Water by itself it basically harmless. But it carries with it all the power of the universe. Even mere drops of water, given enough time, can erode a stone. So, imagine what we can do when we put our minds to it? We are so powerful, and most of the time we don't even know it! *-Lissa Coffey*

**"Drop upon drop collected will make a river. Rivers
upon rivers collected will make a sea."**
-Sa'Di (A.D. 1213? - 1292)

We've been doing WisdomNews for a few years now. It has been a great source of joy for me. When we first started out, there were just a few of us involved, and we basically started the list with our family and friends' addresses. But we persisted, did a little advertising, whatever we could do inexpensively, and the list grew - drop by drop, person by person - we've got a little river going now - or at least a steady stream! Thank you for subscribing, and for contributing to this e-mail community. Someday we hope to be a sea - and we will keep writing and keep persisting because we love doing this! And thanks for sharing this with your friends because every drop counts! *-Lissa Coffey*

**"When you get in a tight place and everything goes
against you till it seems as though you could not hold
on a minute longer, never give up then, for that is just
the time and the place the tide will turn."**
-Harriet Beecher Stowe, 1847

I remember hearing an interview that Jay Leno did once. He was asked what he attributed his success to, and he didn't even have to think about the answer for a second. "I didn't go away!" he said. He explained that there were many comedians who he felt were as good, or better than he was, and they all worked the same clubs, the same circuits, so they got to be friendly. But he said the difference between him and these other guys was that he never gave up. Many of the other guys got worn out, or burnt out, or just plain tired and quit. But Jay loved what he was doing so much that he couldn't quit. He kept going after his dream, even through some pretty bleak times. And now look at him! He could quit anytime he wanted to, because he has so much success that he doesn't need the money. But he keeps going, because he loves it. And that makes all the difference. -*Lissa Coffey*

"You can eat an elephant one bit at a time."
-Mary Kay Ash, 1981

Whatever it is we're up against, no matter how big, or how distasteful, we can handle it. One bit at a time, one day at a time, with persistence. That "elephant" is going to get smaller and smaller, we can mark our progress. And eventually it will be gone, we'll have conquered it. If we try to tackle the whole thing at once it gets overwhelming! But little by little is another story. We can do it. -*Lissa Coffey*

Personality

"The well-developed, well-integrated personality is the highest product of evolution, the fullest realization we know of in the universe."
-Julian Huxley (1887-1975)

All of our life is spent learning who we are, becoming more of who we really are. When we can truly relax, and be comfortable with the knowledge of our self, our radiant personality shows through. We know how we fit in the scheme of things. We recognize our connection to the universe. We appreciate the roles we have to play and understand that we are the ones writing our script. -*Lissa Coffey*

"Personality can never develop unless the individual chooses his own way, consciously and with moral deliberation."
-Carl G. Jung (1875-1961)

There comes a time when we must grow up. Age dictates a lot of what goes on with us physically. Society says when we are "legally" adults. But our personalities can emerge at any time. As we learn, we are gathering tools which will hopefully bring us to spiritual maturity, where we understand who we are, and what we have to share with the world. -*Lissa Coffey*

"Real increase of personality means consciousness of an enlargement that flows from inner sources."
-Carl G. Jung (1875-1961)

As we develop spiritual maturity, we understand that our strength comes from within. We understand that all of our gifts, our creativity, our courage, our intelligence, all of it comes from sources that are found within ourselves. We generate it, and it's up to us to use these gifts wisely and well. -*Lissa Coffey*

> **"I hope that is the keystone of the arch of my teachings – allowing a place for every man's personality, idiosyncrasy."**
> -Walt Whitman

What a varied and wonderful world we live in! Each person is so unique, with so much to offer. We are each here with purpose. We can learn from each other. We can help each other. Thank goodness for diversity! *-Lissa Coffey*

> **"We do not accept ourselves for what we are, we retreat from our real selves, and then we erect a personality to bridge the gap."**
> -Susan Sontag, 1963

In this case, the word "personality" is being used like the word "ego." It is important for us to understand that we are more than the roles we play. Sometimes we lose ourselves in these roles, we identify with our "doing" rather than our "being." Take time in silence to reconnect. *-Lissa Coffey*

> **"I'm not hard, I'm frightfully soft. But I will not be hounded."**
> -Margaret Thatcher

Personality is the image of ourselves that we present to the world. It is how others see us. This is not to be confused with who we really are. Who we really are goes much beyond our personality – we are so much more than that. *-Lissa Coffey*

> **"It is thus with most of us; we are what other people say we are. We know ourselves chiefly by hearsay."**
> -Eric Hoffer

How well do we really know ourselves? How do we define ourselves? When studying a play, actors learn about their characters by reading the script and noting what their character says, and also what the other characters say about that character. In our own script, what are we saying about ourselves? And what are other people saying about us? Let's look at that and see what we can learn about ourselves. *-Lissa Coffey*

> **"The proper time to influence the character of a child is about 100 years before he is born."**
> -Dean Willian R. Inge

History comes into play everyday. Decisions are made based on what has happened in the past. Everything we do has consequences. Every action has a reaction. What happened 100 years ago is influencing us today, and the choices we make today will influence people who are around 100 years from now. Are we setting a good example? *-Lissa Coffey*

**"Individualism is rather like innocence; there must be
something unconscious about it."**
-Louis Kronenberger

When we're comfortable in our skin then our true self shows through naturally – we don't have to think about impressing anyone or doing the "right" thing, we just are who we are and everything is great. We can relax and be ourselves knowing that all is well. *-Lissa Coffey*

"There is a secret person undamaged in every individual."
-Paul Shepard

What are all these masks we wear? This is only the top layer of our disguise. We play roles, we say lines. But as we learn and grow, and get to know who we really are, we discover that strength, that light, that truth that lies within. We are perfect, whole and complete, just as we are right at this moment. *-Lissa Coffey*

Philosophy

**"To teach how to live without certainty and yet without
being paralyzed by hesitation is perhaps the chief
thing that philosophy, in our age, can do for those
who study it."**
-Bertrand Russell (1872-1970)

It seems everyone has a unique personal philosophy, and that's good. Our human existence is filled with uncertainty, and maybe with philosophy we are learning that this is not something that we must fear – in fact, uncertainty is something that we can embrace! *-Lissa Coffey*

"Philosophy is the product of wonder."
-A.N. Whitehead (1861-1947)

It's those big "what ifs" in the world that lead us to great discovery, to great insight. When we let loose our imaginations, when we let our minds wander, and wonder, we can come up with all kinds of amazing theories and philosophies. And yet, how often do we allow ourselves this luxury? Sit in silence and see what happens, see where your mind takes you. *-Lissa Coffey*

"Philosophy is not a theory but an activity."
-Ludwig Wittgenstein (1889-1951)

I like this! Philosophy is active! It takes thought, creativity, and also practice. It's something you can muse over, and explore, and test out. It's a form of expression, a way of living. *-Lissa Coffey*

"As a human being, you have no choice about the
fact that you need a philosophy. Your only choice is
whether you define your philosophy by a conscious,
rational, disciplined process of thought and scrupu-
lously logical deliberation – or let your subconscious
accumulate a junk heap of unwarranted conclusions,
false generalizations, undefined contradictions,
undigested slogans, unidentified wishes, doubts and
fears, thrown together by chance, but integrated by
your subconscious into a kind of mongrel philosophy
and fused into a single, solid weight: self-doubt, like
a ball and chain in the place where your mind's wings
should have grown."
-Ayn Rand, 1982

One of the really cool things about living this life is that we have so much self-responsibility. We think our own thoughts, we make our own philosophy, we live our own life the way we choose to live it. Be aware, think well, live well. *-Lissa Coffey*

"I am open to conviction on all points except dinner and
debts. I hold that one must be eaten and the other paid.
Those are my only prejudices."
-George Eliot, 1857

Having an open mind will get us far. It helps us to learn and to grow. There are so many different experiences just waiting for us. There are times when we need to step up and say "okay, let's go" and see what happens, see where a philosophy takes us. We can always change our mind and try out something else! *-Lissa Coffey*

Poetry

"Poetry is that art which selects and arranges the symbols
of thought in such a manner as to excite the imagination
the most powerfully and delightfully."
-William Cullen Bryant (1794-1878)

Poetry seems to be a lost art sometimes, I don't think we appreciate it enough. I like that with just a few words a poem can illustrate a concept that seems too difficult to explain. It's because we feel the poetry in our heart first, and then think about its meaning and how it applies to our own lives. I like to read a poem out loud every night before I go to sleep. It puts me into that state where I am ready to dream.
-Lissa Coffey

"Poetry begins when we look from the center outward."
-Ralph Waldo Emerson (1803-1882)

Poetry is personal. Whether or not we write the poem ourselves, a poem becomes "ours" by the effect that is has on us. We take it to heart, and bring it forward into our lives. Lyrics to a song work the same way. We remember them, and carry them around with us. The meaning can change from person to person depending upon the interpretation. *-Lissa Coffey*

"Poetry is music written for the human voice."
-Mrs. Flowers, quoted by Maya Angelou

Just as songs are meant to be sung, poetry is meant to be recited. I love that there are poetry readings going on where we can gather and sit and listen to poetry. And isn't it so romantic when your sweetheart reads a love poem to you? The words carry us away to a place beyond the mundane, where music plays, and flowers bloom, and all is right with the world. *-Lissa Coffey*

"Poetry is above all a concentration of the power of language, which is the power of our ultimate relationship to everything in the universe."
-Adrienne Rich

Poetry is just one way to express our connection with the universe. Music does it with sound, art does it with color and texture, and poetry does it with language. While the description is elusive to us in prose, poetry allows us to go beyond mere description, to abandon the confines of "structure" and convey our feelings untethered. *-Lissa Coffey*

"The world is never the same once a good poem has been added to it."
-Dylan Thomas (1914-1953)

One of my very favorite poems is Longfellow's "Psalm of Life" which says:

"Lives of great men remind us
We can make our lives sublime.
And departing, leave behind us
Footprints in the sands of time."

This particular poem is a big footprint that Longfellow left on this earth. He is quoted all the time, because he says it so well. He doesn't have to go on and on with explanations and examples, we know exactly what he means, and we take it to heart. When John Lennon and Paul McCartney wrote: "All you need is love" we listened, and remembered, because those five little words had such an impact in the context of a simple and beautiful song. Poets, and their poetry, change the world. *-Lissa Coffey*

Power

"Power consists to a large extent in deciding what stories will be told."
-Carolyn Heilbrun (1988)

This is where the power of the press comes in. Not just what stories will be told, but how they will be told. Words carry weight. The same holds true in other areas of life. What are our leaders telling us, and what are they leaving out? We exercise our power by becoming more informed, and by voting. -*Lissa Coffey*

"The instruments of power – arms, gold, machines, magical or technical secrets – always exist independently of him who disposes of them, and can be taken up by others. Consequently all power is unstable."
-Simone Weil (1934)

We need to remain unattached to any outside trappings of power – the job title, or money, or whatever it is that "gives" us power. Because when those things go away, as they invariably do, being transitory and unreal, then our power vanishes with them. Instead, recognize that our real power comes from within, and it can never be taken, it can never be lost. -*Lissa Coffey*

"The power of a man increases steadily by continuance in one direction."
-Ralph Waldo Emerson (1803-1882)

We do get a certain momentum going when we work towards something for awhile. We build up steam. We want it more so we pursue it more. And we become more driven, more powerful in our efforts. This focused attention gives us more energy. -*Lissa Coffey*

"Today the real test of power is not capacity to make war but capacity to prevent it."
-Anne O'Hare McCormick (1882?-1954)

This is the same philosophy that Gandhi expressed, and that the Dalai Lama maintains every day. This quiet strength that speaks so loudly. The real power of peace. It takes a spiritual and emotional maturity to put down our toys, set aside our egos, and come to a level of understanding that makes things right, and good, for everyone. -*Lissa Coffey*

"He is most powerful who has power over himself."
-Seneca the Younger (5?B.C. – A.D. 65)

Do we have power over our minds? Can we avoid distractions long enough to sit down and meditate? Do we have power over our desires? Can we steer away from addiction and behavior that hurts ourselves? We have the power, we need to recognize it, and use it wisely. -*Lissa Coffey*

Practice

"We must be the change we wish to see in the world."
-Mahatma Gandhi

Our spiritual practice has purpose. It helps us to learn and grow and feel our connection with the Divine. And it also helps to lift the spiritual energy of the whole planet! The more people who devote time to spiritual practice, the better off our world will be. So, there are two things we can each do, every day, to help ourselves and each other.

1. Continue regular spiritual practices. This includes prayer, meditation, reading spiritual works, serving others, and giving of our time and talents.

2. Encourage others to spend time pursuing their own spiritual practices. This may mean babysitting some youngsters so their mother can spend some time in silence, or sending enlightening e-mails on to friends! *-Lissa Coffey*

"Whoever perseveres will be crowned."
-Johann Gottfried von Herder (German author, 1744-1803)

Remember the old joke, "How do you get to Carnegie Hall?" The punchline is "Practice, practice, practice!" Funny, but oh, so true! How do we reach that peace of mind, how do we get to that spiritual place that we're looking for? The answer is the same: Practice, practice, practice! We're going to get better at seeing ourselves as who we really are the more we practice actually being it. Whatever practice you choose, practice on a regular basis, practice every day, twice a day or more so. *-Lissa Coffey*

"We call prayer... that speech of man to God which, whatever else is asked, ultimately asks for the manifestation of the divine Presence."
-Martin Buber (1878-1965) Eclipse of God:
Studies in the Relation between Religion and Philosophy

The divine Presence is with us always. Here, now and always. It's just that we are not always aware of that presence. We're so busy getting things done and just handling life that our attention is elsewhere. That's why it is so important to spend time on our spiritual practices. During that time, we remind ourselves of who we really are, and of what is really important. Taking some time to center ourselves with spiritual practice helps everything in our lives flow more smoothly. *-Lissa Coffey*

"Never bring the car home without gas in the tank."
-Ron Shelton

Our spiritual practice is as essential to our soul as food is to our body. Practice provides us with the fuel which gets us through those difficult times. It leads us to peace, clarity, wisdom, and so much more. And just like a car, we can run out of "gas" when we're stressed out from going for a lot of miles without a break. Make it a point to incorporate your spiritual practices into your day every day, and watch the difference in how you feel. *-Lissa Coffey*

"Educate the heart - educate the heart."
-Hiram Powers

We know, conclusively and scientifically now, thanks to Dr. Paul Pearsall, that the heart has intelligence. Our hearts can literally "think!" We can listen to our hearts, we can follow our hearts. The best way to become sensitive to the heart's messages is through our spiritual practices. Take time to connect, to settle in and be peaceful. Allow your heart the time and space it needs to communicate! Rather than merely educating our hearts, which intuitively know what is best for us, spiritual practice is about educating ourselves to tune in to that intelligence. -*Lissa Coffey*

Praise

"When you do well, do not praise yourself but the gods."
-Bias (6th cent B.C.) One of the Seven Sages of Greece

We can keep praise in check by understanding that the gifts that we bring to the world do not really come from ourselves, but from God. The good that we do, the light that shines through, is pure Spirit. -*Lissa Coffey*

"The advantage of doing one's praising for oneself is that one can lay it on so thick and exactly in the right places."
-Samuel Butler (1835-1902)

Every once in awhile we need to give ourselves a pat on the back. We're each working so hard, doing our thing, and making our way. Too often we don't get the praise we think we deserve. But that's okay – because we can recognize our accomplishments and praise ourselves! And we ARE doing pretty well with all we've got going on. Kudos to you, dear friend! -*Lissa Coffey*

"The house praises the carpenter."
-Ralph Waldo Emerson (1803-1882)

I guess this is another way of saying that your work speaks for itself. But I think it means more than that, too. It means that when we put the best of ourselves into something, we know it – it shows. And even if no one else can see it, we can be proud of our efforts. -*Lissa Coffey*

"My soul preached to me and said, "Do not be delighted because of praise, and do not be distressed because of blame.""
-Kahlil Gibran (1883-1931)

We must not get too caught up in the teeter-totter of outside commentary on our works. There will always be some who appreciate what we do and others who disparage it. The ego is what gets caught up in this game of needing approval. The soul is wise, and knows that life is a balance of opposites. The soul itself can't be affected by praise or blame. *-Lissa Coffey*

"I do the very best I know how – the very best I can; and I
mean to keep doing so until the end. If the end brings me
out all right, what is said against me won't amount to anything. If the end brings me out wrong, ten angels swearing
I was right would make no difference."
-Abraham Lincoln (1809-1865)

We're bound to receive criticism, either positive or negative, no matter what we do in this lifetime. It's inevitable. So whom do we answer to? Only ourselves! We have to decide what is right, and what is right for us. We're all doing the best we can. *-Lissa Coffey*

Prayer

"Prayer is something deeper than words. It is present
in the soul before it has been formulated in words.
And it abides in the soul after the last words of prayer
have passed over our lips."
-O. Hallesby

We feel our prayers more than we really say our prayers. Prayers become real to us when the emotion behind them, within them, is so strong that the prayer becomes animated – it has life. Our soul houses these prayers before our minds even figure out how to articulate them. Prayers can be silent, yet heart-felt. *-Lissa Coffey*

"You pray in your distress and in your need; would that you might
also pray in the fullness of your joy and in your days of abundance."
-Kahlil Gibran

There is no "right way" to pray. There is no "right time" to pray. Prayer is an ongoing dialogue, a soul connection with spirit, a fusion of physics and metaphysics. Prayer is our expression of gratitude, despair, longing, appreciation. It is one means of com-munication and communion with All That Is. Sometimes we're praying and we don't even realize it. Our actions reflect our thoughts; our thoughts are prayers. What are we thinking? What are we doing about it? *-Lissa Coffey*

"Tomorrow I plan to work, work, from early until late. In fact I have
so much to do that I shall spend the first three hours in prayer."
-Martin Luther

Martin Luther knew that with so much work to do that he needed help. And he knew where to go for help and guidance. The more clear our thoughts, the more direction we allow ourselves to receive, then the faster and easier we will get there, and the more we will accomplish with the least amount of effort. *-Lissa Coffey*

> **"Time spent on the knees in prayer will do more to remedy
> heart strain and nerve worry than anything else."**
> -George David Stewart

Long before Prozac, there was prayer. Can you see the prescription now? "Pray two prayers, twice a day until symptoms subside. Then continue the treatment over the course of a lifetime to prevent symptoms from recurring." Prayer is a remedy. We can turn our burdens over to God and feel the weight drop from our shoulders. Why do we feel the need to carry around all that heaviness? Pray. And then pray some more. And then keep praying. And feel the lightness return. *-Lissa Coffey*

> **"The purpose of prayer is to reveal the presence of
> God equally present, all the time, in every condition."**
> -Oswald Chambers

We have learned, over and over again, that whatever we pay attention to becomes more important in our lives. When we pray, we are paying attention to our relationship with the Divine. With our attention on Spirit, we see the infinite possibilities, the presence of love and light, everywhere we go – because this wondrous spirit IS everywhere and everything! We feel that presence, and it comforts us, and enlightens us.
-Lissa Coffey

Present

> **"No mind is much employed upon the present: recollec-
> tion and anticipation fill up almost all our moments."**
> -Samuel Johnson (1709-1784)

Most of the time, the way our minds work, we're either thinking about something that happened in the past, or thinking about something that is going to happen in the future. Meanwhile, we're missing the present moment, the here and now. We're taking away from the juy that exists only in present moment awareness. It's almost like we need a little alarm to keep us awake. I saw this watch with a great reminder written right on the face: ONE – Only Now Exists! *-Lissa Coffey*

> **"The present is the future of the past."**
> -Karl Popper (1902-1994)

> **"We are tomorrow's past."**
> -Mary Webb, Precious Bane, 1924

We can't change what has happened in the past. We can learn from it, and grow from it, and ultimately go on from where we are now. we cannot predict the future – it is filled with infinite possibilities. the best we can do is to live, and love, the moment we're in. Life is like Disneyland – if we are thinking about the next ride and how we're getting there, we can't enjoy the ride we're on right here and now! *-Lissa Coffey*

"Now or never! You must live in the present, launch yourself
on every wave, find your eternity in each moment."
-Henry David Thoreau (1817-1862)

This is such a powerful concept that entire books have been written on this very topic –
Eckhart Tolle's "The Power of Now" is just one example. Now is the only time there is,
and when we live in this very moment, all of our potential can be realized. -*Lissa Coffey*

"The present is the necessary product of all the past,
the necessary cause of all the future."
-Robert G. Ingersoll, 1899

I love it when I go to a large shopping mall or an amusement park, and there's this
big directory to help us find our way around. It's like a map, and to help us get our
bearings, there's a big arrow that says "You Are Here!" How true is that?! Everything
we've done in the past, every decision we've made, has led us exactly to this place and
time. And from here, we go on. The choices we make now affect our future. When
we live in the present moment, we make better decisions, we know where we are and
where we are headed. -*Lissa Coffey*

"The older one gets the more one feels that the present
must be enjoyed: it is a precious gift, comparable to a
state of grace."
-Madame Curie, 1928

We do become more wise as we get older – and part of that is understanding the
precious value of the present moment. Maybe it is because we have more of a past
to look back on, so we can see just where and when we experienced the most beautiful
times of our lives. And maybe it is because we have had more time to enjoy the
moments, and we know how good that feels. -*Lissa Coffey*

Problems / Solutions

"Problems cannot be solved at the same level of
awareness that created them. "
-Albert Einstein

Although we generally like to look at things in the best possible light, we can't deny
that we live in a world where problems present themselves to us on a regular basis.
Whether the problems are big or small, stretching ourselves to find a solution helps
us in our process of growth. Evading a problem, or trying to pretend that it doesn't
exist, only causes the problem to amplify so that it can get our attention! -*Lissa Coffey*

"Clinging to the past is the problem. Embracing
change is the answer."
-Gloria Steinem

Sometimes it might look like change is the problem. But really it's that we're making change a problem for ourselves because we are resisting it! Change can be a great solution and can open up all kinds of wonderful opportunities for us. There's a time when we need to step outside of the boundaries we have created and just go for it! *-Lissa Coffey*

"All social and political problems are interwoven – that energy, for example, affects economics, which in turn affects health, which in turn affects education, work, family life, and a thousand other things. The attempt to deal with neatly defined problems in isolation from one another … creates only confusion and disaster."
-Alvin Toffler

All problems are interwoven because we are all connected. We function as a society much in the same way that the human body functions as an organism. Each of our organs depends on the others for its well-being. We can't separate out one part without experiencing some consequences in another part, which ultimately affects the whole. So, just as we take care of our bodies holistically, we must care for our communities, and understand how our actions, both positive and negative, affect the world as a whole. *-Lissa Coffey*

"The best way to solve any problem is to remove its cause."
-Martin Luther King, Jr. (1929-1968)

If we don't find the cause and make changes, the same problem is going to keep coming back again and again in different guises. This is true whether we're talking about fixing a leaky faucet, a broken heart, or an unbalanced budget. We have to look at our problems, explore our options, and take responsibility for creating solutions that work. *-Lissa Coffey*

"The real problem of our existence lies in the fact that we ought to love one another, but do not."
-Reinhold Niebuhr (1892-1971)

Love is always the ultimate solution! If we could truly love one another to our full capacity there would be peace on earth. There would be no hunger, no greed, no fear. Imagine what that would be like. Just imagine. *-Lissa Coffey*

Progress

"Frozen food is not progress."
-Russell Baker

Technology has offered us some amazing conveniences – but at what expense? Do we hole up with our computers rather than socialize with our fellow travelers? Do we make

a habit of eating fast food rather than enjoying the wholesomeness of something freshly prepared at home? Where, for the sake of "progress," have we gone awry? When we remember the lessons we have learned in the past and build on them, then we make progress. It's not necessarily about making life "easier" but about experiencing the beauty that is already there. *-Lissa Coffey*

"Our moral progress may be measured by the degree in which we sympathize with individual suffering and individual joy."
-George Eliot (1819-1880)

Progress is learning more about who we are. Progress is understanding and relating and empathizing with other people because we realize that we are all in this together. There is no separation between us. When we can truly experience that Oneness, we will have made real progress! *-Lissa Coffey*

"Each step upward makes me feel stronger and fit for the next step."
-Mohandas K. Gandhi (1869-1948)

One day at a time. One step at a time. Sometimes this journey is a struggle, like we're trying to conquer some huge mountain. But as long as we keep going, we make progress. And our progress encourages us to keep going. We're flexing our spiritual muscles, and getting stronger all the time. *-Lissa Coffey*

"Progress has not followed a straight ascending line, but a spiral with rhythms of progress and regression, of evolution and dissolution."
-Goethe (1749-1832)

Sometimes we need to take a few steps back in order to get a running start. We make mistakes, and as long as we learn from those mistakes, we progress, we grow. Eventually we get to a point where we can look back and see how far we've come. Then we can turn back around and see how far we have to go! *-Lissa Coffey*

"I find the great thing in this world is not so much where we stand, as in what direction we are moving: To reach the port of heaven, we must sail sometimes with the wind and sometimes against it – but we must sail, and not drift, nor lie at anchor."
-Oliver Wendell Holmes, Sr. (1809-1984)

To progress we must make the effort. We must forge ahead. We must put ourselves out there and be open to experiences that challenge us. We can start right where we are, by knowing where we want to go. *-Lissa Coffey*

"All progress is gained through mistakes and their
rectification. No good comes fully fashioned, out of
God's hand, but has to be carved out through repeated
experiments and repeated failures by ourselves. This
is the law of individual growth. The same law controls
social and political evolution also. The right to err,
which means the freedom to try experiments, is the
universal condition of all progress."
-Mohandas Gandhi (1869-1948)

Of course we want to grow, of course we want to move forward and progress. But sometimes we have to go through the whole "two steps forward and one step back" system. As long as we keep going, understanding that the "step back" is not failure, then our progress is inevitable. *-Lissa Coffey*

"We are not going around in circles, we are going
upwards. The path is a spiral."
-Hermann Hesse (1877-1962)

Spiritual growth moves upwards – we see things from a higher perspective as we progress. Spiritual growth also moves inward aw we gain a deeper understanding. When we find ourselves in situations that seem familiar to us, those are markers, and we can compare how we handle things based on our previous experiences. *-Lissa Coffey*

"I find the great thing in this world is not so much
where we stand, as in what direction we are moving:
To reach the port of heaven, we must sail sometimes
with the wind and sometimes against it – but we must
sail, and not drift, nor lie at anchor."
-Oliver Wendell Holmes, Sr. (1809-1894)

If we're planning a journey, whether it's across town or around the world, we map out a route for ourselves. We start with some direction as to which way to go, otherwise we would meander aimlessly not knowing for sure where we will end up. Our inner journey is also served with a destination in mind. We can plot out where we want to be and how we will get there through our own practice of prayer, meditation, study and ritual. Then of course, when unexpected experiences throw us off course, we can make corrections, and keep moving. *-Lissa Coffey*

"No great improvements in the lot of mankind are possible until a great change takes place in the fundamen-
tal constitution of their modes of thought."
-John Stuart Mill (1806-1973)

Everything starts with a thought. Every invention, every recipe, every song, every book. Someone, somewhere thought it up, and now it's here, something tangible in time and space. Whatever it is, if we can see it in our mind's eye, we can make it, we can be it, we can do it. *-Lissa Coffey*

> **"Not fare well,**
> **But fare forward, voyagers."**
> -T.S. Eliot (1888-1965)

As we're on our journey we're meeting other travelers all the time. Some are in our lives for many years, some for just a few moments. Wherever our paths converge, and for however long, these relationships are a gift to us, they help us make progress. So as we travel on toward our own individual paths, we start to understand that we're all eventually going to end up in the same place, together, right where we're supposed to be. -*Lissa Coffey*

Promises

> **"Every organization of men, be it social or political,**
> **ultimately relies on man's capacity for making promis-**
> **es and keeping them."**
> -Hannah Arendt, 1972

It seems like we don't hear that word used as often lately. When we were younger, it was a really big deal to make a promise. And we knew that a promise meant something we could count on. Today there's more hedging... we're reluctant to "promise" results, or overextend ourselves, so we tend to hear: "Well, I can't promise, but I'll do my best." We give ourselves that little "out" so we don't look bad if we don't follow-through. Or we get a "guarantee" that comes with an expiration date or a lot of fine print. But promises, real promises, don't work like that. It's a way of saying: "I mean it" or "I'll do what I say I am going to do." -*Lissa Coffey*

> **"An honest man's word is as good as his bond."**
> -Cervantes (1547-1616)

When we make a promise, it is important that we keep it. When we do, then we are being true to the person we made the promise to, and also true to ourselves. Our words carry weight. And our actions have consequences. It we want to be trusted, we must be trustworthy. -*Lissa Coffey*

> **"Don't ever promise more than you can deliver, but**
> **always deliver more than you promise."**
> -Lou Holtz, 1993

This is good advice for business, athletics, school, for just about every area of our lives! It's always good to give our "all" to a project, to do our best, to go that "extra mile" to make it work. When we do that, it shows, and we feel good about our accomplishments. -*Lissa Coffey*

> **"An ounce of performance is worth pounds of promises."**
> -Mae West (1893-1980)

This has been said a dozen different ways: "The proof is in the pudding," "Talk is cheap," and "Show me the money!" among them. It's the follow-through that really matters. Otherwise our words are meaningless. We've got to "walk the talk" and demonstrate our honesty and integrity. *-Lissa Coffey*

"A contract is a mutual promise."
-William Paley (1743-1805)

The world has gotten complicated. What did we ever do before contracts and attorneys and negotiations? There was a time when we simply made a promise, and that was good enough. Deals were sealed on handshakes. A promise implies trust, and integrity. It can be very simple. *-Lissa Coffey*

Purpose

"Not only to see and find the Divine in oneself, but to see and find the Divine in all, not only to seek one's own individual liberation and perfection, but to seek the liberation and perfection of others is the complete law of the spiritual being."
-Sri Aurobindo (1872-1950)

The more we grow spiritually, the more we realize how we fit into the bigger picture. We're never alone on this journey. We're all in it together. The closer we find ourselves to spirit, the closer we see that we are to each other. *-Lissa Coffey*

"The human soul, the world, the universe are laboring on to their magnificent consummation. We are not fashioned... marvelously for nought."
-Ralph Waldo Emerson (1803-1882)

There is a divine organization, an intelligence to all of creation – and here we are, a part of it all. It makes sense that we are here for a purpose. Life has meaning, and each life is meaningful. *-Lissa Coffey*

"The purpose of life on earth is that the soul should grow - So grow! By doing what is right."
-Zelda Fitzgerald (1900-1948)

We have discovered the truth in this statement. We are actively pursuing our spiritual growth and consciously living our lives in such a way to accelerate that process. We know the importance of prayer, meditation, silence, and wisdom. And we have experienced the growth that comes with doing "what is right." This is our purpose, and we can do nothing less. *-Lissa Coffey*

"Not enjoyment, and not sorrow,
Is our destined end or way;
But to act, that each tomorrow
Find us farther than today."
-Henry Wadsworth Longfellow (1807-1882)

This is from my favorite poem, "The Psalm of Life" which starts "Lives of great men remind us, we can make our lives sublime, and departing leave behind us, footprints in the sands of time." It's about following the examples laid before us, and at the same time, making our own way – becoming a new example, a new light to guide others. Longfellow understood that we need to keep going, to keep pursuing our spiritual growth, because that is our ultimate purpose. -*Lissa Coffey*

"Pursue some path, however narrow and crooked, in
which you can walk with love and reverence."
-Henry David Thoreau (1817-1862)

We each make our own way, even though it might seem like a crazy way around to others! But as long as we're learning and growing and having a good time, that's all that is important. We all ultimately "get there" and realize that our own unique journey was the perfect one for us. We learn to go along purposefully and experience what we need to as we grow. -*Lissa Coffey*

Reality

"There is no reality except the one contained within
us. That is why so many people live such an unreal
life. They take the images outside them for reality and
never allow the world within to assert itself."
-Hermann Hesse

What is "real?" Something we can see with our eyes, feel with our hands? What "makes" something real? With virtual reality and reality-TV, these are tough questions these days! But we know what is really real when we know it in our heart. We know love is real. *-Lissa Coffey*

"Nothing which is at all times and in every way agreeable
to us can have objective reality. It is of the very
nature of the real that it should have sharp corners
and rough edges, that it should be resistant, should
be itself. Dream-furniture is the only kind on which
you never stub your toes or bang your knee."
-C.S. Lewis

We've often heard the phrase "harsh reality." As if reality can smack us in the face. But that smack could just be a wake-up call to alert us to the bigger "reality." When we stub a toe, we're brought immediately to the present moment! Living in present-moment awareness we can more clearly see what is real and what is not, what is important and what is dispensable. *-Lissa Coffey*

"All our interior world is reality – and that perhaps
more so than our apparent world."
-Marc Chagall

Love, joy, bliss, peace – we experience all this in our interior world, yet we cannot draw a picture or take a photo of exactly what it looks like. Our interior world is so vast, so filled with amazing gifts. Yet where do we place our attention? We're busy trying to make our apparent world, our exterior world, look good. When we look within, we find the abundance that we so desperately seek. It is there all the time! *-Lissa Coffey*

"Reality has changed chameleon-like before my eyes
so many times that I have learned, or am learning, to
trust almost anything except what appears to be so."
-Maya Angelou

Appearances change. Nothing in this exterior world stays the same. Have you ever gone to visit a place, only to return several years later and not even recognize it? Buildings go up and down, tenants move in and out, trees grow, signs change. People change, too. We all start out as babies, and our features mature as we age. Our hairstyles and clothes change with the trends. But what stays the same? Spirit. We can trust that love never goes out of style, and never moves away. -*Lissa Coffey*

"We live in a fantasy world, a world of illusion.
The great task in life is to find reality."
-Iris Murdoch

Have you ever been to Disneyworld? It's a beautiful place – colorful, clean, fun, and full of surprises! And when we're there, we know that it is all illusion – that it is all there for our enjoyment. We experience the rides as entertainment, even the scary roller-coasters. Yet when we're in our own "world" we tend to take things so seriously. What would happen if we approached life as our own amusement park? Knowing that one ride takes us for a spin and another shakes us up and another lets us sit back and relax? What a concept! Then we could stop looking for reality all around us and start finding it inside of us. -*Lissa Coffey*

Reason

"Let Reason, not impulse, be your guide."
-Kahlil Gibran (1883-1931)

I like this because Gibran used a capital "R" for reason – and I think that's significant. We have a head, and we have a heart. We are at our best when we can use the two of them together. Reason with a little "r" might just be thinking, using our heads. But Reason with a big "R" connects the heart. Our heart can be impulsive, and our head can be impulsive - but Reason allows us that time for consideration, that time for thoughtfulness. It brings us balance, and peace of mind. -*Lissa Coffey*

"Come now, let us reason together, says the Lord."
-Isaiah (8th cent B.C.) Isaiah 1:18

Reason is calm, rational, and thoughtful. Reason could be called common sense. We are blessed with a thinking mind, which sometimes spins itself into wild imagination. When we bring reason into the equation, it lets us clear our minds, to see the big picture, to hear other opinions, to make sense of the chaotic. -*Lissa Coffey*

"Neither believe nor reject anything because any other
persons or description of persons have rejected or
believed it. Your own reason is the only oracle given
you by heaven."
-Thomas Jefferson (1743-1826)

That still, small, voice of reason sometimes speaks volumes. We don't have to be swayed by incentives or seduced by sales – we know what is reasonable – we know what is True. When we can get past that "noise" and listen to reason, the reason that exists within each one of us, we know what is right for us. -*Lissa Coffey*

"The object of reasoning is to find out, from the consideration of what we already know, something else which we do not know."
-Charles Sanders Peirce (1839-1914)

Part of being reasonable is having an open mind. That willingness to learn, and to share, brings us wisdom. It's information-gathering, and also inspiration-gathering! We each bring something to the table, and when it's all out there, we have a bountiful buffet. -*Lissa Coffey*

"Reason consists of always seeing things as they are."
-Voltaire (1694-1778)

"What is" is the truth. When we start going off on what "should be" or "could be" or "would be" then we're living a life of illusion. Why create confusion and conflict? Accept what is. Love what is. Work with what is. That's reasonable. Yes, we can make changes – but only when we start from a place of clear understanding. -*Lissa Coffey*

Regret

"Never regret. If it's good, it's wonderful. If it's bad, it's experience."
-Victoria Holt, The Black Opal, 1993

Everything we do, everything we go through, has some purpose for us in our life, and in our growth. So if we look at it this way, how could we regret anything that happens to us? It may be terrible at the time, but sometimes it's those really terrible times that give us the biggest spurts of growth. We can look back and see how much we've changed because of the experience – and how much we've learned. -*Lissa Coffey*

"The bitterest tears shed over graves are for words left unsaid and deeds left undone."
-Christopher Crowfield, Little Foxes, 1865

Sometimes the biggest regrets are for things we didn't do, rather than for things we did do. It's important for us to act on our instincts, to pursue our dreams, to say what we feel the need to say. When we live life to its fullest, and not hold anything back, we give ourselves more opportunities to learn and grow. -*Lissa Coffey*

"Regrets are as personal as fingerprints."
-Margaret Culkin Banning, 1958

Regret is personal because it really affects the one who is going through it. And we each experience regret in a different way. Some regrets are offered up with an apology, others eat away at a person. They can be big or small regrets – but we each feel them in a different way. Since we are here to learn and grow, it would be difficult to go through this life without any regrets. As long as we recognize that we are where we are because of everything –what we regret and what we don't – then we will continue to move along the path, learning and growing all the way, -*Lissa Coffey*

"The greater part of what my neighbors call good I believe in my soul to be bad, and if I regret anything it is very likely to be my good behavior. What demon possessed me that I behaved so well?"
-Henry David Thoreau (1817-1862)

It's all a matter of our own unique perspective. No one can make us regret anything. We have our own internal compass which lets us know if we've gone off course. There is always pressure from society, family, peers and associates to act a certain way or to live up to certain expectations. But the only one we answer to in the end is ourselves. We decide what behavior is "regrettable" or not. -*Lissa Coffey*

"Repeated polls over the years have found people's biggest lifetime regret is not getting enough education or not taking it seriously enough."
-Malcolm Ritter "What We Come to Regret," San Francisco Chronicle, 1993

If we look at regret in a healthy way, it would be saying to ourselves: "What could I have done differently?" And in that way we are learning from our experiences. There is also the possibility that we may change our experiences – as in this example, we could still get more education, and take it seriously. We have choices all the time – so maybe regret is a call for us to make another choice. -*Lissa Coffey*

Relationships

"Intimate relationships cannot substitute for a life plan. But to have any meaning or viability at all, a life plan must include intimate relationships."
-Harriet Lerner, Dance of Intimacy (1989)

The purpose of relationships, like just about anything in this life, is for us to learn more about ourselves and who we really are. That is why intimate relationships teach us so much. When we truly open ourselves up and express our feelings we feel closer to God. We become aware of our own vulnerability, and our own divinity.
-*Lissa Coffey*

"Union is only possible to those who are units. To be
fit for relations in time, souls, whether of man or woman,
must be able to do without them in the spirit."
-Margaret Fuller, Women in the Nineteenth Century (1845)

We are each whole, complete, and perfect just as we are. None of us needs another person to be fulfilled. There is no "other half" that needs to be found. Our primary relationship is with ourselves. And we can choose to share our selves, because we know what an unlimited supply of love is available to us! We learn and grow and give and receive from our relationships – and that is beautiful. -*Lissa Coffey*

"Seven years would be insufficient to make some
people acquainted with each other, and seven days are
more than enough for others."
-Jane Austen, Sense and Sensibility (1811)

There are some people we just "click" with. Maybe it's love at first sight, maybe it's some kind of karmic recognition. But when this happens, it is usually a sign to pay attention – that this is an important relationship. We are here for each other. There is so much for us to accomplish together here in this space and time, and we are brought together to do just that. -*Lissa Coffey*

"The biggest mistake is believing there is one right way to
listen, to talk, to have a conversation – or a relationship."
-Deborah Tannen

A relationship is a living thing. It grows, evolves, and no two are the same. We need to care for our relationships, and that can mean different things in different circumstances. We need to pay attention to relationships that are important to us, and know that in return the relationship nurtures us. -*Lissa Coffey*

"The long-term accommodation that protects marriage
and other such relationships is... forgetfulness."
-Alice Walker, You Can't Keep a Good Woman Down (1981)

"Forgetfulness" goes beyond forgiveness. First you forgive, then you forget. This is present-moment awareness in action! The past is history – it's gone, and it can certainly be forgotten. As we grow and change, as our relationships grow and change, forgetfulness can be a welcome accommodation! -*Lissa Coffey*

Reliability

"In helping others, we shall help ourselves, for whatever good we give out completes the circle and comes
back to us."
-Flora Edwards

Reliability means the ability to be relied upon. When we're talking about appliances, that's easy to understand. Flip the switch and if it does what it's supposed to do, it's reliable. With people it's not that different. To be reliable means that we do what we say we're going to do. Our words carry weight because we have proven through our past actions and behaviors that people can count on us. -*Lissa Coffey*

"We seldom stop to think how many people's lives are entwined with our own. It is a form of selfishness to imagine that every individual can operate on his own or can pull out of the general stream and not be missed."
-Ivy Baker Priest

This whole world functions in such a way that we need to rely on each other. We can't go through this life alone – we're all connected. We each have something to contribute to the big picture. It's important to do our part, to be reliable and to know that we can rely on those around us. -*Lissa Coffey*

"You can't build a reputation on what you intend to do."
-Liz Smith

Intention is one thing, action is another. Sure, the thought counts, but isn't it a lot better to have the thought and the follow-through? There are a lot of ideas out there, but the implementation of the ideas is what makes them valuable. Being reliable means taking action, following through on intentions. -*Lissa Coffey*

"Learn to depend on yourself by doing things in accordance with your own way of thinking."
-Grenville Kleiser

Ralph Waldo Emerson wrote several essays on "Self-Reliance" and this quote summarizes one of his themes: when we are true to our own beliefs, our own way of thinking, then we can depend on ourselves, we are self-reliant. We owe that to ourselves, we deserve it from ourselves. -*Lissa Coffey*

"Champions take responsibility. When the ball is coming over the net, you can be sure I want the ball."
-Billie Jean King

Being reliable is being a champion. It's being strong, and confident in our abilities. It's accepting challenges and rising to the occasion. It's taking on life in partnership with the universe knowing that we can handle whatever comes our way. -*Lissa Coffey*

Remembrance

"The world does not require so much to be informed as reminded."
-Hannah More (1745-1833) English author

Those of us who lived through it remember where we were when we got the devastating news on September 11th, 2001. It was such a shock, such a tragedy that affected each of us in some way. Major events jolt our senses into total present moment awareness and the images become ingrained in our memories. Do we remember where we were, or what we were doing, just two uneventful days before that on September 9th? I couldn't tell you what I was doing. It was probably just another day. But those are exactly the kinds of days that we want to, and really need to remember – when things are good, and life is peaceful. *-Lissa Coffey*

"How can such deep-imprinted images sleep in us at times, till a word, a sound, awake them?"
-Gotthold E. Lessing (1729-1781) German dramatist

The images of 9/11 were vividly presented to us on television – so much so that we couldn't get them out of our minds. We were consumed with information, and watched with tear-filled eyes and we tried to make sense of it all. Now some time has passed, and we're starting to feel normal again. But this anniversary has brought up a lot of the same sadness and questions that we experienced one year ago. It is important for us to take time for reverence and remembrance, to acknowledge the events that took place and the far-reaching impact on our lives. And then, as time goes on, it is important for us to move on, too – knowing that the memories remain, there for us to call upon and reflect upon at the appropriate times. *-Lissa Coffey*

"The joys I have possessed are ever mine; out of thy reach, behind eternity, hid in the sacred treasure of the past, but blest remembrance brings them hourly back."
-John Dryden (1631-1700) English poet and author

We remember our sorrow because we felt it so deeply. It is also important to remember our joy. Think back to a time when you felt truly joyful... maybe when you first fell in love? When your child was born? When you accomplished an important goal? Life is filled with these joyful moments, and they are there for us to enjoy not just once, but many times over through our memories. *-Lissa Coffey*

"If there is a single theme that dominates all my writings, all my obsessions, it is that of memory – because I fear forgetfulness as much as hatred and death."
-Eli Wiesel

When we experience a tragedy, we know that we will never be the same. We have changed, and grown from the inevitable changes that occur as a result. We have felt loss, and heartache, and profound grief. We have also felt love for those who share our grief, and gratitude for those who made it through and all those we helped us to get through those trying times. When our emotions come so much to the surface, we can't help but look for comfort. And we can find it from each other, because we're all going through the same thing on some level. *-Lissa Coffey*

**"How we remember, what we remember, and why we
remember form the most personal map of our individuality."**
Christina Baldwin (1977)

Our memories make up a big part of who we are. They help to shape us. We carry our memories with us wherever we go, and we share them with people who want to know us. We can cherish our memories, even the sad ones, because they are ours. *-Lissa Coffey*

Renewal

**"The natural healing force in each one of us is the
greatest force in getting well."**
-Hippocrates

Spring has sprung! Doesn't it feel great? This is a time of rejuvenation and renewal. A new cycle has started. Just as we can shed our winter coats, we can slough off our negativity, wash away our old attitudes, and begin again. Our lives will reflect our new outlook, bright and clear! *-Lissa Coffey*

**"You could not step twice into the same river;
for other waters are ever flowing on to you."**
-Heraclitus

Here on earth, in this physical realm, life is constantly changing. And as people, we are changing and growing and living and learning all the time. This is why we are here! Embrace change, step boldly into the unknown, this is a journey of discovery and self-discovery. *-Lissa Coffey*

**"Create in me a pure heart, O God, and renew
a steadfast spirit within me."**
-Psalm 51:10

Spirit is all-loving, all-encompassing, unbounded, immortal and invisible. And this wonderful energy is available to each one of us, within each one of us! Is it any wonder that we are powerful, beautiful and creative beings? Know it... and enjoy it! *-Lissa Coffey*

"Whatever the mind holds to and firmly believes in, forms a new pattern of thought within its creative mold, as whatever thought is held in the mind tends to take outward form in new creations."
-Ernest Holmes

Who do you think you are? Depending on the tone of the person asking that question, you could choose to be insulted or intrigued. But really, do you know who you are? Are who you know yourself to be and who you think yourself to be the same person? We each create the lives we lead, and we're doing this all the time with our thoughts and our actions. Think about it. *-Lissa Coffey*

"The house of the Divine is not closed to any who knock sincerely at its gates, whatever their past stumbles and errors."
-Sri Aurobindo

Spirit is always within us and all around us, it can't go away. There is nothing that we could possibly do to make it go away! We don't have to knock, we don't have to call, we don't have to call out – it is already HERE! Welcome it, love it, use it, appreciate it. *-Lissa Coffey*

Resolution

"Always bear in mind that your own resolution to succeed is more important than any other one thing."
-Abraham Lincoln (1809-1865)

It's that time again. New Year's Eve, time to make our resolutions. It's tradition. It's one way to keep ourselves on track. Yet how long do we go before letting those resolutions fall by the wayside? Do we even remember what we resolved to accomplish last year at this time? We can choose to do it differently this time. Keeping in mind that we can change or add to our goals at any time, (since every month is a New Month, every week a New Week and every day a NEW DAY!) let's look at this time as a chance to strengthen our resolve! Go for it! Happy New Year! *-Lissa Coffey*

"Resolve, and thou art free."
-Henry Wadsworth Longfellow (1807-1882)

Our resolutions carry power! We can do anything we set our mind to. Ask yourself: do I mean it? Do I want it? Am I committed to taking action to accomplish this? If the answers are "yes" then make that resolution! It's as good as done. *-Lissa Coffey*

"Resolve to perform what you ought; perform without fail what you resolve."
-Benjamin Franklin (1706-1790)

A resolution is a commitment - it's a commitment to ourselves to grow, change, achieve, accomplish. We can make that commitment to ourselves this new year, and we can honor that commitment as time goes on and obstacles are thrown onto our paths. It all starts right here, right now. -*Lissa Coffey*

> "Paths clear before those who know where they're going and are determined to get there."
> -Anonymous

Once we set our minds on something, we make our resolution, then we can just let it go and watch the universe handle all the details. Things just seem to fall into place when we are aware enough to notice. Situations and circumstances orchestrate into one big conspiracy to fulfill our desires, and put us into a position where we can take action. We just need to keep our destination in mind, we don't need to control what happens every step of the way. We will get there. -*Lissa Coffey*

> "He who is firm and resolute in will moulds the world to himself."
> -Goethe

We are blessed with choice, with free will. We are not puppets at the disposal of the planets, but strong, intelligent creatures who are here to learn and grow through our experiences. The more we grow, the more we understand that we are creating our lives every minute of every day. Through our resolve, our will, our intentions, our decisions, we are making and changing our experiences all the time. -*Lissa Coffey*

Risk

> "They are surely to be esteemed the bravest of spirits who, having the clearest sense of both the pains and pleasures of life, do not on that account shrink from danger."
> -Thucydides

Look at the examples we have been given. From the Wright Brothers, to Helen Keller, to Oprah Winfrey, and so many more creative, brave and determined souls. Where would we be today if they decided it was easier to stay home and sit on the couch? They risked! They dared! And they soared! And we can do the same. -*Lissa Coffey*

> "If one is forever cautious, can one remain a human being?"
> -Aleksandr Solzhenitsyn

It is a part of our nature to learn and to grow. And one way we do this is by taking risks. When we learned to walk, we risked falling down. We are constantly striving to better ourselves and our lives, and we can't do that by standing still. Our instincts urge us to move forward, to see what is ahead, to peek around the corner not knowing for sure what we might find. -*Lissa Coffey*

"Without risk, faith is an impossibility."
-Soren Kierkegaard

We often hear: "No risk, no reward!" We know that sometimes we have to step outside our comfort zone to make things happen for ourselves. And yet we hesitate. What is stopping us from taking that risk? If we can get up our courage enough to have faith in the process, we can make progress. Taking a risk is taking that "leap of faith."
-Lissa Coffey

"It is not because things are difficult that we do not dare, it is because we do not dare that they are difficult."
-Marcus Annaeus Seneca

It's so easy to come up with excuses. But what we're really doing is making life more difficult for ourselves. We're hiding from ourselves. What do we want? What do we REALLY want? If we really want it, it is worth the risk. Isn't it better to have that possibility of success by risking, rather than the certainty of failure by sticking with the status quo? I think it is harder to live with "what if" than "I gave it a shot."
-Lissa Coffey

"The important thing is this: to be able at any moment to sacrifice what we are for what we could become."
-Charles Du Bos

And the real truth is that we need to be able to sacrifice at any moment who we think we are for who we truly are. When we can take that risk, and recognize that we are more than the roles we have taken on, that we are defined not by what we do, but by who we are, then we're there. Then we've made it. *-Lissa Coffey*

"Do not be too timid and squeamish. All life is an experiment. The more experiments you make, the better."
-Ralph Waldo Emerson

It's by taking those risks in life that we find out just what we can do, just what we are made of. Taking risks makes life an adventure. Like taking a white water rafting trip, it can be scary, but it can also be exhilarating, and when we come finish and we're still okay it feels fantastic. *-Lissa Coffey*

"All life is a chance. So take it! The person who goes furthest is the one who is willing to do and dare."
-Dale Carnegie

We hear it every day. "Just do it." "Go for it." We are encouraged to tackle that challenge, to take that risk. We are surrounded by examples of people who take chances with no regrets. Where would Lance Armstrong be now if he was content to ride his bike around the block? Where would civil rights be if Rosa Parks hadn't refused to give up her seat on the bus? It's not about going further than other people, it's about going as far as we can go ourselves. *-Lissa Coffey*

"He that will not sail till all dangers are over must
never put to sea."
-Thomas Fuller

The only thing that holds us back from taking a risk is fear. When we let go of fear we let in love. There are risks everywhere, everyday. We have the choice to disengage, to hide in fear – or to embrace the opportunity and see what happens. Life is meant to be lived, and experienced, and embraced. -*Lissa Coffey*

"You can't expect to hit the jackpot if you don't put a
few nickels in the machine."
-Flip Wilson

There's risk, and there's reward. Does reward ever come without risk? Not likely! When we take a risk we put ourselves out there, whether it's in coin or in spirit. And we always get something back, whether it's reward, or experience – which is sometimes the same thing. -*Lissa Coffey*

"Don't be afraid to take a big step if one is indicated.
You can't cross a chasm in two small steps."
-David Lloyd George

There's a reason why it is called a "leap" of faith – it's a big step. You can't take a leap without having both feet off of the ground at some point. That's the risk. What is supporting us? What if we fall? There are a million "what ifs" that we could consider. Instead of focusing on "what if" in terms of failure, let's look at the "what ifs" in terms of success. What if we land on our feet and everything works out great? -*Lissa Coffey*

Science

"One never notices what has been done; one can only
see what remains to be done."
-Marie Curie (1867-1934)

Science makes things look easy. We take for granted that we have electricity now, and telephones, and computers. If we didn't have these things we would miss them. What are we missing now? What inventions are left to be invented? I'm sure some scientists are busy working on them now! *-Lissa Coffey*

"Every great advance in science has issued from a new
audacity of imagination."
-John Dewey (1859-1952)

Where do all these new ideas come from? From someone's imagination! That's where it starts. Backed up by a little bit of wisdom and a lot of determination, we can make great strides in all areas of our life. Science is just one example where we are growing by leaps and bounds. *-Lissa Coffey*

"When you are courting a nice girl an hour seems like
a second. When you sit on a red-hot cinder a second
seems like an hour. That's relativity."
-Albert Einstein (1879-1955)

What is time anyway but some man-made measurement? In Spirit there is no time, that's why time can stand still, or can fly by. Our perception of time is what affects us more than time itself. Look at how some people just don't seen to age. When we feel young, we live young, and look young! *-Lissa Coffey*

"Science is not to be regarded merely as a storehouse
of facts to be used for material purposes, but as one
of the great human endeavors to be ranked with arts
and religion as the guide and expression of man's
fearless quest for truth."
-Richard Arman Gregory (1864-1952)

Ah, science! It had a whole different meaning to me when I was in high school and had to memorize the periodic table. Now I look at science as these amazing discoveries that lead us to the truth. It's not such a big leap from spirituality to science. We can see all of the miracles that exist under a microscope, or through a telescope. And right here we are living miracles, every moment. In the movie "What the Bleep

Do We Know?" several scientists weigh in on the facts of our existence, and what is happening all around us, all the time. *-Lissa Coffey*

"I do not know what I may appear to the world, but to myself I seem to have been only like a boy playing on the sea-shore, and diverting myself in now and then finding a smoother pebble or a prettier shell than ordinary, whilst the great ocean of truth lay all undiscovered before me."
-Isaac Newton (1642-1727)

It is with that child-like heart that all great adventures begin. It's the big "what ifs" in life that spark our curiosity and engage our attention. When we love doing something, it's not work to us, but play. *-Lissa Coffey*

Scripture

"When thy mind leaves behind its dark forest of delusion, thou shalt go beyond the scriptures of times past."
-Bhagavad Gita, 6th cent. B.C.

A lot of times the scriptures tell us stories of things that happened long ago. We are to use these stories not merely as entertainment, but as an illustration of our own lives. When we see the relevancy, and apply the wisdom garnered from those times into our present situations, we can experience tremendous growth. *-Lissa Coffey*

"Search the scriptures."
-Jesus, A.D. 1st cent., John 5:39

When we are looking for wisdom, for guidance, for answers - one place we can go is to the scriptures. The scriptures can give us insight into our situation, and can help us to access our divine intelligence. These are beautiful words which speak to us in a very special way. *-Lissa Coffey*

"There is something nearer to us than Scriptures, to wit, the Word in the heart from which all Scriptures come."
-William Penn (1644-1718)

All scriptures, no matter which religions use them, originated somewhere, and were written by someone, or by many people who were compelled to put those exact words down on paper. The remarkable thing is that they have stood the test of time. Because Truth is Truth, it doesn't change. And what resonated in the heart way back when, still resonates in our hearts when we read the words today. *-Lissa Coffey*

"There is one Lord revealed in many scriptures."
-Saraha, Buddhist saint

I think a lot of us automatically think of scripture as the Bible, but scripture is defined in the dictionary as "sacred writings." So there are many different scriptures from which we can learn: the Bible, the Talmud, the Koran, and the Bhagavad Gita are just a few examples. *-Lissa Coffey*

> **"Obey the Scriptures until you are strong enough to do without them."**
> -Swami Vivekananda (1863-1902)

The scriptures are a kind of guidebook that can set us onto the path. But once we know the Truth, we don't have to keep following the guide, we know the way. It is good to keep it with us, though, to make sure we are going in the right direction at times! *-Lissa Coffey*

Searching

> **"What we seek we do not find - that would be too trim and tidy for so reckless and opulent a thing as life. It is something else we find."**
> -Susan Glaspell, The Morning Is Near Us, 1939

The journey is filled with twists and turns and all kinds of surprises. That's what keeps life interesting. Whatever it is that we seek, we end up finding so much more than we ever could have anticipated. Those unexpected treasures we come across give meaning, and significance, to our experience. *-Lissa Coffey*

> **"We find what we search for - or, if we don't find it, we become it."**
> -Jessamyn West, Love Is Not What You Think, 1959

I think this is another way of saying "be careful what you wish for." Let's keep our "eye on the prize" and keep a look out for those things that make life so precious. Seek love, truth, beauty, wisdom, and peace - for one and for all. *-Lissa Coffey*

> **"When you stop looking for something, you see it right in front of you."**
> -Eleanor Coppola, Notes, 1979

It's interesting how an objective observer can see things for us that we somehow can't seem to see for ourselves. That's just one way that we are here to help each other. We can remind one another of our inherent beauty, of the love we have to offer, of the talents we have to share. *-Lissa Coffey*

> **"Often the search proves more profitable than the goal."**
> -E.L. Konigsburg, From the Mixed-Up Files of Mrs. Basil E. Frankweiler, 1967

There's an old saying that the journey, not the destination, is what is important. What if what we are actually searching for is the search itself? Here we are, somehow we got ourselves at this point in time, at this place on earth, and yet we know there is "more." Just that knowingness leads us to places, both physical and spiritual, that allow us to experience more of our Selves. *-Lissa Coffey*

"You never find yourself until you face the truth."
-Pearl Bailey

Finding yourself. That's what this search is really all about. That's where all roads lead. Look within. Face the truth of your being – your love, your beauty, your wisdom, your peace. We are all that, and so much more. *-Lissa Coffey*

Security

"Our greatest illusion is reliance upon the security and permanence of material possessions. We must search for some other coin."
-John Cudahy

What is secure anyway? And why do we so desperately rely upon it? Anything we can see or touch is impermanent. "Things" come and go. A new car depreciates the minute we drive it off the lot. A gemstone is only worth what someone will pay for it, and prices change all the time. The only permanence, the only unchangeable, is spirit. We can find our security in our faith. *-Lissa Coffey*

"Security can only be achieved through constant change, through discarding old ideas that have outlived their usefulness and adapting others to current facts."
-William O. Douglas

There's an old saying that nothing is permanent but change. When we are flexible and open to change, we can learn and grow through all types of changes. Change offers us newfound freedom, and when we realize that, we are secure in knowing that change is good, and good for us. *-Lissa Coffey*

"Only in growth, reform, and change, paradoxically enough, is true security to be found."
-Anne Morrow Lindbergh

Security could be said to be peace of mind. It's that feeling of being safe. When we know that no matter what happens on the outside, big or small, minor or major, we're always fine, we're always whole, then we have peace of mind – we have security. *-Lissa Coffey*

"Your real security is yourself. You know you can do it,
and they can't ever take that away from you."
-Mae West

There is security in confidence. There is security in knowing yourself, and knowing who you are and what you are capable of. This is an intangible that is more valuable than anything you can put a price tag on. *-Lissa Coffey*

"Be like the bird that, passing on her flight awhile on
boughs too slight, feels them give way beneath her,
and yet sings, knowing that she hath wings."
-Victor Hugo

We have that same freedom of flight – we can rise above adversity, we can let our spirit carry us through any difficulties. That freedom gives us security, something we can count on. *-Lissa Coffey*

Self

"What we must decide is perhaps how we are valuable,
rather than how valuable we are."
-F. Scott Fitzgerald (1896-1940)

When we learn about the world we learn about our self. Any knowledge, any discovery, teaches us more about who we are. And then we can decide just how we can help, how we can serve, how we can be of value to the world. *-Lissa Coffey*

"We never remark any passion or principle in others,
of which, in some degree or other, we may not find a
parallel in ourselves."
-David Hume (1711-1776)

The more we get to know our self, the more we understand that we are so much the same as everyone else. Sometimes it's like we're all living the same life. We have so much in common. There are times when we recognize each other as brothers and sisters, and there are other times when we just say: "That's me!" And that's the truth. We're all connected. *-Lissa Coffey*

"The unexamined life is not worth living."
-Socrates (469-399 BC)

We know that there is so much more to life than the distractions of everyday living. That's why we practice our spiritual rituals. That's why we read books, and meditate, and pray. That's why we strive to learn and to grow. Life is so much more full and satisfying when we look within. *-Lissa Coffey*

> **"Behold, I do not give lectures of a little charity,**
> **When I give I give myself."**
> -Walt Whitman (1819-1892)

The best, most valuable gift we can give is the gift of our self. We know when our heart is in something and when it's not. We feel it when we're just going through the motions. And when we give of ourselves, we're also giving to ourselves, because that feeling of giving is so powerful, and so freeing, that we grow in the process. -*Lissa Coffey*

> **"I can honestly say that I was never affected by the**
> **question of the success of an undertaking. If I felt it**
> **was the right thing to do, I was for it regardless of the**
> **possible outcome."**
> -Golda Meir (1898-1978)

This is conviction. This is instinct. We all have the ability to listen to our hearts, to take on the big undertakings, in spite of any doubts or questions. We just need to summon the courage to do so. When we know our self so well we can't help but do anything less. -*Lissa Coffey*

Self-Awareness

> **"Best to be yourself, imperial, plain, and true!"**
> -Elizabeth Barrett Browning

How many times have we heard someone give us encouragement by saying: "Just be yourself"? When we were young and needed to make a speech in class, or we were a little too shy to approach our secret crush for a date, a friend or parent would remind us that we had what it takes, that there was no need to be afraid. And, still, today, we need to be reminded. We get nervous, feel that we're not "as good as" someone else, or that some silly mistake was made and we weren't supposed to be chosen to give a speech. Self-awareness is knowing who we are, and knowing that we are not only "as good as" or "good enough" but that we are whole and complete, that there is a light within us that shines! -*Lissa Coffey*

> **"When one is pretending the entire body revolts."**
> -Anais Nin

Self-awareness means also being in touch with the signals that our body gives us. We might try to "fake it" on the outside, but we can't fool ourselves. The body doesn't lie. When we get stressed out it can show up in our stomach, or our back, or as a headache. We can use those signals to give our body what it needs to come back into balance – whether it's a glass of water, a massage, or a nap! -*Lissa Coffey*

> "When you affirm your own rightness in the universe,
> then you cooperate with others easily and automatically
> as part of your own nature. You, being yourself, help
> others be themselves."
> -Jane Roberts

We are all connected. We are all living examples for each other. When we are being ourselves, feeling natural and at ease, people can't help but respond in kind. It's beautiful to have this open, honest communication. Being self-aware helps us to relax and be ourselves. We know that when we do that we are happiest, and that we also get the best response from others. *-Lissa Coffey*

> "Nature never repeats herself, and the possibilities of
> one human soul will never be found in another."
> -Elizabeth Cady Stanton

Our individuality is our strength. We don't need to imitate. We don't need to be anything other than who we are. We are blessed with unique gifts that can't be duplicated. The more we get to know ourselves, the more we become self-aware, the more that we will find opportunities to use these gifts to make the world a better place. *-Lissa Coffey*

> "As simple as it sounds, we must try to be the best
> person we can: by making the best choices, by making
> the most of the talents we've been given."
> -Mary Lou Retton

It's these simple things that we need to remember. And if we can remember them every day, and apply them to our lives, then we thrive! We do know what the best choices are for us. We do know what our talents are. When we are self-aware it is natural for us to proceed keeping these things in mind. *-Lissa Coffey*

Self–Determination

> "We make ourselves up as we go."
> -Kate Green, 1983

Determination of the self sounds to me like defining ourselves. Life is a canvas, and we are the artist. Life is a song, and we write the lyrics. Life is a computer, and we are the programmer! There are dozens of analogies, but the outcome is the same. We create our lives. We determine our own destiny. Life is a journey, and we're in the driver's seat! So where do you want to go? *-Lissa Coffey*

> "Can't nothin' make your life work if you ain't the architect."
> -Terry McMillan, 1989

The architect's job is to come up with the plan, to lay out the blue prints. There are all these decisions to made, and you have to start somewhere. Once you've got a plan, then you can lay the foundation, the framework, the whole building can come together. With life, we've got to be the architect. We have to make the decisions that are going to make our life work the way we want it to. When we have self-determination the sky's the limit! -*Lissa Coffey*

"We are not born all at once, but by bits. The body first, and the spirit later; and the birth and growth of the spirit, in those who are attentive to their own inner life, are slow and exceedingly painful. Our mothers are racked with the pains of our physical birth; we ourselves suffer the longer pains of our spiritual growth."
-Mary Antin, 1912

The birth analogy is used often in describing spiritual awakening. I read recently a zen saying that explained that we are actually born twice. Once as an egg out of our mothers. And then again as we break out of our shells we birth ourselves into awakening. Think of what it takes for a bird to break out of its shell. It's hard work, but the bird has to do it all by itself in order to be strong enough to survive in the world. Sometimes our spiritual growth is hard work, and painful. But when we break through we can spread our wings and fly. -*Lissa Coffey*

"Human beings are not so constituted that they can live without expansion. If they do not get it one way, they must another, or perish."
-Margaret Fuller, 1845

We're somehow created with this built in system that spurs us on to growth. Sometimes we can recognize it in our desires. We can't help but go after something we really want. And we learn along the way. The challenges we face help us to figure things out, and to grow on many different levels. We need to move our muscles to stay in shape, or they wither away without use. Our spiritual muscles need a work-out, too. Luckily we have the instinct to search for meaning, to look for wisdom. -*Lissa Coffey*

"A watermelon that breaks open by itself tastes better than one cut with a knife."
-Hualing Nieh, 1981

We can have the best teachers in the world. We can read the most amazing books. We can climb a mountain in Tibet and be blessed by a guru. But when we finally "get it" – it's because we did it. No one can grow for us, no one can learn for us. Life, and its pace, are self-determined. We will get there of our own accord. -*Lissa Coffey*

Self-Knowledge

"Many men go fishing all of their lives without knowing that it is not fish they are after."
-Henry David Thoreau

As a spiritual community, we talk a lot about "who we really are" and becoming "more of our Self." But wanting it and actually achieving it are two different things. The first step is understanding what it is we're really after. And it's not fish! Self-knowledge is something intangible, and invaluable. -*Lissa Coffey*

"Knowing others is wisdom, knowing yourself is Enlightenment."
-Lao-tzu

There are so many things to learn in this life. We spend years in school studying algebra and history, science and literature. All of this is fascinating, and helps us to grow. And yet, when you know yourself, you know everything. It all becomes so simple. We can see the connections, we can feel the balance of it all. Garner wisdom from books and teachings, and also, look within. -*Lissa Coffey*

"No one remains quite what he was when he recognizes himself."
-Thomas Mann

Does the world change when we understand who we are? No, but we see it more clearly. Do we change when we understand who we are? No, but because we can see ourselves more clearly, we may start to make different choices in our lives. So our lives may change dramatically. Once we start this growth process, we can't go back – like a flower reaches toward the sunlight we continue our journey within. -*Lissa Coffey*

"A single event can awaken within us a stranger totally unknown to us."
-Antoine de Saint-Exupery

Sometimes one single event is all it takes to totally wake us up to the Truth that is here all the time. But for most of us, it is a process that gradually unfolds, giving us clues, hints, and glimpses of Reality in small doses so that we can assimilate them into our lives. We become familiar with who we are, we get to know ourselves day by day, as we come to understand and accept that we are much more than the roles we play. -*Lissa Coffey*

"It is not only the most difficult thing to know oneself, but the most inconvenient, too."
-Josh Billings

I guess from one point of view, life would be easier if we just had to get up and go to work everyday – we could pretty much be on auto-pilot and navigate through life without much effort. But what a waste of time and energy that would be. And how boring, too! Sure, spiritual growth takes effort – we need to make time to meditate, read, serve and take care of ourselves and the planet. But isn't that the best part about this life? Once you get started on "the path" and see all the wonders that a spiritual life offers, you want to keep going. Sure, self-knowledge is difficult, messy, challenging, and inconvenient – but it is also the most magnificent and amazing gift that life has to offer. *-Lissa Coffey*

Self-Realization

"I had become a new person; and those who knew the old person laughed at me. The only man who behaved sensibly was my tailor: he took my measure anew every time he saw me, whilst all the rest went in with their old measurements and expected them to fit me."
-George Bernard Shaw (1856-1950) Man and Superman, 1903

Every day we are growing and learning and changing. Physically, our bodies create new cells all the time, renewing each part of us. Mentally, we learn and understand more with every experience we encounter. Emotionally, we grow and mature through our relationships, which come and go and teach us, too. And since we are actively pursuing our spiritual growth, we can see the changes in ourselves spiritually – we are aware of the changes we create in our lives. So, we are new every day – and we can start fresh from right where we are. Since we know that about ourselves, we can also know that for others – we can let go of grievances and allow for the possibilities. *-Lissa Coffey*

"One of the signs of passing youth is the birth of a sense of fellowship with other human beings as we take our place among them."
-Virginia Woolf (1882-1941)

As we start learning more about ourselves, and realizing more and more who we really are, we begin to understand just how much we really have in common with one another. We're all in this together, and there is so much we can each to do help one another. As time goes on, we naturally become more compassionate, because we can empathize with a more broad range of experiences. *-Lissa Coffey*

"King Henry: Presume not that I am the thing I was;
For God doth know, so shall the world perceive,
That I have turn'd away my former self."
-Shakespeare (1564-1616) Henry IV, 1597

I like this because Shakespeare says here "I have made the choice- I have chosen to change" - and that is such a powerful statement. We always have that choice. We can always "reinvent" ourselves. And when we mean it, it works! There are a lot of people in the media who are examples of this – the former "loose image" actress turned mother and Sunday school teacher – the former rock-n-roller who is now a gospel singer. Part of this is knowing who we are – and understanding that how the world perceives us, how we present ourselves, is totally up to us. *-Lissa Coffey*

"Spiritual living is a fulfillment from moment to moment, in which the outer person is in a state of living rapport with the inner being and becomes an extension thereof."
-N. Sri Ram (1889 - ?) Thoughts for Aspirants, 1972

A lot of times we tend to separate our "outer life" from our "inner life." Maybe we're working at a job we hate just for the money, while our heart aches for something more. Or we can't seem to find that certain relationship we're longing. We can come up with all kinds of justifications for these things. But there's always a solution. To fully integrate ourselves, we've got to make our outer life an extension, or an expression, of our inner life. We've got to develop that rapport spiritually within so that we understand how much power we have to create anything in our lives. *-Lissa Coffey*

"Most people are like a falling leaf that drifts and turns in the air, flutters, and falls to the ground. But a few others are like stars which travel one defined path: no wind reaches them, they have within themselves their guide and path."
-Hermann Hesse (1877-1962) Siddharta

You are a star! You are a shining star! I wrote a song once with that title, and the rest of the lyrics in the chorus go: "You are my shining star, you are who you are, you are special to me! No matter where you are, if it's near or far, you shine bright as can be!" *-Lissa Coffey*

Service

"There is no greater satisfaction for a just and well-meaning person than the knowledge that he has devoted his best energies to the service of the good cause."
-Albert Einstein (1879-1955)

All of us who have devoted our time and energy to worthwhile causes know the satisfaction that Einstein wrote about. It's heart-warming. It's validating. And in many ways, it's addictive! There are so many good causes that it would be impossible to contribute to every one. When you find one or two that really speak to you, that you can really get behind, then go for it! Get involved, and be of service. *-Lissa Coffey*

> "Serve self you serve society
> Serve society serve yourself."
> -Ralph Waldo Emerson (1803-1882)

Besides helping other people, service has the added benefit of helping the person doing the serving! How could this be? Because service makes us feel good, it helps us to grow spiritually, it helps us to gain compassion. Service helps to make our society a better place, and it's a place we all share! Because we are all one, what we do for others, we do for ourselves. -*Lissa Coffey*

> "In the time we have it is surely our duty to do all
> the good we can to all the people we can in all the
> ways we can."
> -William Barclay

I believe that it is our duty to serve. I also believe that it is our nature to serve. We are here for each other, we are here to help each other. Many times, I think it is easier for us to help someone else than to ask for help for ourselves. But when we need help, we absolutely should reach out for it. When we need help, we are providing another person with the opportunity to serve, and this is truly a blessing. -*Lissa Coffey*

> "All altruism springs from putting yourself in the other
> person's place."
> -Harry Emerson Fosdick

It's all about empathy. We are all one. We share so much that we can understand another person's heartache or sorrow. We can relate to each other. We want to do what we can to alleviate pain. This is how service begins. -*Lissa Coffey*

> "If we could all hear one another's prayers, God might
> be relieved of some of his burden."
> -Ashleigh Brilliant

We are here as angels, emissaries, to do God's work, to help each other. We can hear one another's prayers if we just listen. We are all one in spirit, and we all want the same things – love, respect, acknowledgment, a purpose. Think about all that we can do for each other to provide those very important things. It could be so simple, and so beautiful, and mean so much. -*Lissa Coffey*

Serving

> "The man who is himself at ease can best attend to the
> distress of others."
> -Adam Smith (1723-1790)

Sometimes to step up and serve, we have to step outside of ourselves. We have to think more about what is going on than how uncomfortable we might feel in the situation. It might involve risk, and it might take courage. This is where heroes come in. A hero is that regular person who sets aside fear and serves because that is what is needed at the time. -*Lissa Coffey*

"The best servant does his work unseen."
-Oliver Wendell Holmes, Sr. (1809-1984)

Seva is a Sanskrit word which means self-less service. This is serving without condition, without expectation of recognition or reciprocation. This is the most pure form of service. When we give of ourselves, with all of our heart, just for the sake of giving, this is when we do the most good. -*Lissa Coffey*

"Serve self you serve society
Serve society serve yourself."
-Ralph Waldo Emerson (1803-1882)

Serving is reciprocal. We give of ourselves, and we receive so much in return. It feels good to serve; it feels good to give. Serving society is really a gift we give to ourselves. -*Lissa Coffey*

"There is no greater satisfaction for a just and well-meaning person than the knowledge that he has devoted his best energies to the service of the good cause."
-Albert Einstein (1879-1955)

The good cause. There are so many good causes. There is so much need. There are so many opportunities to help and to serve that there's really no excuse not to serve. When we see all the good that we can do, the difference that our efforts make, it makes us want to continue to pour our energies into service. -*Lissa Coffey*

"Service is the rent that you pay for room on this earth."
-Shirley Chisholm

Service is a responsibility, and it is also an obligation. We owe it to ourselves to take care of each other – and this is how we do it. It is giving without expectation. It is an expression of love. -*Lissa Coffey*

Sharing

"For we must share, if we would keep,
that blessing from above;
Ceasing to give, we cease to have;
such is the law of love."
-Richard C. Trench

By sharing we recognize the abundance of whatever it is we have and are content to allow others to participate in our good fortune. There's another saying that "love isn't love until you give it away." Blessings, like love, are meant to be shared. And whatever we share we seem to have more of! -*Lissa Coffey*

"Sharing what you have is more important than what you have."
-Albert M. Wells, Jr.

Sharing is not limited to material things. We can share our memories, experiences, and knowledge for example. The beauty in this is that we aren't giving those things away - we couldn't if we tried! But they are so valuable, and they become even more valuable, when we share them other people. The most simple advice can be such a treasure. The fact that we are open and willing to share what we have learned can make this journey more beneficial for all of us. -*Lissa Coffey*

"Friends share all things."
-Pythagoras (580? - 500? B.C.)

True friends share things without even realizing it sometimes. When one of us feels joy, that joy is shared by our friends - we are happy for each other! Whether it is good news or bad news, it feels good to share it with a friend, with someone who will feel the emotions and help us through it. -*Lissa Coffey*

"Imagine no possessions
I wonder if you can
No need for greed and hunger
A brotherhood of man
Imagine all the people
Sharing all the world."
-John Lennon (1940-1980)

With the world in such a state of flux, it might be difficult to imagine ALL the people sharing all the world... but it is not impossible. There's a saying: "Think Globally, Act Locally." If we each started there, kind of a "grass roots" or "backyard" approach, imagine the impact we could make house by house, neighborhood by neighborhood, community by community. -*Lissa Coffey*

"No good thing is pleasant to possess without friends to share it."
-Seneca the Younger (5? B.C. - A.D. 65)

What's the point of having a big screen TV if you can't have some friends over for an NBA play-offs party every once in awhile? I don't think Seneca the Younger had that specifically in mind when he wrote this, but I'm sure they had something of the equivalent in his day! Whatever we have is more sweet when it is shared. -*Lissa Coffey*

**"A decent man at table the other day, taking the only
remaining potato out of the dish on the end of his
knife, offered his friend half of it!"**
-Nathaniel Hawthorne (1804-1864)

Sharing is good manners! We have such an abundant life - there is so much good and so much love to go around. When we share it with other people, we feel it more deeply. We experience the "oneness" because we have something in common. Whether we're sharing a potato or a laugh with someone, sharing brings us together. *-Lissa Coffey*

**"Imagine no possessions
I wonder if you can
No need for greed and hunger
A brotherhood of man
Imagine all the people
Sharing all the world."**
-John Lennon (1940-1980)

I remember a story called "Stone Soup" that my teacher told my class when I was about in the second grade. It talks about a mysterious man who came to a poor town one day and told everyone that he had a magic stone that could turn water into soup. Ah! The town was skeptical, but curious - so one woman let this man in her kitchen and filled a big kettle full of water. The man put the stone in the bottom and brought the water to a simmer. Yes, he said happily, it is happening - but maybe we need just a little bit of flavor. The woman offered a carrot from her garden. And as the story goes on, the man becomes more enthusiastic, and the neighbors begin bringing other things to add to this magic soup: a potato, an onion, a bone, some basil, and other small things. As the smell of the soup wafts through the town, word starts to spread about this magic stone. And of course, because the townspeople share what they have on hand, everyone is able to eat the "magic soup" for dinner that night! I've remembered this story all these years, and the message it conveys about the magic of sharing. *-Lissa Coffey*

"The more we share, the more we have."
-Leonard Nimoy

Dr. Spock was a philosopher on Star Trek, and it sounds like Leonard Nimoy is quite the philosopher in real life. Just the notion of sharing implies abundance. When we can share whatever it is that we have, we have the mindset of generosity. When we are shared with, we feel gratitude. These are all good things! *-Lissa Coffey*

"Friends share all things."
-Pythagoras (580?-500? B.C.)

Friends share sorrows and joys. We can feel for each other, and with each other. It's easy to share sugar with a neighbor, yet more of a challenge for us to share our feelings. But this is why we have friends, so that we can share our support for each other. It's all kind of nature's design for our learning and growth. We are here to help each other. *-Lissa Coffey*

"Sharing is sometimes more demanding than giving."
-Mary Catherine Bateson, 1989

Think about the truth in this simple statement. When we give, we give "away." It goes from being "mine" to being "yours" - we let it go. When we share, it becomes "ours." Sharing requires a closeness, an intimacy, and that can be more difficult to step up to. Just think of all the things we have to share with one another... not just the material things, but also knowledge, and experience. *-Lissa Coffey*

Silence

"Thought works in silence, so does virtue. One might erect statues to Silence."
-Thomas Carlyle (1795-1881)

Silence is the single most important ingredient in our pursuit spiritual growth. Yet how much time do we spend in silence every day? Whether we meditate, or pray, or just sit with nature, silence is like a hallway that we need to go through for the doors of Truth to open to us. *-Lissa Coffey*

"Silence is the mother of truth."
-Benjamin Disraeli (1804-1881)

Silence gives birth to so many wonderful things. It is from this space of infinite possibilities that all great works flow. It is from this realm of vast wisdom that we all learn and grow. *-Lissa Coffey*

"Silence is the language of God."
-Swami Sivananda (1887-1963)

Are we really listening when we are in silence? Or are we "thinking" and listening to our busy minds? Stop the chatter for awhile – breathe – get quiet – and allow those thoughts to pass as clouds drift across a blue sky. Then listen, and hear God. *-Lissa Coffey*

"It [would be] vain for me to endeavor to interpret the Silence. She cannot be done into English."
-Henry David Thoreau (1817-1862)

More can be "said" in a few moments of silence than in volumes of literature. Some things are beyond translation. I could go on and on about this... but I'll be quiet and let you find the silence instead. You'll see. *-Lissa Coffey*

"Quietness is indeed a sign of strength. But quietness may also help one to achieve strength."
-Franz Kafka (1883-1924)

We all have a strength that we may not even realize. But it is there, deep within. It gets us through the most difficult times, it give us courage, and persistence when it seems that all is lost. We can tap into that strength at any time, and use it to achieve our heart's desire. And we can find that strength in silence. *-Lissa Coffey*

"Silence is the perfectest herald of joy."
-Shakespeare (1564-1616) Claudio, in Much Ado About Nothing

Some people might think of silence as empty, or lonely – yet it is anything but! Silence is so filled with love and truth and wisdom that is fills our spirit to overflowing. *-Lissa Coffey*

Simplicity

"In character, in manners, in style, in all things, the supreme excellence is simplicity."
-Henry Wadsworth Longfellow (1807-1882)

Have you noticed that there is a whole industry out there now all about simplicity? There are books and organizers and coaches and magazines all geared towards making our lives more simple. How did this happen? How did our lives get so complex and confused that we forgot how to be simple? It's crazy that we've now created more "stuff" to get ourselves back to basics – it's kind of defeating the whole purpose. Let's just make it simple today: Less "stuff," more love! *-Lissa Coffey*

"When thought is too weak to be simply expressed, it is a clear proof that it should be rejected."
-Luc de Clapiers Vauvenargues (1715-1747)

It's not just our houses and our desks that are cluttered – often times our minds are cluttered, too! Let's treat our thoughts, and our words carefully – let's choose them as we would pick out produce in the market, discarding the ones that are stale or bruised and selecting instead ones that are fresh and fragrant and full of life. And let's just take what we need for now, we can always go back for more. One thing at a time! *-Lissa Coffey*

"Our life is frittered away by detail... Simplify, simplify, simplify."
-Henry David Thoreau, Walden

How many ways can we say this, or hear this? "Don't sweat the small stuff," "Look at the big picture," "All's well that ends well." The beauty of Japanese art is in its simplicity. Artists know that the empty spaces are just as important as the brush strokes. So much can be expressed with just a few lines. Musicians understand that just a few notes can convey an emotion, they don't need a whole symphony every time. And poets need just a few words, not an entire textbook. Is there anything more beautiful than "I love you?" Life can be simple, sweet and oh, so beautiful, if we just allow it to be. *-Lissa Coffey*

> "Manifest plainness,
> Embrace simplicity,
> Reduce selfishness,
> Have few desires."
> -Lao-tzu, The Way of Life

Another word for simple is "easy." With ease, doesn't that sound like a great way to live life? It's our choice. We're the ones who have been complicating our lives. Look at what's really important. Sort things out, give yourself the space to see what is really there. You'll be surprised at just how perfect "simple" really is. *-Lissa Coffey*

> "It is the sweet, simple things of life which are the real
> ones after all."
> -Laura Ingalls Wilder (1917)

What's real? Schedules, deadlines, hassles, arguments, conflicts, "fine print," details? Those things sure command our attention – but are they real? Or do they take us away from what is really real? Where is the love? Put your attention there. Ahhhh, that's better! *-Lissa Coffey*

Sincerity

> "Sincerity is the foundation of the spiritual life."
> -Albert Schweitzer (1875-1965)

A foundation is something upon which everything else is built. So it's a good idea to look at the sincerity with which we live our lives. It seems to me that sincerity is a little bit more than honesty. It's not just the words we say, but the feeling that we put behind those words. There are no "loopholes" with sincerity - it's not just what we say, but what we mean. *-Lissa Coffey*

> "Sincerity is the first characteristic of all men in any
> way heroic."
> -Thomas Carlyle (1795-1881)

Heroism is when you put yourself on the line. And you can't do that without being sincere. It's an "all or nothing" kind of a thing - you can't be a little bit sincere, you have to just go for it all the way to be a hero! *-Lissa Coffey*

> "Individuals are considered sincere when there is little
> or no discrepancy between the goals they seek and
> those they claim to be seeking."
> -Leonard W. Doob

This is basically talking about the difference between what we say and what we do. And this is where I think a lot of politicians get themselves into trouble - and how politicians in general have gotten their reputation of being insincere! We wonder what their true motives are. We wonder if they're just telling us what they think they want us to hear. Trying to sort out the real from the fake, or the sincere from the insincere is a big job. Wouldn't it be nice if we could really just take each person at his or her word? Unfortunately, I think the world has a long way to go in that area. But by understanding the need for sincerity, and practicing it ourselves, we're making a difference that in time will make a big impact. *-Lissa Coffey*

"The most exhausting thing in life, I have discovered, is being insincere."
-Anne Morrow Lindbergh, 1955

Being sincere is being true to yourself. It is hard work being anything less. It takes a lot more mind games and that can be exhausting. What a terrible waste of energy! Being sincere is being genuine, authentic - and that is the more comfortable way to go. *-Lissa Coffey*

"Sincerity is to speak as we think, to do as we pretend and profess, to perform what we promise, and really to be what we would seem and appear to be."
-John Tillotson (1630 -1694)

Remember when we first learned to write letters in school? There was a specific format that we had to follow, with the date, and the greeting and all that. And at the end, we learned to close the letter by writing "Sincerely" and then signing our names. I don't know if way back then we even understood what we were writing, except that it was what we were supposed to do. But now, as adults, we can look at that word and see the significance of closing a letter that way. It's like saying "I mean what I say" or "I am true to my word" - it lets the reader know that the writer knows the weight that the words carry. At least, I'm sure that is how it was intended all those years ago! Think about it the next time you sign a letter. "Sincerely" has meaning, it's not just a formality. *-Lissa Coffey*

"The shortest and surest way to live with honor in the world, is to be in reality what we would appear to be; all human virtues increase and strengthen themselves by the practice and experience of them."
-Socrates (469 - 399 B.C.)

In this kind of strange time in our society where so much is artificial and fake, sincerity is a big deal. I'll admit to watching some of the reality shows that are out now - especially the dating ones - ok, a guilty pleasure, what can I say? But we can learn even from some of those silly things on TV! Since these shows are basically a "game" - the contestants are constantly questioning people's sincerity. They wonder, is this person saying this, or doing this, because they mean it, or because they have a hidden agenda? I think we tend to be on our guards a lot of the time, and when we come across sincerity we find it attractive, and refreshing. *-Lissa Coffey*

Sleep

"Oh sleep! It is a gentle thing,
Beloved from pole to pole!"
-Samuel Taylor Coleridge (1772-1834)

It's morning, but do you feel like you want to go back to bed now? When we sleep well, we feel refreshed, and we can take on the day so much more enthusiastically. We all need sleep, it is a part of being alive! And we do enjoy it – the whole routine of going to bed, getting comfortable. This is a ritual we need to acknowledge and honor. We can prepare ourselves for the night's rest, rather than falling asleep in front of the TV. Take some time to settle in, calm down, and drift off gently and peacefully. Have you ever seen a cat sleep? Cats love their sleep – they relish it, they totally give in to it. *-Lissa Coffey*

"Sleep is that golden chain that ties health and our
bodies together."
-Thomas Dekker

Any doctor will tell you that sleep is an important aspect of our overall health. This is the time when we can really rest and heal. We go, go, go all day long – we put so much stress on our minds and bodies working all the time, and running around everywhere. When we sleep this is the only time we really don't expect ourselves to do anything! And this is the time that our bodies can do the work that it needs to do to keep us in top form. *-Lissa Coffey*

"Sleep is when all the unsorted stuff comes flying out
as from a dustbin upset in a high wind."
-William Golding

Ah! The dreams that we dream! Some outrageous fantasies – some bizarre, seemingly unrelated scenarios pieced together to resemble an unfinished puzzle by Salvador Dali. Just as the body needs rest to repair itself, the mind needs rest, too, and it works things out in our dreams. It doesn't have to make sense – somehow it registers and we figure out just what needs to be done. These little glimpses into our psyche can lead to great wisdom... or it could just be an evening's entertainment! *-Lissa Coffey*

"Of all the soft, delicious functions of nature this is
the chiefest; what a happiness it is to man, when the
anxieties and passions of the day are over."
-Laurence Sterne (1713-1768)

Sometimes it just feels like a big relief to finally crawl into bed at night. Knowing that the day is done, that we've done all we can do with the time that we had, we can sleep peacefully. Tomorrow is another day. The sun comes up in the morning and we begin again. But while we sleep, we can be still. It is a simple pleasure to close our eyes and tie the day up with a sigh. *-Lissa Coffey*

"I believe the greatest asset a head of state can have is the ability to get a good night's sleep."
-Harold Wilson

We could take this quote a couple of ways. When we sleep well, we are strong, and we make good decisions. And when we have done our best, and made what we feel are good decisions, we have a clear conscience, so we can get a good night sleep without having nagging thoughts keeping us up at night. This is true for anyone, not just a head of state. -*Lissa Coffey*

Solitude

"Solitude is as needful to the imagination as society is wholesome for the character."
-James Russell Lowell, Among My Books

Solitude, time spent alone, nourishes our soul. And yet, some of us associate time by ourselves with loneliness. Maybe it's that we're afraid of being bored, or that we're so used to having company that the silence seems awkward. Yet solitude is necessary for our spiritual growth. This is where we learn, this is where we receive those valuable insights. Make a date with yourself today – and spend some time in glorious solitude! -*Lissa Coffey*

"Solitude gives birth to the original in us, to beauty unfamiliar and perilous - to poetry. But also, it gives birth to the opposite: to the perverse, the illicit, the absurd."
-Thomas Mann, Death in Venice

To appreciate solitude we need space and time. We need space to be by ourselves and time to enjoy our own company. And from there we can experience silence, and go beyond space and time! Here there are infinite possibilities for us; here is where we find inspiration and creativity. Here there is peace, and joy, and bliss. -*Lissa Coffey*

"I have never found the companion that was so companionable as solitude."
-Henry David Thoreau, Walden

No one can know you as well as you know yourself. And yet, how well do you really know yourself? Are you your own best friend? Spend some time with yourself, just you, and pretty soon you'll discover just how wonderful you really are! -*Lissa Coffey*

"We're all of us sentenced to solitary confinement inside our own skins, for life!"
-Tennessee Williams, Orpheus Descending

There comes a time when we realize that there's no escaping it, we have to live with ourselves! How do we treat ourselves? Are we kind and loving, do we show appreciation and forgiveness? Too often we're our own worst critics! We're hard on ourselves when we really need a break once in awhile. Let's work on being the kind of person whom we want to be with – and spend some time being ourselves, by ourselves. -*Lissa Coffey*

> "The secret of solitude is that there is no solitude."
> -Joseph Cook, Conscience (1880)

So the secret is out! When we understand that we can never be "alone" because God is always with us, then we will never be lonely. We will cherish our solitude, and consider it time alone with God. -*Lissa Coffey*

Soul

> "The growth of the soul may be compared to the growth of a plant. In both cases, no new properties are imparted by the operation of external causes, but only the inward tendencies are called into action and clothed with strength."
> -George Ripley (1802-1880)

Oftentimes when we talk about spiritual growth we compare it with the growth of a plant – planting the seed, allowing it space and time to grow with its own innate intelligence. We use this example because we understand how the growth of a plant "works." We've seen seedlings sprout, we've had potatoes take root in glasses of water in our fifth grade science classes. And we need this kind of illustration because spiritual growth is not something we necessarily "see." It is an internal phenomenon, something we feel, something we experience, something that goes beyond words or pictures. -*Lissa Coffey*

> "The soul of man ... is a portion or a copy of the soul of the Universe and is joined together on principles and in proportions corresponding to those which govern the Universe."
> -Plutarch (AD 46?-119?)

Any attempt to define the soul inevitably brings with it a connection with the Universe. So it follows that each soul, while connected to the Universe, is also connected with each other soul – by association, if nothing else! We're more than family, we are all One. -*Lissa Coffey*

> "All religion, all life, all art, all expression come down to this: to the effort of the human soul to break through its barrier of loneliness, of intolerable loneliness, and make some contact with another seeking soul, or with what all souls seek, which is (by any name) God."
> -Don Marquis (1878-1937)

Yes! Our connection with one another is there, and we are seeking to experience it. And by experiencing our connection with one another, we can experience our connection with God. God expresses through each one of us. Do we notice? Are we listening? Each person we come into contact with has something for us, some piece of the puzzle large or small. We are searching for ourselves, so why don't we make it easier and stop hiding from ourselves? *-Lissa Coffey*

"The soul of man is immortal and imperishable."
-Plato (427-347 B.C.)

The physical world is temporary and transient. It is ever changing. What is true and constant and utterly reliable is that God is ever-present. And our connection with that Source remains even when the physical fades away. *-Lissa Coffey*

"The soul unfolds itself like a lotus of countless petals."
-Kahlil Gibran (1883-1931)

Our spiritual growth is such a beautiful thing. We bloom into ourselves and extend loveliness and sweetness out into the world. Like the lotus, we become more soft and gentle as we unfold into more of who we are– and we also become more "layered" in our experiences and challenges. *-Lissa Coffey*

Speech

"Think all you speak, but speak not all you think. Thoughts are your own; your words are so no more."
-Patrick Delany (1686-1768)

Our words come from us, and go out into the world. Once they are said, we can't take them back. Remember when we were little, our mother's used to say: "If you can't say something nice, don't say anything at all." If we speak impulsively, we may come to regret it. Our words carry weight, and when we think about what we are going to say, we can make better choices about how to say it so that it is received in the best possible light. *-Lissa Coffey*

"Speech is silvern, silence is golden; speech is human, silence is divine."
-German Proverb

Sometimes we can't help ourselves, we go on and on thinking we need to fill the empty spaces with words. But the truth is that a lot of communication happens in the silence. We relate to each other on a whole different level when we have time to just "be" with each other. Silence invites God to be a part of the conversation. *-Lissa Coffey*

> **"Let us say what we feel, and feel what we say; let speech harmonize with life."**
> -Seneca the Younger (5? B.C. – A.D. 65)

One way that we can be true to ourselves is with our speech. Are we saying what we mean? Are we meaning what we say? When we are in harmony with our words and our actions, we are in harmony with life. It takes too much time and energy to say things just because we are "supposed to." It has to feel right, it has to resonate within us, for it to be real. *-Lissa Coffey*

> **"Speech is a mirror of the soul; as a man speaks, so is he."**
> -Publius Syrus (85-43 B.D.)

I think this is really quite interesting. The words we speak come from within us. We think them, we articulate them. They come up with our breath, through our throats and over our tongues. They have an impact on us. It is important to speak truthfully, kindly, and with clarity. Are the words we use "nutritious" – or are they "toxic?" What are we feeding ourselves? *-Lissa Coffey*

> **"Violence of the tongue is very real – sharper than any knife."**
> -Mother Teresa, 1983

We used to hear "sticks and stones may break my bones, but words can never harm me." Well, forget about that one! Words can hurt – terribly! And it's okay to admit it. The good news is that words can also heal. Think about how good if feels to hear "I love you." Look at the way a person's face lights up when you say "You look so beautiful!" The world needs to stop using words as weapons, and work more on using words as medicine. *-Lissa Coffey*

Spirituality

> **"The spiritual quest begins, for most people, as a search for meaning."**
> -Marilyn Ferguson, The Aquarian Conspiracy, 1980

We talk a lot about spiritual growth, but lets look a little deeper into what that really means to us. I think it's true that most of us found ourselves on a spiritual path because we were looking for "more," because we instinctively knew that there was something beyond the material world that could sustain us, nourish us, and fill our hearts. And perhaps all of our questions aren't answered, but we catch glimpses of profound peace, and joy, and that keeps us going. Each day is new, each day we learn and grow and bask in the glow of spirit. *-Lissa Coffey*

"Peace is a necessary condition of spirituality, no less
than an inevitable result of it."
-Aldous Huxley (1894-1963)

Peace is reason enough for each of us to pursue our spirituality, and to encourage and support others who wish to do so, also. We experience inner peace through prayer, meditation, and spiritual activity. And that peace radiates outwards to affect our homes and communities. The more of us who live spiritually, the more peace there will be in the world! *-Lissa Coffey*

"Nothing in all nature is so lovely and so vigorous, so
perfectly at home in its environment, as a fish in the
sea. Its surroundings give to it a beauty, quality, and
power which is not its own. We take it out, and at
once a poor, limp dull thing, fit for nothing, is gasping
away its life. So the soul, sunk in God, living the life of
prayer, is supported, filled, transformed in beauty, by
a vitality and a power which are not its own."
-Evelyn Underhill, The Golden Sequence (1932)

We are spiritual beings, and in this human existence, where we encounter conflict and stress, we often feel like a fish out of water. We must immerse ourselves in our spirituality, and let it be our home. We find solace in our spiritual practices, whatever they are for each one of us. And then we can bring that good energy into all aspects of our lives, so that feeling of spirit is always with us. *-Lissa Coffey*

"Although I try
to hold the single thought
of Buddha's teaching in my heart,
I cannot help but hear
the many crickets' voices calling as well."
-Izumi Shikibu (c 1000)

Sometimes following our spiritual practices can be a challenge because we are so distracted by the demands of everyday life. This is true for everyone – there never seems to be enough time, or enough quiet, to set aside for prayer, meditation, or contemplation. It is so worth it when we do! And yet, spirituality does not have to be a separate experience from the rest of our lives. We can choose to hear the beautiful song of the crickets' voices as a gift from God. We can choose to express gratitude for the full and exciting lives we lead, however busy we may be! *-Lissa Coffey*

"We cannot take a single step toward heaven. It is not
in our power to travel in a vertical direction. If however we look heavenward for a long time, God comes and
takes us up."
-Simone Weil, Waiting for God, 1950

Spirituality takes less effort than we think. We don't have to try and try – we just have to commit to it, recognize it, embrace it! It's all about connecting with God, and knowing that God is the One really doing all the "work." *-Lissa Coffey*

Study

"No matter how occupied a man may be, he must
snatch at least one hour for study daily."
-The Bratzlaver (1770-1811)

This is good advice. Meditation might be called a form of study. It's allowing the wisdom of the universe to come to us. We can also read, or write, or take classes, or talk with wise people. Study can be pleasurable, it doesn't have to be a chore, like doing homework! Somehow everything we learn helps us to grow. -*Lissa Coffey*

"Study the teachings of the Great Sages of all
sects impartially."
-Gampopa (A.D. 12th cent.)

All of the Great Sages would say the same thing. Would a Sage be a Sage if he or she said: "I know everything, look no further"? No! We'd laugh! The brightest, most intelligent people know that there is always more to learn. They know that there is always knowledge to share. And they know that wisdom can be found anywhere, that there is not one particular place that we need to go to attain it. "Impartially" is a great word – without judgment, without bias – and with an open mind. -*Lissa Coffey*

"Just as eating contrary to the inclination is injurious
to the health, so study without desire spoils the
memory, and it retains nothing that it takes in."
-Leonardo da Vinci (1452-1519)

A computer is impartial. It will save and store anything, and we can retrieve it from the computer just as we put it in there. But our minds don't work that way. If something doesn't matter to us, if it has no relevance to anything in our lives, then there is no reason for us to remember it, and we usually don't. But when we choose to study something that is important to us, when we have that desire, then what we learn becomes a part of who we are. We make room for the memory in our mind, and we use the information in context with what we already know. -*Lissa Coffey*

"The great business of study is for a mind adapted
and adequate to all times and all occasions; to which
all nature is then laid open, and which may be said to
possess the key of her inexhaustible riches."
-Sir Joshua Reynolds (1723-1792)

Study is exercise for the mind. And what happens, is that just like when we exercise our body and we discover how strong we are, when we exercise our mind we discover how wise we are! The muscles were there all the time, but when we work them, and pay attention to their development, they serve us by being able to lift weights, or hike a mountain, or run a marathon. And our mind is there for us to use the same way.

We can be creative, we can be problem-solvers, we can be wise. Our strength, both in body and mind, comes from within. *-Lissa Coffey*

"Every great study is not only an end in itself, but also a means of creating and sustaining a lofty habit of mind."
-Bertrand Russell (1872-1970)

It seems like we are studying all the time. We have aspirations for spiritual growth, so we soak up all the wisdom that comes our way, and we seek out wisdom as we go. And yes, we learn from all of these sources. And one of the great things that we learn is that the process of study itself is good for us, and makes us more wise ourselves. So we want to do more, and it becomes a good habit! *-Lissa Coffey*

Style

"To me style is just the outside of content, and content the inside of style, like the outside and inside of the human body – both go together, they can't be separated."
-Jean Luc Godard

In this quote Jean Luc Godard is talking about writing style in particular, but it can really be applied to any kind of style. We always hear: "You can't judge a book by its cover" and yet, it happens all the time! Even if we don't "judge" a book, or a person, by appearance, experience tells us that certain expectations have been set up for us. What does this mean to us spiritually? We understand that mind and body, inside and outside, are intricately linked. We need to take care of both. Our style reflects the person we are, it's what the world experiences of us. The way we present ourselves is the way we see ourselves. *-Lissa Coffey*

"Style is the garb of thought."
-Seneca the Younger (5? B.C. – A.D. 65)

What we say, the content, is important, and the way we say it, the style, is important, too. I saw a television movie about the life of Mother Teresa and one scene really stuck with me. Of course, her whole life was beautiful, and everything about her was beautiful. But we don't really associate Mother Teresa as someone who was concerned with style. Ah, quite the contrary! She knew that her appearance was going to make an impression on the people she served. She chose her habit very carefully. She did not want it to be too fancy, or bright, and she didn't want it to be too plain, or drab. She went through several different designs before choosing the one that she felt was just right. And when she found that one, she stuck with it. She didn't have to think about it anymore. This was a woman of style. She knew what was right for the occasion and she got just what she wanted. *-Lissa Coffey*

"The style is the man himself."
-George-Louis de Buffon (1707-1788)

This quote is talking about writing style. He is saying that the style in which a person writes is how his personality shines through. Look at how many times, and how many ways, we have heard the same spiritual lessons. There are so many good spiritual teachers out there, with books and videos and classes and ministries. And yet they're really essentially all saying the same thing when it comes down to it! But we each respond differently because we have different styles of our own, and different styles resonate with us in different ways. Said with a certain style we hear the messages better, understand them more, relate to them more personally. *-Lissa Coffey*

"Styles, like everything else, change. Style doesn't."
Linda Ellerbee, 1991

There are so many different fashion trends and fads – they come and go as quickly as the magazines appear and disappear on the newsstands! We couldn't possibly follow each one. And we wouldn't want to! At a certain point in our lives, we find that all this is fun to observe, but we have to develop our own sense of style. We have to refer to ourselves to know what we like and don't like, what works for us and what doesn't. Being confident is always in style. *-Lissa Coffey*

"Fashion is general; style is individual."
-Edna Wolman Chase and Ilka Chase, 1954

We have choices all the time, and fashion is just one of them. The choices we make help to define our style. It's interesting to think about the Dalai Lama in terms of style. He wears the traditional garb of a Buddhist monk, like many other Buddhist monks do. And yet, somehow just the way he smiles, or carries himself, or speaks, defines the Dalai Lama's style. His clothes have very little to do with it! Style is much more than what we wear; it's our attitude. *-Lissa Coffey*

Success

"Self-trust is the first secret of success"
-Ralph Waldo Emerson

Since this is the time of year that many people are graduating from school, or just finishing up the school year before summer break, I thought we'd look at "success" and see how that relates to our spiritual growth.

Everyone seems to have a different definition of success. It means so many things, and each one of us relates to the word in our own way. For some, success might mean the attainment of goals. For others it might be fame or fortune. However you describe it, success, like spiritual growth, is an ongoing process. It is more a journey than a destination. *-Lissa Coffey*

"If a man wants his dreams to come true, he must wake up."
-Anonymous

Dreams might come to us, but success is something we must go after. Inspiration strikes, then it's up to us to take action. We could buy all the great works of literature, but it we don't actually read them, what is the point? If we feel that success is eluding us, then now is the time to evaluate our activities. *-Lissa Coffey*

"I am not the smartest or most talented person in the world, but I succeeded because I keep going, and going, and going."
-Sylvester Stallone

There is a lot to be said for persistence and perseverance. How much drive and enthusiasm have we put into our efforts? When we pursue something "whole-heartedly" then we simply can't give up. When we invest our Selves into our plans, we can't help but succeed! *-Lissa Coffey*

"Success is peace of mind, which is a direct result of knowing you did your best to become the best that you are capable of becoming."
-John Wooden

With this definition, it doesn't matter what industry you work in, or how much money you make. It doesn't matter where you grew up or who you know. This says that success is all a matter of our own efforts, and how we see how we are doing. And it leaves room to say that we are "becoming" – which is great, because we are all changing, and growing, and succeeding every day, every minute! *-Lissa Coffey*

"Life is a succession of moments. To live each one is to succeed."
-Corita Kent

Present-moment awareness. Being awake and aware and alive to the beauty and abundance in and around us at all times. Wow. How could that be anything less than success? *-Lissa Coffey*

Talent

> **"We can't take any credit for our talents. It's how we use them that counts."**
> -Madeleine L'Engle (1962)

Talent. Are we born with it, or do we develop it – or is it a little bit of both? This is an interesting theme for the discussion board, and I'd love to hear what you have to say about it. I think skill is something that is developed. Talent is another matter. Perhaps we are born with certain gifts, certain aptitudes that come more easily for us. But those gifts must be nurtured, and honed, if we are to use them well. *-Lissa Coffey*

> **"Talent is like electricity. Electricity makes no judgment. You can plug into it and light up a lamp, keep a heart pump going, light a cathedral, or you can electrocute a person with it. Electricity will do all that. It makes no judgment. I think talent is like that. I believe every person is born with talent."**
> -Maya Angelou, 1983

Every person is born with talent, talents that are unique to that individual. When we can figure out what our talents are we can use them for our own growth, and to make the world a better place. This journey is about self-discovery, and discovering our talents is a big part of that. *-Lissa Coffey*

> **"Patience is an integral part of talent."**
> -Vicki Baum, 1964

The old line about "How do you get to Carnegie Hall? Practice, practice practice" holds a lot of truth to it. Talent alone is not as valuable to us as talent with practice, and patience, and persistence. The three P's. *-Lissa Coffey*

> **"The only thing that happens overnight is recognition. Not talent."**
> -Carol Haney, 1957

We often see these people who just come onto the scene seemingly out of nowhere. But when we look further we find that they have been working on their talent without that recognition for a long, long time. When you really love to do something, you do it for the love of it, the joy of it, not for the recognition. And when the recognition comes it's like frosting on the cake – an added sweetness to the substance that was already there. *-Lissa Coffey*

> **"Talent develops in quiet places, character in the full current of human life."**
> -Goethe (1749-1832)

So much of the time when we're working on our talent we're all by ourselves. It's just us and the computer, or the canvas, or the kitchen, or whatever tools we need at hand. That takes a lot of diligence, and self discipline. But at the same time we need balance in our lives. We are not alone in this world, as much as it may feel like it at times! We need to get out there and socialize, and connect, and share our talents with other people. -*Lissa Coffey*

Teachers

> **"It is the supreme art of the teacher to awaken joy in creative expression and knowledge."**
> -Albert Einstein (1879-1955)

We can all look back and remember some of our most favorite teachers over the years. And chances are, what made them so memorable to us is not the subjects that they taught, as much as the way they taught. I still remember Dr. Herriot in 10th grade math. She knew I was slacking off and she challenged me to do better. I was so surprised that someone actually called me on it, and decided to give it a shot. Dr. Herriot handed the next test back to me with a big smile on her face - I got an A. It felt great for me to see that grade, and that smile! She helped me to understand that when I put my mind and my efforts into something, I can achieve. That's a good teacher. -*Lissa Coffey*

> **"The teacher is no longer merely the-one-who-teaches, but one who is himself taught in dialogue with the students, who in turn while being taught also teach."**
> -Paulo Freire (1921-1997)

It is true that one of the best ways to learn is to teach. It gives us a better understanding of the material from the ground up. If we can take something complicated and distill it down so that someone else can learn it, we are mastering the concept ourselves. In addition, in the role of teacher, we are asked questions - questions we might never have thought of on our own. In finding the answers, we learn more about the concept, and about ourselves. So the students become the teachers as well. We are all teachers, just as we are all students. -*Lissa Coffey*

> **"When the National Science Foundation asked the "breakthrough" scientists what they felt was the most favorable factor in their education, the answer was almost uniformly, "Intimate association with a great, inspiring teacher.""**
> -R. Buckminster Fuller (1895-1983)

I think we all need some sort of a mentor, or a role model, or an inspiring teacher in our lives. We may have one, or we may be fortunate enough to have several. Great teachers can give us more than we can get from books or history lessons. When we form a personal connection with a teacher, we also learn from that teacher's life experiences. It is meaningful to us because we understand that the teacher is invested in our learning, he or she cares. That inspires us. -*Lissa Coffey*

"No man can reveal to you aught but that which already lies half asleep in the dawning of your knowledge. The teacher who walks in the shadow of the temple, among his followers, gives not of his wisdom but rather of his faith and his lovingness. If he is indeed wise he does not bid you enter the house of his wisdom, but rather leads you to the threshold of your own mind."
-Kahlil Gibran (1883-1931)

All of the knowledge and wisdom of the world is available to us at all times. We have only to tap into it to make use of it. The truth is that we don't need anyone to tell us anything! But... until we can fully make use of our gifts, we could use someone to show us the way. Life is hard enough trying to make it on our own. Thanks goodness that we have teachers to guide us and give us some direction. -*Lissa Coffey*

"An understanding heart is everything in a teacher... One looks back with appreciation to the brilliant teachers, but with gratitude to those who touched our human feelings. The curriculum is so much necessary raw material, but warmth is the vital element for the growing plant and for the soul of the child."
-Carl G. Jung (1875-1961)

We have teachers all throughout our lives. I can remember just a handful of the ones I had while I was in school, and that is because I knew that they cared about me. As an adult, I studied at The Healing Arts Center, and my teacher there was Louise Taylor. I am so grateful to Louise for sharing so much of her knowledge and wisdom with me. And she taught me, and all of her students, by example as much as by her classes. Louise is a wonderful, caring, compassionate mother, friend, and businesswoman. She radiates integrity, creativity and love. Those are qualities of a good teacher! -*Lissa Coffey*

The present

"The secret of health for both mind and body is not to mourn for the past, nor to worry about the future, but to live the present moment wisely and earnestly."
-Buddha (563-483 B.C.)

"Live the present moment." It sounds so simple, doesn't it? Yet we seem to have a very difficult time doing that, indeed! Right now, right where you are, focus on this moment, and this moment alone. Experience the wholeness of it, the completeness of it. When we are in present moment awareness, we are not worried, we are not stressed – we simple ARE. -*Lissa Coffey*

> "Stay present. You'll always have time to worry later
> on if you want to."
> -Dan Millman

Do we worry because we want to? If everything is a choice, and it is, then why would we choose to worry? When we stay present, we can't be worried, because this moment is all there is. One moment at a time, we allow ourselves to see the perfection of the Universe, in all its glory! The present moment is where we are, it's where we find out who we really are. -*Lissa Coffey*

> "For you, the world is weird because if you're not
> bored with it you're at odds with it. For me the world
> is weird because it is stupendous, awesome, mysterious,
> unfathomable. I want to convince you that you must
> learn to make every act count, since you are going to
> be here for only a short while; in fact, too short for
> witnessing all the marvels of it."
> -Don Juan (Carlos Castaneda)

That's the kind of world I want to live in, one that is "stupendous, awesome, mysterious and unfathomable!" Imagine having that on a travel brochure? We'd all want to go to a place like that! And here we are! Do we recognize it, do we experience it every day? Do we make every act count? Every moment count? This is our world, this is our moment. Embrace it! -*Lissa Coffey*

> "On Arturo Toscanini's eightieth birthday, someone
> asked his son, Walter, what his father ranked as his most
> important achievement. The son replied, "For him there
> can be no such thing. Whatever he happens to be doing
> at the moment is the biggest thing in his life – whether it
> is conducting a symphony or peeling an orange."
> -Ardis Whitman

When we live in present moment awareness we're living with heightened senses. We're awake to the many miracles all around us, all the time. We can find joy in peeling an orange: filling our nostrils with the sweet and tangy fragrance, feasting our eyes on the brilliant fiery color, coating our fingers with the sticky and succulent juice. The orange is a gift, and we are blessed. When we are grateful, we are in the moment, and life is good! -*Lissa Coffey*

> "Every moment is a golden one for him who has the
> vision to recognize it as such."
> -Henry Miller (1891-1980)

How many golden moments have gone by while we were worrying about the future or fretting about the past? If these moments were our nourishment, how well fed would we be? Now is the time, this is the moment, to begin living in present moment awareness. Before we starve ourselves, let us partake of each moment as if it were a divine delicacy, because that is exactly what it is! -*Lissa Coffey*

Thinking

"In this world, if a man sits down to think, he is immediately asked if he has the headache."
-Ralph Waldo Emerson (1803-1882)

A little bit of humor from Emerson, a favorite of mine! His point is that we are so much on "auto pilot" that we rarely take time out just to think. There is a lot of busy-ness, or business, going on, all the time, and we tend to jump right from one thing to the next with barely a breath in between. How rare, and yet, how wonderful, to take a moment, or two, or twenty, to just sit and think. -*Lissa Coffey*

"A man is but the product of his thoughts; what he thinks, he becomes."
-Mohandas K. Gandhi (1869-1948)

Do we think "good" thoughts? Or do we worry, and stress, and speculate? When we hold in mind where we want to go, we get there. Our mind finds ways to overcome the obstacles and make our thoughts, or our visions, a reality. We can elevate ourselves with our thinking. -*Lissa Coffey*

"Right living is a way to right thinking."
-Abraham Joshua Heschel (1907-1972)

It all works together. Just like diet and exercise – we need both to stay in shape! How we live and how we think are intricately linked. Are we living the life we want to live; are we thinking the thoughts we want to think? "The good life" to me is living in integrity, in love, in balance. Thinking thoughts that encourage those things helps to strengthen them in our lives. The diet is our thoughts; the exercise is our actions. -*Lissa Coffey*

"Few people think more than two or three times a year; I have made an international reputation for myself by thinking once or twice a week."
-George Bernard Shaw (1856-1950)

Shaw was a prolific writer, and so funny! He shows us how to laugh at ourselves. It is truly amazing what we can do when we put our minds to it. Whether it is writing plays like Shaw, or theory like Einstein, or music like Mozart – there are examples of brilliant ways to use our minds to create, and to change, the world. -*Lissa Coffey*

> "To have ideas is to gather flowers. To think is to
> weave them into garlands."
> -Anne-Sophie Swetchine, 1869

I love this! We gather ideas all the time, yet if we do nothing with them, they whither and die like flowers do over time. But if we take the time to do something with them, something creative, organized, and original – then we are taking our ideas to a new level, where they live on and bring extended benefits to the world! It's the "what if" the "how" and the "why" that gets our juices flowing. -*Lissa Coffey*

Thoughts

> "The game of life is the game of boomerangs. Our
> thoughts, deeds and words return to us sooner or
> later, with astounding accuracy."
> -Florence Scovel Shinn

We've heard it time and time again, in a million different ways: we reap what we sow. When we plant apple seeds, we get apples. When we plant broccoli seeds, we get broccoli. It's the law of nature and we all understand it! Now we need to take it to the level where we understand that when we plant seeds of encouragement, that's what we receive in return. When we spread happiness, we get happiness back. When we give love, we get love. There's no mystery to it, that's just the way it is! -*Lissa Coffey*

> "As a man thinketh in his heart, so is he."
> -Proverbs 23:7

Even way back when the bible was written people were talking about the heart's intelligence. What do we KNOW in our heart? What conviction do we carry with us? It is important to recognize these thoughts, because they make up how we are, and who we think we are. -*Lissa Coffey*

> "All that we are is the result of what we have thought.
> The mind is everything. What we think, we become."
> -Buddha (563 - 483 B.C.)

Our thoughts direct our lives. The path we are on begins in our heart and in our mind. Each step we take moves us toward our greater purpose if that is where we want to go. We can become the person we want to be, the person we know that we truly are. -*Lissa Coffey*

> "When you rule your mind you rule your world. When
> you choose your thoughts you choose results."
> -Imelda Shanklin

Our minds are so constantly busy that we often forget that we actually have a choice in the matter. We can choose our thoughts! And by choosing our thoughts, we are choosing our experiences and creating our futures. And we need to remember that our reactions are thoughts, also. Instead of letting our emotions ride on auto-pilot, we can choose to take a breath and take inventory rather than giving in to an impulsive reaction. In this way, our thoughts can lead us in a much more productive direction, one that creates solutions rather than problems. *-Lissa Coffey*

"The happiness of your life depends upon the quality of your thoughts."
-Marcus Antonius (A.D. 86-161)

How often do we think about the QUALITY of our thoughts? We obviously have an abundant quantity of thoughts – but how many of those are thoughts of absolute quality? Which thoughts are like little gemstones that we want to treasure and save, to bring out again and again to wear with pleasure? Maybe it's time to do some mental housekeeping. All those old, dusty, dinghy, non-productive thoughts that just end up making us feel bad - throw them out! They are no longer useful to us! Now, replace those old thoughts with new, efficient, beautifully clear thoughts. And watch how our outside lives begin to reflect the shiny new thinking that is going on inside.
-Lissa Coffey

Time

"If we take care of the moments, the years will take care of themselves."
-Maria Edgeworth (1801)

We don't need to plan too far ahead, sometimes it's better to go with the flow. If we are living in the now, doing good work and making good use of our time, everything is going to unfold exactly as it is meant to. It's the same thing as "you reap what you sow." Invest minutes and reap hours – Sow kindness, love and compassion and reap those rewards - an abundant harvest awaits! *-Lissa Coffey*

"Time and space are only forms of thought."
-Edith Nesbitt

"Measure, time and number are nothing but modes of thought or rather of imagination."
-Benedict Spinoza

Whether analog or digital, clocks and watches are man-made inventions. We follow along, agreeing to the certain standard measurements of time, when it is really only a perception of what has transpired. When we understand that there is no such thing as time, we will stop running out of it. We have all the time we need. Just as we have all we need in every area of our live, if we'd only recognize it! *-Lissa Coffey*

> **"I grew up in a gentler, slower time. When Ike was president, Christmases were years apart, and now it's about five months from one to the next."**
> -Garrison Keillor

There is so much truth in this... I've been getting Christmas catalogs in the mail since August! Our society has gotten so retail oriented, so marketing savvy, that we're always months ahead of ourselves. Whether it's holiday sales, or movie previews, or upcoming specials, we've been trained to think ahead or be left behind. So we can't really enjoy the moment we're in because we're too busy planning for the time that's yet to come. How sad. But we can do something about it! Resolve to live in the now. Experience this moment of time fully. Now is the only time there is. *-Lissa Coffey*

> **"As every thread of gold is valuable, so is every moment of time."**
> -John Mason (1706-1773)

Some might joke that John Mason was a lawyer, but he was actually part of the clergy. Lawyers tend to bill by the fraction of the hour, and literally, their time is money. If you think about time that way, you get a different perspective. Every moment that we spend here on earth is precious. Not so much for the money that we can make, but for the lessons and experiences that we go through which help us to grow. It is important to be respectful of people and their time, to arrive promptly for meetings and not keep someone waiting. This is just part of being a responsible spiritual citizen. And, if we are the ones who are kept waiting, we know that we can use that time and not waste it. We can take a few moments to notice things, to breathe, to feel gratitude. No moment is ever wasted when we are living in the now. *-Lissa Coffey*

> **"There is a time to be born, and a time to die, says Solomon, and it is the memento of a truly wise man; but there is an interval between these two times of infinite importance."**
> Leigh Richmond (1772-1827)

How do we live our lives? How do we spend our time? Are we learning and growing, serving and loving? We are given this magnificent gift of time, and how we use it is up to us individually. We're making choices constantly. Choose wisely, with intention. *-Lissa Coffey*

Transformation

> **"The sacred call is transformative. It is an invitation to our souls, a mysterious voice reverberating within, a tug on our hearts that can neither be ignored nor denied. It contains, by definition, the purest message and promise of essential freedom. It touches us at the center of our awareness. When such a call occurs and we hear it - really hear it - our shift to higher consciousness is assured."**
> -David A. Cooper, 1994

In this passage, David Cooper writes about the shofar, the ram's horn sounded in synagogue services during the Ten Days of Penitence. But there are a lot of different ways that 'the sacred call' may be expressed. The fact that we are pursuing our spiritual growth, that we are allowing ourselves to be more of who we really are, shows that we have heard that call! We know that life has meaning, and we are transforming our own lives to reflect that. *-Lissa Coffey*

"Transformation means replacing old values with new ones in the evolution of conscious life."
-Kazimierz Dabrowski, 1964

Things change. That's for sure! 'Things' change – and times change... but spirit remains the same. And our values, as we come to a higher consciousness, must necessarily change as we experience this. That's evolution. We're getting better as we grow! *-Lissa Coffey*

"You don't go through a deep personal transformation without some kind of a dark night of the soul."
-Sam Keen

Heavy, dark experiences change us. They shake us to our core and cause us to re-evaluate our lives and our values. So, it is understandable that a transformation can come out of that. And sometimes it works the other way around. Sometimes a transformation occurs – maybe we've been working on it for a long time but then suddenly there's a shift – and we need some time and space to assimilate it into our consciousness. We need to see how we can fit our new selves back into our old lives. It can feel like a dark night of the soul – but it's only temporary. The light shines through. *-Lissa Coffey*

"Any transformation of one person invites accommodating transformations in others."
-R.D. Laing (1927-1989)

We're all connected. There is a unity that can't be denied. When one person changes, it can dramatically affect those around him or her, causing more changes, more transformation. Our lives impact each other; we can't help it! So, let's make it work for the good of all of us. *-Lissa Coffey*

"An underlying urge to self-transformation possibly lies at the basis of all existence, finding expression in the process of growth, development, renewal, directed change, perfection."
-Lewis Mumford (1895-1990)

We are wired to grow and improve and to experience more of our true selves. This is something we crave! It is our instinct, and it leads us towards transformation. *-Lissa Coffey*

Travel

> **"The traveler was active; he went strenuously in search of people, of adventure, or experience. The tourist is passive; he expects interesting things to happen to him. He goes "sightseeing.""**
> -Daniel J. Boorstin

Without even going anywhere, we can live like a traveler, or live like a tourist. I like the idea of getting out there and having an adventure, setting out to discover new people, places, and things. That sounds more fun to me than looking out the window at things going by, just happening without any actual involvement. We can plan our days with the same enthusiasm that we do when we are traveling - finding interesting things to see and do, and new people to meet, any time we want to! *-Lissa Coffey*

> **"Why do you wonder that globe-trotting does not help you, seeing that you always take yourself with you? The reason which set you wandering is ever at your heels."**
> -Socrates (470? - 399 B.C.)

Even Socrates was saying, way back when, that we can't run away from our problems, we can't run away from ourselves! We may end up in totally different surroundings, but we don't change just because the scenery has changed. Travel doesn't change us, we change ourselves because we choose to do so, by facing our issues and dealing with them. Travel can help us to learn and grow, and we can choose to take that "new and improved" version of ourselves with us. *-Lissa Coffey*

> **"This is what holidays, travels, vacations are about. It is not really rest or even leisure we chase. We strain to renew our capacity for wonder, to shock ourselves into astonishment once again."**
> -Shana Alexander, 1967

One of the benefits of travel is that it gets us out of our routines. It stretches us to try new things, to expand our horizons. It allows us to experience the world first hand, rather than from the comfort of our homes watching the Discovery Channel. Sometimes it's good to get out of that comfort-zone, to challenge ourselves, to wake ourselves up! *-Lissa Coffey*

> **"To me travel is a triple delight: anticipation, performance, and recollection."**
> -Ilka Chase, 1961

Travel is something that sticks with us. We look forward to, and plan the trip, learning about where we're going and how to get there. And then just being there - soaking up all there is in unfamiliar surroundings, exploring new territory. It excites our senses! And most importantly, there are the memories we bring home with us, which we can revisit at any time. *-Lissa Coffey*

"Through travel I first became aware of the outside
world; it was through travel that I found my own
introspective way into becoming a part of it."
-Eudora Welty, 1984

I know that some people have always had that kind of wanderlust, a curiosity that compels them to go out and see the world. When I was younger I felt I had all I could handle right here at home, I didn't have any burning desire to go someplace else. But now I feel differently. I have traveled a little bit and "caught the bug" I guess! Travel is just so eye-opening, so revealing. And it's not just in discovering different places and cultures, it's about how much we can discover about ourselves just by being in a different environment. -*Lissa Coffey*

Trees

"Every time I meet a tree, if I am truly awake, I stand
in awe before it. I listen to its voice, a silent sermon
moving me to the depths, touching my heart, and
stirring up within my soul a yearning to give my all."
-Macrina Wiederkehr, A Tree Full of Angels (1988)

I can pretty safely guess that we've all seen a tree or two in our time. But can we say we've actually met a tree? Trees are incredibly beautiful living beings. We can learn so much from their inherent wisdom. My teacher, Louise Taylor, taught me that spirituality is like the trunk of a tree. From there strong branches can grow, our career, health, relationships and everything else. But if we get caught out on a limb, we become off balance. Our spirituality is our strength, our core. -*Lissa Coffey*

"She had so deep a kinship with the trees, so intuitive
a sympathy with leaf and flower, that it seemed as if
the blood in her veins was not slow-moving human
blood, but volatile sap."
-Mary Webb, Gone to Earth (1917)

Some people have this innate connection with the plant world. I guess those would be the same people who have "green thumbs." There is a definite communication that goes on between plants and animals, whether we are aware of it or not. We can find peace in nature. We can find ourselves in that peace. -*Lissa Coffey*

"I like trees because they seem more resigned to the
way they have to live than other things do."
-Willa Cather, O Pioneers! (1913)

Trees are patient. They are resilient. They don't try to be something they're not. They don't get jealous of faster growing varieties. They bloom where they are planted, and make the best of it. They don't make any demands. There is a children's book called "The Giving

Tree" which really explains generosity. Freddy got this book from his aunt when he was little and it was always one of his favorites. We can learn a lot from trees. -*Lissa Coffey*

"When you look up from your typewriter, look at the trees, not the calendar."
-Mary Virginia Micka, The Cazenovia Journal (1990)

That's good advice for all of us these days! We're on the computer so much. When we get a moment's break, what do we do? If we can just take some time to re-connect with nature, to remember the beauty that surrounds us, we will be so much more natural and relaxed. There is a tree right outside my office window. It looks so calm, and it makes me feel calm to just sit and look out the window for awhile. -*Lissa Coffey*

"Trees are the lungs of the earth. Just as we breathe oxygen into our lungs and exhale carbon dioxide, so trees breathe carbon dioxide into their leaves and exhale oxygen."
-Helen Caldicott, If You Love this Planet (1992)

Reciprocity. There is a science to it. We're here for a reason. Trees are here for a reason. We can learn from each other, grow with each other, help each other breathe! -*Lissa Coffey*

Trust

"Self-trust, we know, is the first secret of success."
-Lady Wilde (1891)

That's the lesson we learn over and over again. It all comes back to the self. We must trust ourselves. We must trust our instincts. We must trust our connection with the universe enough to take the steps necessary to make progress in the direction of our success. -*Lissa Coffey*

"Trust one who has gone through it."
-Virgil (70-19 B.C.)

Experience speaks loudly. When we seek advice, don't we trust someone who has had experience with a subject more than one who merely has an opinion? Experience educates a person in such a way that when that person shares the experience, they can help us to learn, too. -*Lissa Coffey*

"Trust, which is a virtue, is also a habit, like prayer. It requires exercise. And just as no one can run five miles a day and cede the cardiovascular effects to someone else, no one can trust for us."
-Sue Halpern (1993)

Trust. It's a little one syllable word that carries with it a lot of meaning, and responsibility. And it's really different for each one of us. Some people trust easily, others are more cautious. Why is this? Trust seems to be a learned behavior. If we've had good experiences with it, then trust comes more readily. If we've been burned then we might hesitate to trust. On our American money it says "In God We Trust." That's a good place to start. *-Lissa Coffey*

"Those who trust us, educate us."
-George Eliot, 1874

We learn that to be worthy of trust, or trustworthy, is a good feeling. It's an honor, really, to have earned someone's trust. We experience the responsibility that comes with that trust, and we fulfill it, because trust is something we know that we can lose as well as gain. *-Lissa Coffey*

"The soul and spirit that animates and keeps up society is mutual trust."
-Robert South (1634-1716)

As human beings we really do rely on each other. There are many situations where we have no choice but to trust each other. When we drive on the freeway, for example, we trust that each driver will adhere to the traffic laws and do his or her best to avoid an accident. We trust that when we wait for a bus, that the bus will show up approximately when the schedule says it will do so. Parents trust schools to educate their children, and schools trust parents to get the kids to school on time. Customers trust businesses to provide the products they need, and business trust their customers to keep coming back when they give good service. Love makes the world go 'round, but trust definitely makes society go 'round! *-Lissa Coffey*

Truth

"This is the character of truth: it is of all time, it is for all men, it has only to show itself to be recognized, and one cannot argue against it"
-Voltaire (1694-1778)

Truth is the great clarifier. I think of Jack Nicholson in "A Few Good Men" being grilled on the witness stand by Tom Cruise – it's obvious that Jack's covering something because the pieces aren't falling into place. And he gets frustrated and yells at Tom: "You want the truth? You can't handle the truth!" It's one of those great moments in film where you get that "ah-ha!" and then the truth comes out. The truth might not always be pretty – but it is what it is, and it wants to be discovered. *-Lissa Coffey*

> **"Truth is stranger than fiction, but it is because Fiction is obliged to stick to possibilities; Truth isn't."**
> -Mark Twain (1835-1910)

Of course, we know that there are infinite possibilities, but in our human experience we can only conjure up a portion of the possibilities based on what we've been exposed to. That's why when some things happen we just can't believe it – we can't comprehend how such a thing could happen. But when we seek the truth, through prayer and meditation and spiritual practices, we see many more possibilities. We open up to answers and solutions that were once beyond our realm of understanding.
-Lissa Coffey

> **"We know truth, not only by reason, but also by the heart."**
> -Blaise Pascal (1723-1662)

In many ways, truth is intuitive. We know it when we see it. We recognize it, we feel it. There may be no hard evidence to back something up, but when it is the truth, we don't need evidence – we understand it without explanation. *-Lissa Coffey*

> **"There are no new truths, but only truths that have not been recognized by those who have perceived them without noticing. A truth is something that everyone can be shown to know and to have known, as people say, all along."**
> -Mary McCarthy (1912-1989)

Truth is beyond time and space. Truth is always available to us, now, and wherever we are. Truth is unchanging and eternal. Truth is not biased or preferential – truth is the same for each one of us, it is there for all of us. *-Lissa Coffey*

> **"Truth - is as old as God -**
> **His Twin identity**
> **And will endure as long as He**
> **A Co-Eternity -"**
> -Emily Dickinson (1830-1886)

Truth – just five little letters and yet such a big word. It's so powerful, and so real. Truth is something we all revere – we all search for it, we all believe in it. Truth is pure and simple. It makes everything make sense. Truth is a guiding principle that can't steer us wrong. *-Lissa Coffey*

Uncertainty

"If we insist on being as sure as is conceivable...
we must be content to creep along the ground,
and can never soar."
-John Henry Cardinal Newman

"Playing it safe" is a choice – but if we make that choice every time, life could get boring. Sometimes it's good to take a risk, to leap into uncertainty with both feet! Maybe we'll fall, and maybe we'll fly- but we won't know "for sure" until we've actually done it! *-Lissa Coffey*

"Every area of trouble gives out a ray of hope, and the
one unchangeable certainty is that nothing is certain
or unchangeable."
-John F. Kennedy

Isn't this uncertainty such a great concept? It sure helps us out when we make a mistake! We can change things, make them better. Nothing is set in stone, that's just the way it is – life is fluid, moving, changeable – and that is good for us. There is great potential in uncertainty- it means that ANYTHING, and everything is possible. *-Lissa Coffey*

"The unknown is what it is. And to be frightened of
it is what sends everybody scurrying around chasing
dreams, illusions, wars, peace, love, hate, all that...
Accept that it's unknown, and it's plain sailing."
-John Lennon

Why is it so difficult for us to just accept the unknown? We tend to feel like we have to "make" things happen. Sure, we must take action, and work towards our goals – but at the same time if we could also relax and know that however things turn out, that's the way they're supposed to be. The process itself is really where we learn. And at the same time, since everything is changeable, and everything is possible, we can always start again! *-Lissa Coffey*

"Uncertainty and mystery are energies of life. Don't
let them scare you unduly, for they keep boredom at
bay and spark creativity."
-R.I. Fitzhenry

We live in a world of uncertainty. No matter how hard we plan or schedule or try to control things, the truth is that anything can happen, at any time! We can embrace that, and take what comes- or we can live in a state of apprehension. But we can't change the "unknowingness" – that's just a part of life, so we might as well enjoy it! *-Lissa Coffey*

"The quest for certainty blocks the search for meaning. Uncertainty is the very condition to impel man to unfold his powers."
-Erich Fromm

I think this is kind of like "necessity is the mother of invention." What makes us learn and grow and propels us forward is uncertainty. If everything were certain we would get lazy pretty quick- Instead we are constantly challenged to find solutions and better our conditions. *-Lissa Coffey*

Understanding

"Those who understand only what can be explained understand very little."
-Marie von Ebner-Eschenbach (1830-1916)

There is so much more to this world that what we can actually see and hear and feel. There is so much that is without explanation, but that is beyond explanation. There are unlimited possibilities all around us, at all times – how could we even venture to guess what they all could be? When we realize that our lives can open up to these possibilities, we allow understanding to pour in and nourish us. *-Lissa Coffey*

"Sometimes it proves the highest understanding not to understand."
-Baltasar Gracian (1601-1658)

Some things seem beyond our understanding. Certain algebraic formulas, for example – or the mentality of terrorists. This is a complicated world we live in. And we may not understand all of it. But we can expand our faith to accept what understanding we do have, and to build on that. We can take what we know, and learn and grow from here. *-Lissa Coffey*

"In what we really understand, we reason but little."
-William Hazlitt (1778-1830)

True understanding is knowingness. We don't have to be able to put it into words, we just know. In our heart, in our mind, in our very being, some things just ARE, and we understand. It's kind of like how we can feel when someone loves us. We know it without that person having to say it. We don't have to think about it and analyze the situation, there is just this understanding that is there. That same understanding, that same knowingness, comes with the presence of Spirit, omnipotent and omnipresent. *-Lissa Coffey*

"Much learning does not teach understanding."
-Heraclitus (540?- 480?)

Where do we find understanding? It doesn't just come from education. It isn't just in books. How easy that would be it if were so! Understanding is not something that is generated in our minds. It starts with our mind, but whatever it is becomes understood when it finds its way into our heart. We understand because we can relate, we can identify, we can see that we are not separate from that which we seek to understand. *-Lissa Coffey*

"You never really understand a person until you consider things from his point of view – until you climb into his skin and walk around in it."
-Harper Lee,To Kill a Mockingbird, 1960

For all of us to get along and live together in this world requires a certain amount of understanding. The more we learn and discover and understand about ourselves, the more we can understand other people. We are really all much more alike that we are different. Given our different circumstances and situations, it's easy to forget that. *-Lissa Coffey*

Universe

"Had I been present at the creation, I would have given some useful hints for the better ordering of the universe."
-Alfonso X, King of Castile and Leon, attributed

We have to laugh at ourselves sometimes. We think we know better. This is the premise behind the movie "Bruce Almighty." God needs some time off so he gets Jim Carrey to take his place for awhile. And, of course, hilarity ensues! At some point we need to stop trying to control the universe and understand that there is perfect order in all things. Always has been. Always will be. *-Lissa Coffey*

"A man said to the universe:
"Sir, I exist!"
"However," replied the universe,
The fact has not created in me
A sense of obligation."
-Stephen Crane

The universe doesn't give us an engraved invitation to participate in life. And just showing up to the party doesn't guarantee us a good time. The universe responds to our actions. We get out of it what we put into it. *-Lissa Coffey*

**"Always think of the universe as one living organism,
with a single substance and a single soul."**
-Marcus Aurelius (A.D. 121-180)

The universe is not something "out there" beyond our reach. We are an essential part of the universe. It is within us, and all around us, not separate from us, but one with us. We are sustained by the universe, and each of us contributes to the wholeness, and wellness of the universe. Uni-verse: one song. We sing; we harmonize.
-Lissa Coffey

**"The universe is represented in an atom,
in a moment of time."**
-Ralph Waldo Emerson (1803-1882)

I think I quote Emerson more than any other single person. I like the way he expresses himself so succinctly, yet so profoundly. Great scientists have said this same thing, it is the whole theme of the movie "What the Bleep Do We Know?" When you think of it this way, every atom is precious, every moment is precious. *-Lissa Coffey*

**"Gazing up at the stars, for the first time, the first, I laid
my heart open to the benign indifference of the universe."**
-Albert Camus (1913-1960)

The universe is vast, indifferent and impartial. It can't play favorites because it doesn't recognize the separateness of any particular individual. We're all in this together, equally. We see the same stars; we feel the same sun. *-Lissa Coffey*

Value

"To gain that which is worth having, it may be necessary to lose everything else."
-Bernadette Devlin

To gain peace of mind, it is necessary for us to step away from fear, doubt, and anxiety. To gain love, we must give up grudges, and resentments. Let's look at what is worth having, and what we are willing to give up to get it. *-Lissa Coffey*

"The Worth of a thing is best known by the want of it."
-James Kelly (18th cent.)

It's that insatiable desire for something that keeps us at it. It's that burning passion that compels us to work hard, to not give up, to stay focused and on target. We can cite countless examples of people who have worked to build their own businesses, or buy their own home. It works the same way with our spiritual growth. Do we have a burning desire for it? Do we work at it every day? Do we make it a priority in our lives? *-Lissa Coffey*

"Labor is the true standard of value."
-Abraham Lincoln (1809-1865)

How much do we want something? How much is it worth to us? How hard are we willing to work for it? The more thought and effort we put into something, the more the universe picks up on our desire and intention and works with us to turn our dreams into reality. Sitting around and wishing is one thing, but going out and making things happen is something else altogether! *-Lissa Coffey*

"A thing is worth precisely what it can do for you; not what you choose to pay for it."
-John Ruskin (1819-1900)

If we take the example of a car – a car is not just transportation. If it were, we'd all be driving very fuel-efficient, non-descript vehicles. A car has become a symbol – of our wealth, our style, our priorities. A Mercedes costs more money not just because it is more expensive to produce, but because people are willing to pay more for the prestige associated with the name. So, the car is providing necessary transportation, but also the "image" that the driver wants to project. Is the image worth the price? It's just a matter of personal preference. We have choices, in cars and in everything. *-Lissa Coffey*

> **"There is no such thing as absolute value in this world.
> You can only estimate what a thing is worth to you."**
> -Charles Dudley Warner (1829-1900)

A lot of times we thing of value in terms of money. On "Antiques Roadshow" we watch with interest as various pieces are given a certain dollar value. But that dollar amount is only one measure of the item's value. If some heirloom has been in the family for generations, and represents a kind of family history, then the sentimental value for its owner may be much more than the dollar amount. He may not be willing to part with it for any sum of money! There's an old saying that "one man's junk is another man's treasure." -*Lissa Coffey*

Vegetarianism

> **"I have known many meat eaters to be far more
> nonviolent than vegetarians."**
> -Mohandas K. Gandhi

Vegetarianism is just one choice we can make in our lives. But just being a vegetarian doesn't make a person a saint. We are faced with many choices every day of our lives. Yes, it is important to treat animals with love and respect. It is also important to live in peace among our fellow human beings. The kindness and compassion we feel for one friend, or pet, or family, or species, can extend out into the world to all living creatures, and create peace and harmony for all of us. -*Lissa Coffey*

> **"It is nearly 50 years since I was assured by a
> conclave of doctors that if I did not eat meat,
> I should die of starvation."**
> -George Bernard Shaw (1856-1950)

This discussion came about by the suggestion of one of our subscribers, and I think there is a lot to say about it. Now before all our meat-eating readers take offense, rest assured that I am not trying to convert anyone! I believe that diet is a choice. I have made the choice to be vegan - that's the vegetarian without eggs or dairy. It can be challenging at times, particularly when dining at restaurants that do not provide such an enlightened menu - but I have found the benefits, both in terms of health and spiritual growth, to far outweigh the inconveniences. -*Lissa Coffey*

> **"It is a part of the destiny of the human race, in its
> gradual improvement, to leave off eating animals, as
> surely as the savage tribes have left off eating each other
> when they came into contact with the more civilized."**
> -Henry David Thoreau (1817-1862)

There are many reasons for choosing a vegetarian lifestyle. Here is just one: As we're on this spiritual path, and begin to assimilate higher knowledge, we lose sight of separation. We experience more and more the "oneness" of the universe. It seems

only a natural extension of our spiritual growth to adopt habits that allow ourselves to express more love and compassion for the world of which we are a part.
-Lissa Coffey

"The road to health is paved with vegetables, fruits, beans, rice and grains."
-Polly Strand, 1993

Nature's bounty is plentiful! The food with which we are provided is nature's medicine cabinet. We have everything we need to keep ourselves healthy and fit. Nature's intelligence works with us to sustain life. *-Lissa Coffey*

"Anyone who cares about the Earth - really cares - must stop eating animals."
-Linda McCartney, 1990

It all begins with each one of us. There are many small things we can do to make this world a better place - and when we start doing them in large numbers, it makes such a difference. The world has gotten more environmentally conscious - out of necessity! There are many more people here, and that puts a tremendous burden on our planet. But we have become aware of using environmentally friendly materials, and recycling more, and carpooling. Living a vegetarian lifestyle is another choice that can make a positive impact on the world in so many ways. *-Lissa Coffey*

Victory

"Victory comes, at times, just when one no longer expects it."
-Martin Buber (1878-1965)

Have you ever had those times where you're trying to think of a word, or a person's name, and no matter how much you search your brain you can't seem to find it? And then later, when you relax, when you've given up and let it go, it comes flooding back to you clear as day! That's the law of detachment at work. Whatever you are striving for, release and let it go, then it is free to be yours. *-Lissa Coffey*

"The greatest of victories is the victory over oneself."
-The Dhammapada: The Path of Perfection (1st Cent. B.C.)

Sometimes it seems that the mind is in constant turmoil. It's always racing from project to problem, keeping us busy, making us stressed. To be able to still the mind, to find that calm and quiet place within, is a true victory, one that rewards us with health, happiness, and peace of mind. *-Lissa Coffey*

"The real and lasting victories are those of peace and not of war."
-Ralph Waldo Emerson (1803-1882)

The word victory is often associated with a competition, or battle. But a victory doesn't have to mean that there's a "winner" and a "loser." A successful negotiation, where both parties feel that a fair resolution has been reached, is a victory. When peace reigns, that is a victory. *-Lissa Coffey*

"Do not scorn little victories."
-Andre Gide (1869-1951)

Can we leap to the top of a mountain? That would be a difficult task. But what we can do is to climb a mountain, one step at a time. Each step that brings us toward that peak is a victory in itself. It takes effort, it takes vision, and it takes persistence. When we get discouraged, thinking the goal is too far off in the distance, we can look back and see just how far we've come. *-Lissa Coffey*

"The first step towards victory is to gain courage."
-Plutarch (A.D. 46? – 119?)

Whenever we embark upon any endeavor, there's always a first step. To reach a goal we must take action. To take action we must have courage. When we set our minds to it, we can achieve success, we can be victorious! *-Lissa Coffey*

Virtue

"If self-knowledge is the road to virtue, so is virtue still more the road to self-knowledge."
-Jean Paul Friedrich Richter (1763-1825)

We're here to learn and grow, to know more about our selves. Virtue is something we have to define individually. It's natural evolution for us to become more virtuous as we move along the path because we understand more about ourselves and our true nature. *-Lissa Coffey*

"Virtue is nothing else but action in accordance with the laws of one's own nature."
-Baruch Spinoza (1632-1677)

When we are tuned in and going with the flow, we allow ourselves to be who we really are. There's no faking it, no play-acting, just instinct and authenticity. Our virtues come shining through because we can't help it. That's who we are. *-Lissa Coffey*

> "By virtue I mean nothing arcane or obscure. I mean
> good citizenship, whose principal components are
> moderation, social sympathy and willingness to
> sacrifice private desires for public ends."
> -George F. Will

Being virtuous isn't necessarily being angelic. It's not that complicated, or perfect. It's simply living up to what we know and trust to be good and just. It's looking at the big picture at times, rather than our own individual needs and desires. *-Lissa Coffey*

> "A noble spirit will seek the reward of virtue in the
> consciousness of it, rather than in popular opinion."
> -Pliny the Younger (A.D. 62? - 113?)

There's a saying that virtue is its own reward, and it probably came from this quote. As we learn and grow, we understand that we really answer only to ourselves. We can't please everyone, and we can't go against what we know in our heart to be right. All we can do is the best we can at any given moment. *-Lissa Coffey*

> "Society can only be happy and free in proportion as it
> is virtuous."
> -Mary Wollstonecraft (1759-1797)

Happy and free. Sounds good, doesn't it? In any society growth starts with the individual. One by one, each of us contributes to the whole in our own unique way. By being virtuous we're helping ourselves, and also helping the entire world. *-Lissa Coffey*

Vision

> "We are all visionaries, and what we see is our
> soul in things."
> -Henry Amiel (1821-1881)

Ah! This is something to think about - what we see is our soul in things... not necessarily that we are seeing with our soul, but that we relate, we identify, with our visions. When we have a vision, we become a creative force, bringing that vision into reality. We see that the vision is not only a "thing", it is a part of who we are. *-Lissa Coffey*

> "The idea is to seek a vision that gives you purpose in
> life and then to implement that vision. The vision by
> itself is one half, one part, of a process. It implies the
> necessity of living that vision, otherwise the vision will
> sink back into itself."
> -Lewis P. Johnson, 1987

I think we all have lots of visions throughout our lives. Some we shrug off, we're not attached to. Others seem to come to us easily. And then there are those that give

us a purpose in life. Those are the ones that are important. Those are the ones that push us to learn and grow. We can't just let those visions go, we have to do something about them. Those are the visions that are life-changing, world-changing!
-Lissa Coffey

"Visions are like dreams, only they occur in the waking state."
-Carl G. Jung (1875-1961)

Are we awake? Are we thinking clearly? Are we seeing clearly? When we can answer these questions affirmatively and have a vision that has caught our attention, we need to do something about it. There's a reason why certain visions come to us at certain times in our lives. And there's a reason why certain visions come to certain people and not others. It doesn't matter where this vision comes from, once we have it, it is ours. And it is up to us to act on it, to do what we can to make this world a better place.
-Lissa Coffey

"Visionary people are visionary partly because of the very great many things they don't see."
Berkeley Rice

Isn't this so true! Visionary people don't seem to see obstacles - or at least, they don't see them as obstacles, maybe just as challenges. I've heard so many successful business people say that when going in, they didn't even know what could go wrong. They were so focused on looking at their vision that all the obstacles were a blur. They were so committed to following through with their vision that they couldn't even imagine anything stopping them. And they turned something that vision into a reality.
-Lissa Coffey

"Vision is the art of seeing things invisible."
-Jonathan Swift (1667-1745)

Like this quote says, it's the kind of vision that goes beyond just what the eyes can see. It's seeing with the heart. It is seeing possibilities. It is seeing what could be. Sometimes it's something that we can see, but no one else can. That doesn't make it any less real. Vision is powerful, and a shared vision is even more so. *-Lissa Coffey*

Waiting

"There is a difference between the waiting of the
prophet and the standing still of the fool."
-Ralph Waldo Emerson (1803-1882)

This is an issue we all struggle with at one time or another. It can be difficult to wait, it can be difficult to be patient. And yet, it is so often necessary! Everything has its own time, its own season, and more often than not we are the ones who have to adjust to fit in with the grand plan. But waiting doesn't have to mean standing still, or wasting time. We can use our time wisely, even when we are waiting. *-Lissa Coffey*

"A man watches his pear tree day after day, impatient
for the ripening of the fruit. Let him attempt to force
the ripening of the fruit and he may spoil both fruit
and tree. But let him patiently wait, and the ripe pear
at length falls into his lap!"
-Abraham Lincoln (1809-1865)

Ah! We are rewarded for our patience! There's another saying that "good things come to those who wait." Even if we pluck a pear straight from the tree, that doesn't make it ripe. It is ripe only in its own time. We can apply the concept to our ideas and projects, our relationships and job searches. We know when the time is right to proceed, to take action. We don't need to rush. *-Lissa Coffey*

"Let us, then, be up and doing,
With a heart for any fate;
Still achieving, still pursuing,
Learn to labor and to wait."
-Henry Wadsworth Longfellow (1807-1882)

This is just part of a longer poem by Longfellow called "A Psalm of Life." Its message is simple. Work – and wait. It's a balance. Put in the effort, and put in the thought. Take time for action, and take time to be quiet. This is the formula for success in any endeavor. *-Lissa Coffey*

"All good abides with him who waiteth wisely."
-Henry David Thoreau (1817-1862)

This scenario is familiar. Have you ever been in a long line, and the person serving customers is just doing the best that they can. Maybe the place is understaffed, or unexpectedly busy. There always seems to be someone who complains, who is impatient, and who makes the experience more aggravating for everyone around. And then there's the kind-hearted person who uses the time to chat with the other people in line, who steps up and smiles and thanks the person doing the work. That person makes the experience much more pleasant! Next time you're in line, observe. And choose to wait wisely! *-Lissa Coffey*

"Everything comes to him who hustles while he waits."
-Thomas Alva Edison (1847-1931)

I love this! Whistle while you work, and hustle while you wait! The world doesn't stop moving just because we have to wait. We can work on so many things, even on our patience! These are times when we can accelerate our learning and growing by reading books, listening to audio recordings, and meditating. When we are committed to learning and growing, there is never a dull moment to be had! *-Lissa Coffey*

Winter

"There is a wilder solitude in winter
When every sense is pricked alive and keen."
-May Sarton, "The House in Winter" 1966

I know that we have readers all over the world, and for those in the southern hemisphere, this is actually summer time! My step-children live in Australia, and they have been writing me about how hot it is there now. But here in the U.S., where I am, we are in the midst of winter. Even in California, which is known to be pretty "season-less," the temperature has dropped. That nesting instinct kicks in; we want to be warm and cozy. The weather brings us indoors, and like hibernating bears, it is a time for us to be still. *-Lissa Coffey*

"There is a privacy about it which no other season
gives you. In spring, summer, and fall people sort of
have an open season on each other; only in the winter,
in the country, can you have longer, quiet stretches
when you can savor belonging to yourself."
-Ruth Stout, 1955

In other seasons we are more outwardly oriented, we're playing sports or running around outside. In the winter we tend to spend more time going inward. This is a time for reflection, and contemplation. In places where there is snow, the snow tends to make everything more quiet. It's as if we are meant to listen more closely, to listen to our hearts. *-Lissa Coffey*

"In a way winter is the real spring, the time when the
inner thing happens, the resurge of nature."
-Edna O'Brien, 1978

In the winter, on the outside, it looks like nothing is happening. The trees are bare. The ground is cold. But growth is taking place. Inside things are happening. We don't see the results of that growth until the spring, but that doesn't mean that something wasn't taking place every moment. The tree is bare, but it is very much living. It's like when we're meditating – we look like we're asleep because on the outside we are still, but major growth is happening on the inside. *-Lissa Coffey*

"The cold was our pride, the snow was our beauty. It fell and fell, lacing day and night together in a milky haze, making everything quieter as it fell, so that winter seemed to partake of religion in a way no other season did, hushed, solemn."
Patricia Hampl, 1981

Snow seems to make everything seem to clean, so pure, so peaceful. Utah is one area where they get a lot of snow in the winter. The kids love it because they can go skiing and snowboarding. But every time I go to visit it amazes me just how different the landscape is from season to season. It's really a different world in the winter. You have to move more slowly, to be safe. You have to take more time getting places. The snow makes you stop to think, you can't help it. *-Lissa Coffey*

"Perhaps I am a bear, or some hibernating animal, underneath, for the instinct to be half asleep all winter is so strong in me."
-Anne Morrow Lindbergh, 1971

It is our instinct to go within, to seek warmth, to find that inner light. It's more dark in the winter, so we turn within for that light, and it's there, like it always is. That feeling of wanting to "cocoon" in winter is strong because it feels good. We all need that, and the season provides it to us. *-Lissa Coffey*

Wisdom

**"Wise men hear and see
As little children do."**
-Lao-Tzu (6th cent. B.C.)

Children see things with an open mind and an open heart. Wisdom is not being childish, but rather it is being child-like in our curiosity and wonder. It allowing possibilities to present themselves in front of us. It is marveling at the grandeur of life. *-Lissa Coffey*

"The invariable mark of wisdom is to see the miraculous in the common."
-Ralph Waldo Emerson (1803-1882)

Since this newsletter is called WisdomNews I thought we'd start off the new year talking about wisdom. Wisdom goes beyond knowledge. We often hear wisdom associated with sages, people who seem to know and understand those things that sometimes have no explanation. Maybe it is recognizing that connection between all things that makes everything miraculous. Wisdom is attainable, all the wisdom of the universe is at hand right now. *-Lissa Coffey*

**"The first step in the acquisition of wisdom is silence,
the second listening, the third memory, the fourth
practice, the fifth teaching others."**
-Solomen Ibn Gabirol (A.D. 1021? – 1069?)

Hard to argue with that, huh? Silence, meditation, time with nature, self-reflection... all of these things lead us to wisdom. Have we taken that first step? Do we listen? Do we remember? Do we practice? Do we teach others? We all know what we must do, yet how often do we really do it? We get so distracted by our daily activities that we forget how important it is to just sit down and be quiet for a change! Yes, it is important – wisdom is important! Wisdom is necessary to lead the kind of lives that we say we want to lead. The first step is silence. *-Lissa Coffey*

"It is easier to be wise for others than for oneself."
-La Rochefoucauld (1613-1680)

This is so true! Don't we all give better advice than we take from ourselves? Because we can look at someone else's problems objectively, and we are so caught up in our own emotions that it's hard to step back and look at our own problems with the same wisdom. But it is possible! As we learn and grow and spend more time in silence, we make better decisions, we become more wise. *-Lissa Coffey*

**"Wisdom cannot be pass'd from one having it to
another not having it.Wisdom is of the soul, is not
susceptible of proof, is its own proof."**
-Walt Whitman (1819-1892)

This is another example of the more that you give, the more that you have. One of the best ways to learn is by teaching! Wisdom is not something that can necessarily be measured, but it can be felt, and it can be shared. *-Lissa Coffey*

Women and Men

**"I object to anything that divides the two sexes.
My main point is this: human development has now
reached a point at which sexual difference has become
a thing of altogether minor importance. We make
too much of it; we are men and women in the second
place, human beings in the first."**
-Olive Shreiner (1884)

The "battle of the sexes" was an issue back in the 1800's and we're still talking about it today. Clearly, there is a difference between men and women. But maybe we've come to the point where we can understand that our similarities far outweigh our differences. Rather than look at what divides us, let's look at what binds us. We aren't Martians and Venusians, we're here together on the same planet. *-Lissa Coffey*

> **"The basic discovery about any people is the discovery
> of the relationship between its men and women."**
> -Pearl S. Buck, 1941

This whole subject has been the basis for many sociological studies. A recent reality TV show had several men live as women for a few weeks, just to see if they could do it, and who get away with it the longest. Of course, it made for many comical moments, but the deeper lesson was that at the end of the exercise these men had a newfound respect for women, particularly the women in their lives. And this is a basic truth that carries over into every area. If we want to know how someone lives, we need to walk a mile in their shoes, or in this case, their high-heels! *-Lissa Coffey*

> **"Sometimes I wonder if men and women really suit
> each other. Perhaps they should live next-door and
> just visit now and then."**
> -Katharine Hepburn, 1980

The most successful relationships are the ones where there is interdependence. If two people are so independent that they live separate lives, and they don't come together as a unit, then the relationship suffers. If two people are so dependent on one another that they have no life outside of the relationship, then there is no growth, just stagnation. But when each person has a life of their own, and they come together out of mutual choice to share their lives, then lots of learning and growth takes place. There needs to be a nice balance of space and coming together to really flourish. *-Lissa Coffey*

> **"My research suggests that men and women may speak
> different languages that they assume are the same,
> using similar words to encode disparate experiences of
> self and social relationships. Because these languages
> share an overlapping moral vocabulary, they contain a
> propensity for systematic mistranslation."**
> -Carol Gilligan, In a Different Voice (1982)

Communication. Ask any relationship expert and they will tell you that the major issue between men and women is communication. But this is true in just about any relationship. Parents and teenagers, employers and employees, teachers and students. We need to really listen, to make sure that we understand and are understood. *-Lissa Coffey*

> **"The sexes in each species of beings are always true
> equivalents – equals but not identicals."**
> -Antoinette Brown Blackwell, The Sexes Throughout Nature (1875)

Isn't it great that we're not identical? We complement each other. It's the yin and yang, the shiva and shakti, not opposites but an energetic combination of elements. We each do our part in sustaining the species. We're here with each other, and for each other. -*Lissa Coffey*

Wonder

"Wonder is music heard in the heart, is voiceless."
-Rosemary Dobson, 1973

We can't hear wonder with our ears, or see it with our eyes. It's something that goes on in our hearts. It's the process of translating something that might ordinarily seem mundane into something spectacular. It's recognizing the divine within everything and everyone. -*Lissa Coffey*

**"If a child is to keep alive his inborn sense of wonder...
he needs the companionship of at least one adult who
can share it, rediscovering with him the joy, excitement
and mystery of the world we live in."**
-Rachel Carson, 1965

Children have this wide-eyed sense of wonder, everything is new to them, everything is a surprise. If we could just see through their eyes again for a day... look at a line of ants as a parade rather than a nuisance, see the clouds as dancing rather than threatening rain... how might this change our perspective? Wonder brings with it a sense of contentment, the world looks good and we feel good in it! We can learn a lot from our kids. -*Lissa Coffey*

**"Everything has its wonders, even darkness and
silence, and I learn, whatever state I may be in,
therein to be content."**
-Helen Keller, 1902

We see what we choose to see. Helen Keller could not physically see with her eyes- and yet she could see with her heart, she could experience wonder. Her life, and the way she chose to live her life, is such an inspiration to us. There is wonder all around us, but do we choose to see it? -*Lissa Coffey*

"Men love to wonder, and that is the seed of our science."
-Ralph Waldo Emerson (1803-1882)

Emerson always states it so well. Wonder is that "what if" that spurs us on to progress. It is the seed of science, but also the seed of creativity. We come up with ideas before we can make them into a reality - and those ideas come from wonder. Let's make it a point to spend some time just wondering today. -*Lissa Coffey*

"Wonder is a state of mind in which... nothing is
taken for granted... Each thing is a surprise, being is
unbelievable. We are amazed at seeing anything
at all; amazed not only at particular values and
things but at the unexpectedness of being as such,
at the fact that there is being at all."
-Abraham Joshua Heschel (1907-1972)

Wonder is wonderful! I like Heschel's definition of wonder - it shows the freshness, the newsness, associated with wonder. Wonder is just one of the things that makes life so beautiful. *-Lissa Coffey*

Words

"The more perfect the understanding between men,
the less need of words."
-Ralph Waldo Emerson (1803-1882)

Have you ever noticed how, with a really good friend, the silences are completely comfortable? It's as if you don't need words to communicate. There's an unspoken communication that allows space to just be. Sometimes words aren't enough to express how we feel. If you've ever said "I love you more than words can say" you know how that feels! You can write songs and poems and letters, and somehow it just can't quite sum up that feeling you get when looking into that person's eyes, completely silent. *-Lissa Coffey*

"You can stroke people with words."
-F. Scott Fitzgerald (1896-1940)

What would we do without language? This is how we communicate. Words by themselves are so innocuous, but when we put them together, combine them together in such a way, they can be bitterly poisonous, or powerfully healing. Words can carry with them so much meaning. Through words we can express tenderness, and compassion. *-Lissa Coffey*

"Words make another place, a place to escape to with
your spirit alone."
-Robert MacNeil

We all know what it feels like to get lost in a really good book. What magic there is in that! What a gift that is available to us, to be able to share our thoughts and feelings and experiences with each other – to express our concerns and joys. All this is possible because we have the words to do it. It doesn't matter if it is the spoken word, or the written word – written on a computer or by hand – in block letters, a smothe cursive, or even Braille! Words help us to learn more about ourselves, and about each other. *-Lissa Coffey*

"You may choose your word like a connoisseur,
And polish it up with art,
But the word that sways, and stirs, and stays,
Is the word that comes from the heart."
-Ella Wheeler Wilcox, 1906

When we communicate, we want to choose our words carefully to be sure that we are completely understood. And yet, when we want to express our feelings, sometimes it helps to just let those feelings flow, to think with our hearts more than with our heads. The words that come from our hearts are so true and real that they can't help but have an effect on anyone who hears them. *-Lissa Coffey*

"Words and eggs must be handled with care.
Once broken they are impossible things to repair."
-Anne Sexton, 1975

Another way of making a promise is by saying: "I give you my word." When you do what you say you are going to do, you are being true to you word – you are being honest, and showing integrity. It is important for people to be able to trust each other. And when once a word is broken, the trust that comes with it is broken, too. We can gain trust, and show that we are trustworthy, by being true to our word. *-Lissa Coffey*

Work

"I believe in hard work. It keeps the wrinkles out of
the mind and the spirit."
-Helena Rubinstein

"To find joy in work is to discover the fountain of youth."
-Pearl S. Buck

Helena Rubinstein is the famous cosmetics mogul. She is a great example of a businesswoman ahead of her time! It is obvious that she enjoyed her profession and was very successful with it. It is true that doing work that we love helps to keep us young and feeling good about ourselves. *-Lissa Coffey*

"The man [or woman!] who does not work for the love
of work but only for money is not likely to make money
nor to find much fun in life."
-Charles M. Schwab

That's quite some advice from one of the top businessmen in American history! Yet how many of us really take this to heart? I've heard so many times from people who say that they are working just for the money and that what they REALLY want to do is something else entirely. This isn't productive. So our choice is to either find a way to love the work that we are at least temporarily required to do, OR find a way to make money doing what it is that we love to do.

Both of these are valid options. Work can be a ministry. No matter where you are or what you're doing, there are people you can reach, people you can help. And we also know that when you truly love what you are doing, nothing can stop you from doing it! *-Lissa Coffey*

"Working is so satisfying that if we didn't have to work to eat, we'd have to invent some other reason for doing it."
-Andrew S. Rooney

"It's not work, if you love what you're doing."
-Steve Sears (1941-1996)

Can you just picture Andy Rooney sitting on the set of "60 Minutes" and talking about his topic of the week? I can hear his voice saying just what he said above! Aren't we funny about our work? When we enjoy what we're doing there's this timelessness about it. It is satisfying and gratifying. It is fun! *-Lissa Coffey*

"If a man [or woman!] love the labor of any trade, apart from any question of success or fame, the Gods have called him. [or her]"
-Robert Louis Stevenson

"Dharma" is a Sanskrit word that loosely translated means "purpose in life." To have found our dharma is indeed a beautiful thing! Dharma can be more than one thing, and dharma can also change and evolve as we do. But basically, we know that we're in our dharma when we love what we do, when we feel fulfilled, when we are unaware of the time that goes by when we are working. True dharma is work that we enjoy and that also helps people in some way. *-Lissa Coffey*

"All growth depends upon activity. There is no development physically or intellectually without effort, and effort means work. Work is not a curse; it is the prerogative of intelligence... the measure of civilization."
-Calvin Coolidge

It's great to plan, to pay attention, to have intention, to dream, wish, and visualize. Yet there comes a time when we must take action! Work is how things get done. Because we live on this human plane, work is how we learn and grow. Whether it is by studying or through our experiences, our activities take us to new places mentally, emotionally, and spiritually. *-Lissa Coffey*

Also By Lissa Coffey

Bhakti: 108 Prayers of Devotion

Ananda: Discover the Vedic Way to Happiness & Bliss

Awakened Parenting: Family Life as a Spiritual Path

The Perfect Balance Diet: 4 Weeks to a Lighter Body, Mind, Spirit & Space

What's Your Dharma: Discover the Vedic Way to Your Life's Purpose

CLOSURE and the Law of Relationship: Endings as New Beginnings

What's Your Dosha, Baby? Discover the Vedic Way for Compatibility in Life and Love

Getting There With Grace: Simple Exercises for Experiencing Joy

The Healthy Family Handbook: Natural Remedies for Parents and Children
(co-authored with Louise Taylor)

Freddy Bear's Wakeful Winter

Feng Shui For Everyday: Easy Ways to Bring Abundance Into Your Home and Workplace

Acknowledgements

I have to thank all the amazing voices throughout the book. Each of these quotes has inspired me, and taught me in it's own special way. We learn and grow every day. It happens gradually, over a lifetime, with the various experiences and challenges that come our way. And it happens when we seek it out, through books, and classes, and teachers. I've been so fortunate to have some wonderful teachers in my life. Deepak Chopra introduced me to Vedanta and it changed my life. I think I was a Vedantin before I ever knew what that meant, so in finding Vedanta I felt like I had come home. Much love and gratitude goes to my community at the Vedanta Society of Southern California, and especially my teacher, Swami Sarvadevananda.

Of course, I continue to learn so much from my children, who are adults now. With any relationship we can learn and grow, but being a parent opens up the heart in a way like no other. I remember writing in the car while waiting to pick my kids up from school, or in the karate studio while they were in class. My family has expanded over the years, and for that I am so grateful. These wonderful people inspire me every day.

A big thank you goes out to the super talented Ray Mawst. Ray makes my work look good. I'm so lucky to have found him, and now I'm obsessed with his art and lettering. Check out his website and you will be, too! RayMawst.com

Greg, my husband, my love, my companion in this journey of life – you have my gratitude, and my heart.

My CoffeyTalk team has my love and gratitude: Eric, Josh, Nancy, Lindsay, Emma, Jon and Freddy. Thank you!

To my global family, those I have connected with over the internet and social media, people I wouldn't have known had we not been here at this particular juncture in technology – thank you for your constant support and encouragement. I feel so blessed!

Resources

Lissa's Website	www.CoffeyTalk.com
DharmaSmart: Purposeful Living Essentials	www.DharmaSmart.com
What's Your Dosha? Quiz and more	www.WhatsYourDosha.com
What's Your Dharma? Your Life Purpose	www.WhatsYourDharma.com
All About Meditation	www.PSMeditation.com
Dosha Design: Vastu & Feng Shui	www.DoshaDesign.com
The Ayurveda Experience	www.AyurvedaECourse.com
The Ayurvedic Balance Diet Club	www.PerfectBalanceDiet.com
The Kindness Movement	www.EverythingKind.com

Social Media

YouTube.com/coffeytalk
Facebook.com/lissacoffeytalk
Twitter.com/coffeytalk
Instagram.com/lissacoffey
Pinterest.com/lissa_coffey
HuffingtonPost.com/lissa-coffey

www.ingramcontent.com/pod-product-compliance
Lightning Source LLC
Chambersburg PA
CBHW051413090426
42737CB00014B/2653